They Call Me Grandpa

ISBN: 978-0-578-24143-2

Cover and book design by Taodesigns

First printing edition 2020 in United States.

Randy "Grandpa" Jones

Grandpa Jones Book Publishing
Milwaukee, Wisconsin
grandpajonesbook@gmail.com

They Call Me Grandpa

Randy "Grandpa" Jones

Foreword

There are a few people that could have written this forward who have a pretty good idea why I wrote this book. I thought about it and decided the best person to explain WHY would be me...so here it goes.

For many years I have been taking the young ones to a wide variety of different places from the mall to restaurants, from Tae kwon do class to county parks and from weddings to birthday parties. People from waitress' to preachers, to young parents, to teachers, to other grand parents and friends have been telling me, you are a "GREAT GRANDPA"

I take being a grandpa very seriously, so when people go out of their way to tell me what a good job, I am doing I accept the compliment with great pride.

I work very hard to watch what I say, how I say it and make sure they stay safe both physically and emotionally when in my care. As I get older, hopefully wiser, I wanted to know what exactly makes a great grandparent. It is not just buying candy and toys then sending them back home to mom and dad. Yes that is part of it, but I wanted to see why nobody, and I MEAN NOBODY says "You are such a good grandpa" whenever anyone compliments me, it is ALWAYS; *"YOU TREAT THOSE KIDS SPECIAL, YOU ARE SUCH A GREAT GRANDPA."*

People want to know what I do and what I continue to do that earns the respect and admiration of my grandkids. They want to know *WHAT MAKES A GOOD GRANDPARENT IN TODAYS BRAVE NEW WORLD.*

IT WAS FOR THIS REASON THIS BOOK WAS WRITTEN!

Table of Contents

OLD SCHOOL SHENANIGANS THAT WERE NOT P.C.

Being a "GREAT GRANDPA" means knowing what kind of a kid you were. The things you were allowed to do not because it was right or wrong but because it was the sign of the times. We grew up in a time when boys were still allowed to do boy things and girls could be girls. Boys played with toy guns, played war and cowboys and Indians. Girls played with dolls, had EZ bake ovens to learn how to bake, and even wore dresses. Kids respected their elders and at times felt the sting of a leather belt or wooden paddle across our backside. We were exposed to rooms painted with lead paint our parent's cars had no seat belts and car seats and cell phones were not even invented yet. Believe it or not when we had to use a public restroom EACH & EVERY ONE OF US KNEW THE CORRECT BATHROOM TO WALK INTO. WOW, WHAT A CONCEPT FOR TODAYS YOUTH TO GRASP.

Some of the stories in this chapter may offend certain people Then this book is not for you... ENJOY

Today kids have to deal with rules and restrictions that would have emptied every seat in my grade school. These kids have a zero-tolerance policy for sexual harassment, weapons, and a plethora of other offenses they could get kicked out of school for. When I was a young one and in school, we had a game at recess that by the standards set down after 1989 would get kids both boys and girls expelled for sexual misconduct and 3rd-degree rape but when I was a kid it was allowed and permitted by the playground supervising teachers.

At recess, we knew who liked who and our games of tag were not just tag it was if you caught them you could kiss them. Now at 5-6-7 years old back in the '70s & '80s would run around trying to get away unless you were being chased by someone you wanted to catch you then slow down a little get caught a quick peck on the cheek a few giggles and you would take off running again. We had no idea about sexual harassment or even thought about doing something wrong we were just a bunch of kids having fun at playtime.

Could you imagine that the same game being played in the new millennium? OH MY GOD, some little boy chasing a little girl with the full and premeditated intention of kissing her on the cheek. That poor kid would be expelled from the school probably some sort of charges would be filed and no doubt he would be placed on a sexual predators list and the little girl he was chasing had every intention of slowing down and when it was her turn chase him down and return the peck on the cheek. Not in today's politically correct world.

You need to keep your hands to yourself and if you don't someone will be screaming RAPE.

Another zero-tolerance policy today's kids have to deal with that we played daily is war games with pretend or toy guns. When I was in grade school in the winter months it was common practice to build snow forts in the front yard and have wars with snowballs, cap guns, and plastic army riffles could you imagine driving through a neighborhood in the 2000s and seeing a snow fort in someone's front yard and another one next door or across the street and there were boys playing war or having a snowball fight dressed in army gear or heaven forbid they were PRETENDING to be cops and robbers. The people in the neighborhood, their heads would explode and the ones that didn't would be on the phone and the police and S.W.A.T. Would be called to the scene and the game would be ended. Now that would happen in a private neighborhood and we used to do this on a PLAYGROUND at school. Could you even imagine the repercussions of the building of snow forts and playing cops and robbers on the school property today? I have read stories of kids getting expelled for pretending a stick was a gun or some little boy was kicked out of school for bringing a water pistol to school. I am all for a safe school environment, especially because in the next couple of years I will have a good number of grandkids in the public school system but political correctness has gone way too far in my opinion.

There are things that we survived as kids that are not only not PC but in some cases are now laws. Could you imagine in the year 2020 a pickup truck heading up Hwy 41 with 2 pre-teen boys sitting in the box with play plastic machine guns shooting at cars wearing no seat belts and having people pretend to be shooting back. We did that. More times than not whoever was driving the other vehicle would be the one shooting back. If we were lucky enough that there were other kids in the car we would have shoot outs for miles. No way would that happen today

First, it is VERY illegal to ride in the box of the truck now seat belts and car seats are required for every passenger depending on weight and height.

Second, In today's road rage and the gun-happy world there is a very good chance that your game of pretend war may escalate into someone shooting back with live ammo.

Third, even if sitting in the back was ok and legal aiming a toy gun at another car would no doubt because for arrest or at the very least a huge ticket.

Not only did we play with guns in trucks but we played war games and cowboys and Indians in our yards. Yes, I said cowboys and Indians. Back in the day stores sold full toy outfits that consisted of a bow and arrow, a rubber knife, and a headband with a feather and yes you were the Indian. The cowboy outfit may have consisted of a holster, a pair of 6 shooters a cowboy hat with a lone ranger mask. Were we as kids trying to disparage a nation of people, of course not, we were doing what we have seen on T.V. The Lone Ranger was the good guy or John Wayne and how he fought the Indians. We meant no disrespect we were kids and kids do what they learn, and television learned us that cowboys were the good guys and Indians weren't. when we were little the code of honor was in place. As your enemy rode or ran away you would be like "phew..phew..phew I got you."

"No, you didn't you missed by a mile."

Then as we got older we used dart guns and there was no denying when you were hit. As pre-teens into our early teens, we used BB guns. Growing up a good friend of mine had a piece of land that was owned by the city as his back yard. It was a square mile of woods, bushes, hills, and a small creek that ran right through the center. So as we got older and bolder, we had helmets and swim goggles and some of us had gardening gloves and long sleeves and jeans. The rules changed just a bit and you had to stay a relatively safe distance and no intentional face shots, but we used BB guns way before anyone ever thought about making money letting kids shoot each other with paintballs. This would never happen in today's world because.

First, I doubt that you could even go into a store anymore and buy a cowboy outfit for sure an Indian outfit would be completely out of the question as completely racist and unacceptable.

Second, weapons...although they are toys finding bow & arrows and toy riffles and 6 shooters are very tough to find. To be honest I am not sure if they even sell BB guns anymore.

Third, Today's politically correct parents simply WOULD NOT allow their kids to play cowboys and Indians. I would guess they would consider it to offensive and hand them a switch or cell phone to play with.

COULD YOU EVEN IMAGINE YOU AS A GRANDPARENT HEARING YOUR GRANDSONS WERE ENGAGED IN A GAME LIKE THIS? ME... I'D BE GIDDY WITH PRIDE BUT THEIR MOTHER WOULD HAVE TO BE PUT ON AN OXYGEN TANK.

MORE THAN JUST WAR! These woods that we played in were used for far more than cowboys and Indians. As I said there were dirt trails and a creek that ran through the property. As older teenagers, we had minibike races through there but before that, we had motor cross bicycle races. Back then the bike of choice was a 20" dirt bike or if you were one of the cool kids you had a tricked out 20" bike with a banana seat and small front tire. These bikes were the racers' choice for 1-1 sidewalk racing but for the dirt track, you needed the dirt bikes. So not only did we race bikes we raced them wearing NO HELMETS OR PADS and not one of my friends ever passed away from a bike accident. Some bad bumps and bruises a few scraped knees or elbows maybe even a broken bone or two but never a death. In the middle of this young people's wonderland, there was a creek that ran through a ravine and that ravine was anywhere from 2-6ft across at different points and I would say about a 3-foot drop. Some areas had dirt mounds but, in most cases, we had to use at least 1 ramp to jump the creek. We had jumping contests for distance. At the beginning, a two-foot jump was a scary adrenaline rush because if you missed you either crashed into the other bank or fell 3 feet into the water. As the competition heated up the jumps got further and further apart until we were jumping the maximum distance which was about 6 feet What's that you say 80s kids played outside took risks and had fun? We rode bikes and had races jumped ramps and lived our life, not this boohoo we're so sensitive please don't offend us CRAPOLA!

I know that seems hard to believe with today's "BOYS" struggling to figure out what restroom to use or what color ribbon matches their eye shadow that in one generation could make such a mess of things.

THE NEIGHBORHOOD. In the neighborhood I played in everyone on the block knew everyone else. Baseball games were a very common thing most of the time if you were up and out at the baseball field by 8 in the morning there was a good chance that you would be playing ball and if you showed up after 8:30 more than likely you would be waiting for the second game because there were so many kids that played together if you were not there for picks all the positions would get filled and you would have to wait to the next game and 9 times out of ten everyone playing game 1 would also just stay and play in game 2.

We were just kids, but we knew the pecking order of the neighborhood. Two brothers were the leaders of the neighborhood not because they were gang leaders or bullies but because they were the best ballplayers and had dreams of going pro someday. We did not fear them we respected them so every morning they were the first two at the school baseball field and as soon as they got there other kids started to flock over and without exaggerating there would be 20-25 kids within 15 minutes waiting to get picked. I was not a very good athlete when I was young. I did have friends that enjoyed playing so I was happy to go watch and cheer for my friends. This was a daily occurrence all day every day all summer long.

After the baseball games, everyone went home for dinner for me the evening playtime was much better. We played a game called HUNTERS which is a team game of hide n seek and tag. The rules were very simple there are two teams of 5 or 6 kids and we were allowed to hide in 4 yards my grandma's, her neighbor, who by the way had 5 kids 3 of which usually played with us the other two older brothers were in college and too old to play kid games. The house on the corner across the street also had 2 players and their neighbor that had no kids but was just a cool neighbor. The corner house had a free-standing fort that was the safety zone for team 1 and my grandma had an old shack in her back yard which was the safety zone for team 2. both teams Start at one safety zone and one team counts while the other scatters to hide. Then the games begin...one team is hidden throughout the yards and the other team searches when found you either run and make a break for your safety zone which would be guarded by someone or you are tagged out. When all the members of the hiding team are found and captured the roles switch. Although I did not get picked to play baseball I was always either captain or first picked for hunters because I was small, which meant I could hide well and I was also quick which meant I made it back to our safety zone freeing my team and hiding again.

Another yard game we played as kids was a game called kick the can which should be relatively self-explanatory. This game however was played after dark. The rules again very easy you would take a large can, most of the time for us it was a coffee can and place it in the middle of the yard and someone would guard it. Hidden around the yard the kickers would have to try and sneak up and kick the can as you tried if you were tagged you were on the protector's team the game would end when all were captured, and the can remained unkicked.

The big one for us as kids that is now illegal was Yard Jarts. Now for those of you who don't know what a jart is let me try to explain. It is a very large oversized yard dart. Only it does not get thrown at a board its target is a plastic circle 24" in diameter. The jart itself was about 18" long with the tip being about 4" of blunted steel designed to bury itself in the ground. The handle was 4" of plastic, wrapped in rubber for a better grip and the center was 3 fins that very much resembled the feathers on an arrow for the aerodynamics needed to play the game. The rules are very similar to the game of horseshoes, the plastic rings were 30 ft apart and the object was to toss the jart like pitching a softball high in the air with a significant arc allowing it to stick in the ground. A circle hit scored if not keep going until how many points were scored to win the game. Now although the jarts were not sharp they were 3 or 4 pounds of metal coming down from 10-15 feet in the air and if someone was not paying attention could and did do some serious damage. At some point the powers that be changed the game from a fun family activity to a dangerous menace to society and pulled it off the shelves and out of the stores.

Being part of the neighborhood allowed us to do other things besides play games with the other kids. It allowed us to feel safe to go door-to-door. When I was 6 or 7 years old someone gave me a kit for making hot pads. It simply consisted of a 12" x 12" plastic loom and a bag full of colorful nylon bands that one side stretched across and the other side you would lace them across then one at a time loop them over tying off the last one making a very nice very colorful hot pad. The first bag of nylon loops produces 10-12 pads which I went door-to-door selling in my neighborhood. Another money-making venture that I did at a very young age was collect newspapers. Back in the day junkyards were paying 1 dollar a pound for old paper to recycle so some people had stacks and piles of papers in their garage and basements so as kids my cousins and I would walk around the neighborhood knocking on doors asked for old papers. Almost every house had at least a few to give but every once in a while, we would hit a huge load and have to go back and ask my dad to go with his truck and we'd load them up. Otherwise, we would walk around with our wagon fill it stack it the best we could until full bring it home load the truck until it was full then mom or dad would take us in and we'd cash in and split the money.

In today's electronic age and with news and information being so accessible with the touch of a button it would be hard for some people especially kids to visualize newspapers but back in the day, there were 2 newspapers the Milwaukee Journal and the Milwaukee Sentinel. One was printed and delivered in the morning and the other was the afternoon paper. For 2 ½ years I got up at 4:30 A.M. To deliver the morning paper before school and I did not do it alone for those same 2 ½ years my dad also got up to drive me not because the area was not safe at 4:30 in the morning but because I was a little entrepreneur and the fact that I was out making my own money was something he could get behind so he drove me on my route every day.

One final area I would like to touch on about making money and safer neighborhoods back in the day were the holiday season and Christmas caroling. From Thanksgiving until Christmas eve 3,4 sometimes 5 or more kids would go out at night after dinner for a few hours and ring doorbells and when the family answered we would sing. YES, WE WENT DOOR-TO-DOOR SINGING FOR GRATUITIES. The holiday season is a time for celebration and giving so when we sang, we were a group of kids with no adult supervision singing carols to bring cheer to the family and hoping for a cash tip.

WATER IN A BOTTLE WELL PLAYED. Who would have guessed that kids who brought empty gallon jugs full of tap water to drink at the ball field would be the same generation that convinced the world they needed to filter the water from the tap and that evolved into a billion-dollar business selling bottled water convincing the world tap water would potentially kill us or get everyone very sick. When we were kids playing in the yard not only would we take a break from playing to run in for a glass of water. I have been on bike rides in the summer and drove by someone watering a lawn with a garden hose and trigger and we would be hot and sweaty asking for them to spray us down with the hose or I have even had people take the trigger off and take a drink straight from the hose.

I know a woman who happens to be a friend of my daughter which would put her being born somewhere in the mid-90s and she has a son somewhere around 6 years old. This kid NEVER had a drink of city water. Not out of his kitchen sink, mom has a bottled water service that brings the 5-gallon jug whenever they need it. He is homeschooled so never had bubbler water, if they go shopping or if he is sent by a friend, he is sent with bottles of water with very CLEAR instructions he is only to drink his water.

Now in my opinion this woman takes things to the extreme but there are 100s of thousands of people that believe tap water is harmful to your body. Now I a not sure if that is advertising hype or not but for someone who grew up and never had to be rushed to the hospital for sipping out of a hose I do find myself treading in the world of buying water when all I care to drink comes out of my faucet.

Taking things one step further than chemicals in the water when we were kids there were and are chemicals in the water we drank, if you went fishing and ate the fish you caught the possibilities of chemicals in your food. Paint and varnish if ingested could and does cause brain damage. This chemical was in huge supply and very easily accessible to everyone especially little kids. What is this killer chemical? This chemical is LEAD. Yep back in the day, every house was painted with lead-based paint and in certain area lakes the lead content was considered toxic.

DRESS CODES. There are things we did as kids that would have some parents of the new millennium in tears worrying that their precious little young ones would get a scratch but the reality is that there are things allowed today that would have been not even close to allowed when I was in school. Some days when I pick my grandkids up from school I sit and chuckle to myself first with some of the outfits some of the boys wear to school. Man buns and skinny jeans, both ears pierced and wearing eyeliner and/or lipstick and the **REAL COOL BOYS** are wearing their pants around their knees walking around with their boxers completely showing. I always wondered every time I see these guys walking around like that if they know how that started.

The thing that is confusing to me is when these boys say they identify as girls and the schools are putting gender-neutral restrooms in schools. What does that even mean they identify as a female? If you were born with male plumbing, you are a boy and use the boy's bathroom how hard is that?

Boys back in the day had fashion statements and we knew who you were by what you wore. If you wore an army jacket had long hair and jeans you would have been a freak someone who smoked and partied on the weekends. Letterman jackets and sweaters, class rings, and short hair you would be a jock. Someone that either played football, baseball, or basketball for the school. The third major group was the greasers these were the kids trying to relive the 50s they would wear black or white solid T-shirts with leather jackets and blue jeans with motorcycle boots. All the other students were just students and had no stereotype they were just there to go to school.

What shocks me about today's young mothers is that they are screaming that everything and everyone needs to be politically correct, yet they find it acceptable to send their 8th grade or younger daughters to school looking like they will be standing on the corner after school soliciting dates. Girls are allowed a whole lot more freedom on what they are allowed to wear. Although I did go to public school there was a somewhat dress code back then.

PARTIES. When we had parties as kids, we had outdoor parties. The popular thing for us was to get a bunch of kids together and by kids, I mean 14-17. When I was a teenager I hung out with kids on a Friday or Saturday night. Most of these kids I knew by name and that was it. I had no idea what school they went to if they had any siblings or anything about them. All I needed to know was my friend and I would meet them at the mall someone would tell us where the party was and we'd give our few bucks then meet the gang in the party place with a quarter or a half barrel of beer and someone always had a bag of marijuana to share. There was a group of 8 of us that met every weekend, but that number could go as high as 20 depending who brought who and how many friends were invited. Now, these were all guys, not just any guys we wore long hair with bandanas with pocket chains, and army coats either waste long or trench coats. The old saying goes good girls like bad boys and I have to believe that to be true because every weekend no one came with a girl but every week we left with an eager and willing female to party with.

Most of the time these parties happened down in a remote area by the lake or we had a couple of isolated spots in the woods that were also a favorite. We would have a decent bonfire, a kegger, and a doobie or two to share. No one would get so shit-faced things would get out of hand. We had these parties every weekend outside over two years but Every once in a while, someone's parents would be gone on vacation or away for the weekend so we could be in a garage or basement which was always nicer in the winter months.

Even back then the police had a bad reputation for being more forceful with lawbreakers than need be but as always there were a couple of very cool cops that let us slide. One night we were just cruising for girls and decided to see what was happening around our high school sometimes after a game people hand around and chill. Not tonight, however, we drove around the school 2 or 3 times and no one was anywhere around so we just decided to go around the back and park in the teachers parking lot and toke a quick doobie before heading home. There was my friend James driving, I was sitting in the passenger seat, and a couple of friends in the back. We drove to the back, parked, and rolled our doob. On the second pass around, I rolled down my window to blow out the smoke and as I blew someone was standing right next to the car. I blew the smoke square in his face so I quickly rolled up the window cause it sounded like he said "you're BUSTED" with the window up and a lit doobie in the car with nowhere to get rid of it the 4 of us were a tad bit freaked out. Tap...Tap...Tap I slowly rolled the window down and all the trapped smoke made its way out and yes it was a cop standing there fighting back the laughter and he simply said, "you can't park here" and walked away. He did not walk to a squad car or a motorcycle he walked into the precinct that was 15' away from the parking lot we were blazing a joint. He was one of the cool cops of the day and he did not have to fill out a report we did not have to go to court he got a good laugh that night and the story made its way into this book. A WIN-WIN-WIN situation if you ask me.

OLDER=RISKIER As we got older the risks and daredevil stunts grew at the same pace we did. When I was 12 years old, I had a paper route. Unfortunately, at 12 years old I could not drive a car, but we had a cabin up north, so I was allowed to drive a minibike. At the time I only had my paper route a very short time with very little money saved. The nice thing was our neighbor up north was a very nice old lady who had grandsons that came up from the Chicago area to visit almost every weekend and when they were there I was there. They brought toys not the kind of toys that fit in the car but the kind of toys that required a trailer to haul. They would bring a 4-wheel ATV, a 3-wheel ATV and 2 50cc minibikes. Now there were only two grandsons and 4 toys so guess who got to ride whichever one they didn't? You got it...ME! At the time, the older boy was 13, I was 12 and his younger brother was also 12. When up north we had no adult supervision. We would fill the gas tanks and head into the woods for a day a bike riding and racing. Now keep in mind there were no cell phones no gas stations on these trails and quite literally if we took a wrong turn we be on our way to Canada. The north woods of Wisconsin is 100s 0f miles of wilderness and very easy to get turned around and lost. For over a year we drove the trailer around the cabin and never got lost. We put 100s of miles a weekend on those bikes and not once had been lost which while thinking about it was pretty impressive for a couple of kids.

After a little over a year, I was able to save enough money to buy my own motorcycle. I was able to purchase a 90cc Harley Davidson. I was almost 14 when I bought that bike and believe me, we had some fun together. As with riding our pedal bikes as kids helmets were recommended by not required. In both cases, we were not allowed on the road, so we felt helmets were unnecessary. Although I had my own bike, I still spend most of my time with the neighbor boys. There was a dirt road right next to our cabin that led down to a creek which was about a mile away so we had many races to the creek and back, we had wheely contests to see who could hold the highest and longest wheely. But the most intense things we did were the jumps. We did not use ramps or man-made objects we would simply find a hill in nature that was at the end of a straightaway and have at it. My Harley could easily hit 40MPH so trust me when I say I flew a loooong way and landed flush. If there would have been any sort of social media back, then we would all have been stars.

Now that was our summer fun. What pray tell did we do in the winter because our bikes would be stored until spring. This was Northwoods Wisconsin every kid old enough to see over the dash had some kind of snowmobile and my family was no different. We had a Rupp machine that I was not allowed to drive alone but we did go on many trail rides and the best were at night when we had the best chance to see deer out in the wild. The trail rides were fun but too calm for us so we would take the 3-wheeler ATV and tie a plastic saucer to it. Now back home in Milwaukee, we did go sledding but the most thrilling thing we could do is ride the sled down a long high hill. Yes, that was fun and somewhat exciting reaching a top speed of maybe 10 mph doing nothing but rolling down the hill getting wet if the saucer tipped over. Now up north, the ATV could do 25MPH in 2nd gear. Driving an ATV through roadside drainage ditches is much more exhilarating and a tad more dangerous than simply sliding down a hill. In a 1-mile stretch, there was a house, our cabin, and our neighbor's trailer all having ditches about 2 feet deep and a hill of about 30 degrees that went up and over the driveways. So imagine this... an ATV in the middle of the ditch then a 20' rope tied to the back and the other end attached to a plastic snow saucer with your butt on the sled...the driver takes off and hits the 2nd gear and you are swooshing from side to side in the ditch and then the ATV goes up and over the driveway with you know what is coming and WWEEEE you hit the hill flying as high as 5' in the air and a distance of 15' or more...3xs no helmet, no pads, NO FEAR just a completely pure adrenaline rush.

COMPETITION. At age 13 I was given my first BB gun. Over a short amount of time, I became I very good shot. Shooting soda cans off the post was always a way to show off our skills. The farther back you were the trickier the shot because the BB gun had the same amount of power if you shot the can from 5' or 25' the shooter would have to adjust the arc of the shot to score a hit. Well, one weekend my parents decided that I could bring a friend from home to the cabin. This turned out to be a very, very bad idea. I remember this day like we just did it yesterday. My friend and I could not sleep for whatever reason that part I do not remember but I do remember going in the basement with my BB gun a box of bb's and some empty soda cans. After about 15 minutes of shooting cans, my friend was like;

"I wonder if this gun is strong enough to go throw a pane glass window?" me being just as curious said;

"I don't know...try it"

Then the fun began. Yes, the gun was strong enough to go straight through a window. Then like the competitive person I am I said;

"I bet I can shoot a bb through the same hole."

I did not; He shot then I would try to hit the exact same hole before we knew it, it was 4 A.M. And we shot out every piece of glass in every window. I suppose it would be pointless saying how pissed my folks were and what kind of ass beating I got. And yes that too was the first and last time I was allowed to bring a friend.

TEACH THEM - EVERYONE HAS SOMETHING TO TEACH

Being a GREAT GRANDPA means you know, respect, and accept the responsibility of the task at hand. It is going to be you and the other adults they interact with daily that will be teaching them hot from cold, good from bad, and right from wrong. Teaching them about their family tree. Who they are, where we came from. Setting examples and showing them how to live and love. You are teaching them how to be a good human being.

Over the past couple of years, I have had some very interesting conversations with other grandparents my age or older that feel they have nothing to teach today's young people be it their grandkids or not.

One fella, I spoke with felt that because he worked a factory job recapping semi-truck tires which to him was a dirty meaningless dead-end job. He felt he has nothing to teach. His opinion was that he went to work at 5 A.M. Worked on his machine for 8 hours came home dirty and sweaty making just enough to put food on the table and a nice roof over his head with a little extra for bowling night and dart leagues.

As he continued to speak, I just sat and listened, when he was finished, I just smiled and said, "so you're a bowler? WOW, are you any good?"

"YES SIR, I WOULD SAY I AM BETTER THAN AVERAGE."

"So you never took them grandkids to watch you bowl or better yet took them to practice during open bowling? What about darts have you ever tossed a double in-double out or maybe needing 98 points to win the night and tossed a 20/20/double 19 to snatch victory away from the opponent when on his next turn only needed 18?"

"As a matter of fact, something like that just happened about a month ago."

"So you toss a decent game of darts?"

"Yes sir I am always in the top 10 in my league."

"THEN MY FRIEND LET ME TELL YOU, THERE IS PLENTY YOU HAVE TO TEACH."

"Like what?"

I went on to explain to this gentleman first and for most, in today's world, he was showing his grandkids that an honest job for an honest wage is a good thing. Secondly, I explained that I can't bowl it is a skill that I do not have. It is something one must learn so if it must be learned someone needs to teach it. Darts? Did you just stand in front of the dartboard and wall a you were an expert? No, you didn't. You either watch someone throw darts or chances are someone taught you how to hold it, someone taught you how to aim, and maybe even taught you speed and technique. Depending on what game you played adding or subtracting. So just imagine if you took the time to teach them how to play darts you unknowingly giving them lessons in physics, aerodynamics, and math. "Pretty important things to know don't you think?"

I spoke to a grandma who was a wife and mother from a very young age and she only had grandsons and felt she had nothing to teach them because they were boys. She was very proud of the fact she was able to pass her mothering skills to her daughter and she took great pride in the outstanding wife and mother her daughter had become. This woman had the good fortune of being a grandma at a very young age. Her daughter got pregnant, had her first son, got married had son number 2, and became a military widow all before the age of 23. Because she was a very recent college graduate and found herself a working career mom. My friend, the grandma, decided to allow her daughter and two young sons to say with her and she volunteered to babysit while Shelly was working.

Mary knows she is a very loving and caring grandma but she felt because she was a mom with only 1 daughter and the male role models in the boy's young lives were either permanently out of the picture or dead she had nothing extra to offer as far as teaching them. "Well, Mary lets think about that. Do either one of the boys like vegetables? What about raspberry pie or strawberry jelly?"

"Yeah, as a matter of fact, they both like many veggies and of course they like pie and jelly why do you ask?"

"Well I remember last year you brought me a jar of homemade jam and for last year's Christmas party you brought a veggie tray from your garden."

"YEAH AND?"

"Well, I was just thinking if the boys enjoy eating veggies and jam maybe they would like to see AND learn how it is done. You can maybe grab a couple of sprouts from your vegetable garden and put them in a cup of dirt or bowl until they were ready to plant and show the boys how veggies are prepared, nurtured then planted for the season."

"I was also thinking that I too have 2 young grandsons that LOVE raspberry jam. I do not know how to make homemade jelly and that is a skill I think would be very interesting."

"I also bet that my grandsons would be interested in learning how jam is made. I'm thinking that if my grandsons would like learning how to make homemade jam chances are yours will too."

She quickly replied; "You know that's a great idea, Now I know why people call you a GREAT GRANDPA."

Last spring my daughter and I were at a park we like going to early one morning fishing off the pier. An older gentleman was sitting on the other end of the pier and he was alone sitting in his wheelchair fishing for BASS. Knowing that bass fishing takes a lot of concentration and patience nobody said anything to anyone for a good two hours.

Then he finally broke the ice", "Anything biting on your side?"

"Yeah as a matter of fact we caught quite a few pan fish. How are you doing on that side?"

"Nothing yet. I am thinking about packing up and heading home."

"Already? It is still early"

"I know but I like to get home so my granddaughter and I can watch tennis on Saturday morning sports."

"My granddaughter is 10 years old and is fascinated with tennis. Unfortunately, my son, her daddy, has a job that requires him to work every Saturday. His wife - her mama, has to take care of the younger kids but she has no interest in tennis, so I make it a point to be there by 9, so we can grab a breakfast and head to my apartment to watch tennis uninterrupted".

This nice man told us how his granddaughter Maggie was amazed at the speed the ball is served the pinpoint accuracy of the return shot, and a gooooood volley. "She loves watching a few good back and forth shots."

"Really? Where does she play?"

"SHE DOESN'T. But, She would love to."

He continued; "We are a members of a club that has both indoor/outdoor courts. She will also be going to a school next semester that has a tennis team. The problem is we have the ability for lessons, I have the time and transportation to take her and she definitely has the desire to learn and be GREAT but how would she practice to improve?"

She could play against other kids her age and maybe even older kids while at the gym but how does she improve?" "YES, I know they say practice makes perfect but they also say the devil is in the details."

"Yes, all that is true but, listening to you talk you sound very passionate about helping her. Am I right?"

"YES, yes you are, but it makes things rather difficult sitting here in this chair. I would love to just get up and watch, critique, and help her hone her game."

"Let me ask you this, you speak very fondly of Maggie so I am betting she has been here with you and you taught her how to fish. She knows how to cast her line out, she no doubt can put a hook, sinker, and bobber on her line and get it ready. And if I was to be a betting man I would bet that she can even bait her hook. Depending on the time of day and the type of fish you were trying to catch she knows EXACTLY where to throw her line. Am I right?"

"YES, yes, you are. Maggie and I have been fishing off this pier since she was old enough to walk and hold a fishing pole"

"Then I am also willing to bet that you came out here took her MINNIE MOUSE fish pole out of the package and away she went! AM I RIGHT?"

"Of course not first I had to put a hook sinker and bobber on the line then bait the hook and toss the line by showing her how to reach back and release at the correct time. After she crawled up on my lap and we watched the bobber for movement..."

"Yeah, yeah, I get it you taught her how to fish one step at a time. So let me ask you something. When you watch tennis on Saturday morning do you understand the mechanics of movement? What movement generates the most power? How to prepare for a backhand return? Are you strong enough to hold a tennis racket? Do you own a cell phone with a decent camera? And finally, do you have access to the internet?"

"If you answered yes to ALL these questions I would suggest to you that you are in a GREAT position to teach — YES I SAID YOU CAN TEACH your granddaughter how to play and excel at the sport of tennis from your wheelchair."

"Let me suggest this to you, while your granddaughter plays take a video then take that video to her coach ask her to analyze it and give the both of you pointers on what needs to be improved." "Then after the coach shows you the technique she needs to practice you can also go to YOUTUBE and find videos that run in slow motion — As they say, where there is a will there is away."

"Video does not lie it does not discriminate it shows you exactly what you are doing either right or wrong. As a grandpa, you look like a genius to both the coach and Maggie. The upside is that you stay involved with an activity that your granddaughter is passionate about and helps build a life long bond."

"What a wonderful idea. THANK YOU"

THESE ARE ACTUAL CONVERSATIONS I HAD WITH OTHER GRANDPARENTS AND THE FACT I SHOWED THEM EVERYONE HAS SOMETHING TO TEACH MADE ME EVEN MORE AWARE OF WHAT I SAY AND DO AROUND MY GRANDKIDS.

As I wrote these few stories to share it dawned on me that no matter who you are or what you may think you have or have not done in your life EVERYONE has something to teach SOMEONE. If you are a grandparent EVERY time you are asked a question and give an answer you've just taught something.

For example, I have been teaching my grandkids for years without even thinking about it. Think about this, you are on your way to play at the mall. Your grandson is buckled safely in the back in his car seat. He can barely see out the window and is only 3 years old but EXTREMELY curious.

"WOW grandpa , what dat?"

"Well buddy that is called a SEMI TRUCK."

"COOOOOOL!"

A few minutes later while sitting at a red light some Harley guy revs his motor - "OOOWWWWWWW!" Aspen exclaimed, "Neat Grandpa was is dis?"

"Well little man that is called a MOTORCYCLE"

"COOOOOL a mo-mo sickle. Is it BLUE?"

"No, that is a BLACK motorcycle"

"BLACK OK, IT IS A BLACK mo-mo sickle"

Without thinking and certainly without realizing it you just taught your young grandson 3 things in the last minute and a half. Things he did not know before but was curious enough to ask about. Things that were insignificant to you but knowledge that will stay with him for the rest of his life. Just imagine all the life lessons you can teach those kids if you simply make yourself aware. Over the past decade, I have taught my grandkids dozens of things both intentional and unintentional.

The rest of this chapter are stories that I hope inspire you to realize EVERYBODY HAS SOMETHING TO TEACH SOMEBODY.

While writing this section I asked my grandsons what is the number 1 coolest thing I taught you so far? Their answers completely floored me.

"Aspen grandpa taught you how to do lots of things but what is your favorite so far?"

"How to swing on the swing."

"What do you mean swing on a swing?"

"You showed me how to pull the chain and pumped my feet. I tried and tried and tried but I wasn't swinging." "Then I asked you 'grandpa how are you going so high?, I am trying but won't move."

I was swinging on the swing next to his. So I started scraping my feet on the ground — unintentionally teaching him how to stop a swinging swing — "I'll be right there buddy."

I sat on the swing sat Aspen on my lap he grabbed on the chains I grabbed his hands and showed him that when we pull back and the chain at the same time stretch our legs forward-pointing our toes forward aiming at the treetops off in the distance. Once we were at the top stop pulling the chain let our legs down and back into a sitting position let gravity do its job and swing us backward. When we as far back as we were gonna get, "OK BUDDY, DO IT AGAIN, PUULLL, KICK AND POINT THOSE TOES!" As he did it I could feel the adrenaline rushing through his little body then we hit the pinnacle of the swing and we relaxed our legs let gravity do its job again and went further back than the time before. "OK, YOU READY...PULL...KICK"

We did this maybe 4 or 5 times and we were at the top end of both sides of the swing. Being maybe somewhere between 3 ½ and 4 years old and the very first time he was this high and swinging this fast I thought maybe just maybe he would be freaking out a bit. Boy was I wrong not only was he not freaking out, but he was also Screaming - "HIGHER GRANDPA CAN WE GO HIGHER?"

We swung together for 5-10 minutes or so than my legs started to fall asleep. After we came to a stop this crazy little dude wanted to do it alone. As I said he was maybe 4 at most and going that high being his first attempt my head went right to IF HE FALLS OFF HIS MOM WILL SHIT HER PANTS AND IF HE GETS HURT I WILL FEEL BAD. Well thankfully those thoughts went away quickly and I turned back into grandpa and let the boy be a boy.

"You sure your ready for this bud?"

"YES SIR"

"All righty then jump on up - would you like a push to get going?"

"No thanks, grandpa...I GOT THIS"

And away he went.

He stayed on that swing for hours trying to go higher and faster than everyone else.

That day in the park was over 4 years ago. Since then he has logged 100s of miles swinging on different swings and 1000s of feet flying through the air jumping off said swings marking distance jumps in the sand daring anyone else swinging to BEAT HIS JUMP. To this point with no broken bones.

Who would have thought that an innocent play day at the park would have been such a turning point in a young boy's life? What else did he learn besides simply how to swing on a swing? He learned self-confidence. He learned to believe in himself and he learned he can trust in ME.

The play area and the swing set was only the beginning of lessons learned that day. Not only for Aspen but for grandpa too. As I watched him swing and the smile on his face with the out-loud laughs. At that moment I had an epiphany not only do I have things to teach them BUT, I HAVE been teaching them, all along. Learning how to swing was Aspens number 1 thing he remembers me teaching him but when I asked Effers he said, "learning how to play GO FISH."

I have always enjoyed and understood card games. I also fancy myself very good at math and numbers so a deck of cards was always a natural learning tool for me. How I would use the cards is first we would learn the numbers. (At this point Aspen was already in K5 and learning how to count learning his colors which he already knew well because of the work we did with him at home).

Ethen and I sat down and he recognized a few numbers maybe 6-7 from 1-10. He would get confused because a 6 was an upside-down 9 and vise-versa. 7 s & 8 s also threw him off but going through the deck over and over and over made him more confident and Aspen already knowing the numbers and blurting the answer didn't hurt either. So there we sat, shuffle the deck flipping over the top card;

"6"

"Aspen please be quiet and let your brother tell me — Effers what number is this?"

"6"

"Very good... Do you know what color it is?"

"it's RED grandpa. It's a red 6!"

"VERY GOOD BUDDY A RED 6 YOU ARE CORRECT."

We would sometimes practice for an hour or more because even at a young age the boys were motivated by money. After we went through the entire deck a few times with minimal mistakes I would ask "ARE YOU READY TO TRY?"

Our deal was if he could make it through the entire deck and tell me the correct number and color error-free he earned himself a dollar if not we were done for the day and he would have to try again tomorrow. He was ready. I grabbed the deck shuffled and flipped a JACK I could see in his face he thought he knew but wasn't positive so counting on Aspen to help I said: "Effers just give it your best guess." Without missing a beat Aspen was like "IT'S A JACK."

"Jack? Yeppers little man, it's a jack but ETHEN, can you tell me what color it is?

"IT IS RED."

That was the first, last, and only mistake he made. Now he knows all 13 cards and what colors they are either black or red tomorrow we work on suits.

Again, I shuffled the cards and we divided it into two/two piles one stack for red which would either be hearts or diamonds and the second stack which was for spades and clubs. It only took 3x to get the two separated correctly then we moved on to separate the deck into all 4 suits. I was very impressed and surprised how fast he caught on got them ALL correct. After we did the practice decks 3 or 4 times with no mistakes I asked him if he was ready for the money challenge —

"SHOW ME THE MONEY GRANDPA hahahahahahaha".

PERFECT SCORE no mistakes... no hesitation. He called out the deck and earned himself a crisp 1 dollar bill that lasted about 15 minutes until we drove to the dollar store for a pack of Pokémon cards. On the way back from the store Effers asked if we would teach him how to play go fish. Believe me, it was a special feeling spreading out the cards and knowing he knew the cards and how to play because of what I taught him.

Since that day he has played many, games of GO FISH and every time we play together I smile a little inside.

THAT DAY I TAUGHT HIM ABOUT FAIR PLAY, SELF CONFIDENCE AND I BUILT A SOLID FOUNDATION FOR LEARNING.

At this time Ethen was too young to go out with me and those two were the only grandkids I could see at the time so Aspen spends A LOT of GRANDPA time with me until Ethen was old enough to join the party.

As they got older we became an inseparable trio. Where you found me you would find Aspen, and where you found Aspen you would find his little brother, following behind like a little puppy dog.

For most people and I am included here is when someone asks 'WHAT'S THE MAGIC WORDS?' for 99.9% of the courteous and English speaking population the correct answer would be 'PLEASE' or 'THANK YOU.'

For me the magic words are: *"WOW GRANDPA THAT WAS COOL! HOW'D YOU DO THAT?"*

Each and every time I knew I was about to teach them something new and at the same time re-enforce my GOD-LIKE status. For the most part, we spent a good deal of time playing at the play area of the mall but as they got older our mall time transitioned into park time. Our favorite park was Grant park because it has everything we enjoy. It has an 18-hole golf course with a putting green, there are at least 4 nice sized play areas, large steep bluffs to climb, and a beach right on Lake Michigan.

While going through my Facebook videos I realized I have been teaching them boys lessons about LIFE, SELF CONFIDENCE, and SELF IMPROVEMENT way longer than I thought.

June 3, 2015, The boys and I were driving through the park enjoying the day and Aspen noticed a play area we never played at before. Even though Aspen had just turned 4 and Effers was just over 2 I knew it would be a challenge to keep tabs on two very active young ones in an outdoor play area but I was willing to deal. After I parked the van and unbuckled both car seats BOTH boys made a break for the playground (I WAS ABLE TO RUN ALONG WITH THEM. ANOTHER REASON TO BE THANKFUL I AM A YOUNG GRANDPA) When we got there this playground had all the typical playground toys but it also had a small obstacle course that included a zip line. Ever since Aspen was able to walk he was intrigued with speed and how fast he could run. So after I explained what an obstacle course is and how it works he wanted to run it. But because this play area was designed for kids 8 and under I was not able to "SHOW" him how to run it but I could certainly explain what to do.

Here is how it was laid out. from the starting line the first obstacle is a balance beam you need to navigate then at the end of the beam there are 6 red rings approximately three feet apart with a circumference approximately the size of a manhole cover. All 6 were secured to the ground and frame tightly with chains which means there was some wiggle but not much. The first two rings were designed so that the participant had to climb up to the next ring, the middle two were flat and you could crawl straight through. the last two on a downward climb. After the rings came a 10x10 spiderweb looking challenge made of thick cargo rope with a center hole to crawl through. then when on the other side there were 3 swinging cones with a rope going through the center connect at the top and bottom by a very thick rope with about 12 inches of movement the challenge was to hop from cone to cone hanging on to the ropes without falling off. After the cones was a three-step ladder that got you up to the monkey bars. Swinging across the monkey bars to a platform then up the ladder down the slide, sprint across the play area up on a picnic table to the zip line grab on and swing to the other side. Once you hit the bumper the course was finished, and the clock stopped. The magic words were altered just a bit. It wasn't... 'GRANDPA THAT WAS COOL, HOW'D YOU DO THAT?' It was 'GRANDPA THIS LOOKS COOL. CAN YOU SHOW ME HOW TO DO THAT?'

And away we went.

The first thing I did was walk him through it explaining what needed to be done and how. We did that only twice and I asked if he understood and of course, he said yeah. I knew right from the jump I wanted to make this a VERY positive learning experience. How? By teaching the boys self-confidence and self-improvement. But at the same time, I made a very hard effort not to criticize anything. If they made a mistake and they no doubt will because they are 4 and 2 Years old. Mention it, correct it, practice the corrected method and PRAISE, PRAISE, PRAISE.

"OK BUDDY get on the starting line — READY. ON YOUR MARK, GET SET, GO!"

Off he went. Up and across the balance beam, standing at the end of the beam reaching for the first ring with a somewhat confused look not exactly sure how to get up. "Reach, step, pull, COME ON LITTLE MAN YOU GOT THIS, Reach, step, pull."

That confused look went away and a devious grin took its place because now he knew exactly what to do. He was a tad short for his age so he had a bit of a tough time but he DID NOT QUIT. Through the rings, he went onto the spiderweb rope scurried across easily and through the center hole. The moving cones were a bit of a challenge and he did fall a time or two but soldiered on.

Up the ladder but not strong enough to swing on the monkey bars so I held him by the waist "HAND, HAND, HAND" swung across with some help to the platform up the ladder than down the slide raced across the playground up on the picnic table to the zip line.

"GRANDPA NOW WHAT?"

"You put one hand behind the other jump as far as you can kick your feet and zip to the end."

That turned into a bigger challenge than anticipated. When he jumped and kicked his feet he would make it about half way but if I was there to give him a push he would sail across hitting the bumper no problems. Again and again, we tried and every time on his own NOPE with a push no problem.

Other kids were starting to join the challenge and soon there were 5-6 kids in line waiting for a turn. Some kids made it on their own yet others like Aspen needed a push. I was trying hard to figure it out and then I noticed something interesting ALL the kids that made it had their left hand in the front and ALL the kids that needed a push had their right hand in front. That made no sense to me why hand position would matter but just for giggles I told Aspen to switch his hands, and son of beech he EASILY made it across on his own. To this day I am not sure of the physics behind that zip line but hand position makes all the difference.

 When we finally left and I dropped them off with mom I was driving home reflecting on our day and feeling pretty good. I felt that I taught those boys a few very important life lessons that will stay with them for the rest of their life.

1. I taught them the value of self-confidence don't just THINK you can KNOW you can don't let ANYONE tell you that you can't do it NOT ME, NOT YOUR MOM, NOT GRANDMA, NOBODY. IF YOUR DREAMS ARE TAKING YOU TO THE MOON, THAN BUILD A ROCKET SHIP.

2. I taught them a "never quit" attitude if you keep trying the wrong way don't quit simply change your approach and keep trying until you get the results you want.

3. Aspen from that day until today knows how important it is to set a good example for his younger siblings. Ethen was following him like a little shadow wanting to do everything big brother was doing from swinging across the monkey bars to riding the zip line.

At the time of writing this that day in the park was over 5 years ago. We still go to that play area a couple of times a month they still enjoy it and more importantly remember and use the lessons they learned that day

May 19, 2013, When Aspen first learned to walk he liked to run. He also enjoyed grandpa time. Even at this very young age, he was a very social kid. We spent a lot of time together when he was young and before he had siblings that could come with. This particular day we happened to be at the mall because it was the day after his birthday and I had to work yesterday so I took him for a GRANDPA DAY just he and I. He was two and the traditional mode of transport for a two-year-old in my family was riding up on my shoulders. The tradition was not gonna stop with the grandkids especially my first grandson. As we walked around the mall I asked what we should do. Again only being 2 years old words at times were hard to understand but I did make out EAT. So off to the food court we went. After lunch and on the way to the play area we stopped for a sample of cookie dough, Ice cream then some frozen yogurt by the time we got to the play area the boy was jacked on sugar. Even at the early age of 2, Aspen had a special gift for being the leader of the pack. Within 30 seconds of taking his shoes off, he had the other kids(even older kids) organized and playing tag. We stayed at the mall for a couple of hours that day and we had a blast. Whenever I am with them I make it a point to try and encourage good behavior point out and correct misbehavior. Teach them life lessons when the opportunity to do so presents itself. However today I was the one who was taught a life lesson... The boy is a natural leader.

Some parents or grandparents may have looked at this as "showing off" or perhaps they prefer to play alone stopping or discouraging him. But for me, I just let him do his thing and watched how it played out. When we left and I was talking to him and recapping the day I made sure he knew I was very impressed with the way he played and organized the other kids.

I TAUGHT HIM HOW TO BELIEVE IN HIMSELF. THAT SELF CONFIDENCE IS A GOOD THING & LEADERS NOT FOLLOWERS WILL GO FAR IN THIS WORLD.

That day at the mall was over 7 years ago and since then he has organized 100s of kids at many different playgrounds, played tag, hide-n-seek even building a sandcastle or two along the way. He is a leader at school organizing kids for basketball, kickball, and a new game the call GAGA ball which I believe is just dodge ball but played in a pit. He is often picked to demonstrate techniques and is a role model in Taekwondo. Most importantly a GREAT big brother.

August 23, 2017, with summer winding down and the boys and I spent quite a bit of time together we were trying to think of different things to try. During the summer we spend time playing in the mall and at different parks. Although the playground equipment was fun it was also very similar in all the parks so at times it could be somewhat boring especially if there were no other kids to play with. While driving around we drove by Dunham's sporting goods store so we decided to stop and maybe get some ideas. We walked by golf equipment, tennis stuff, weight sets, boating and swimming area ALL of may have been fun but unfortunately nothing we could do TODAY. As we were getting ready to walk out the door I happened to see a clearance sign and went to check it out. A multi-colored flashing battery-operated, glow in the dark FRISBEE for $ 5. I believe we just found our next toy.

"Grandpa, what is that?"

"You guys never played with a Frisbee before?"

"NOPE" they both replied.

Well, it indeed looks like we found our new toy. Paid the lady and headed straight for a beach.

The rest of the day turned out to be very interesting indeed. As I said it was a day late August mid-afternoon so the temp was extremely hot so we headed to the beach with our new toy.

Teaching the boys how to toss a Frisbee was EASY they both caught on quick and were tossing like old hippies in no time. Traditional toss, reverse wrist snap toss, and of course the from behind your back softball pitch toss. Me to Aspen, Aspen to Ethen, then Ethen back to me.

The game went for 45 minutes or so then they both got overheated and decided the waves of Lake Michigan looked pretty inviting so they both jumped on in. I on the other hand am not at all fond of cold lake water. I much prefer the heated pool at my gym or the very least water temps above 70 so jumping into icy cold water is not for me. The boys both ran in to the water waist deep and did a headfirst dive. As they splashed and played I was walking along the waterfront looking for smooth flat rocks to skip. I think they both thought I was gathering rocks to see how far I could throw. They both know I have a great arm and they expected to see I long toss into the water. But when they saw me lean sideways and fling the rock sidearm skipping across the top of the water I heard those ever magical words; "WOW GRANDPA THAT WAS COOL, HOW'D YOU DO THAT?"

"Well fellas come on over and I'll show ya." "First we need to find rocks. What I want you to look for are rocks that are just a bit bigger than a .50 cent piece. They should be flat and smooth and round as Possible."

We walked the edge of the lake looking smooth flat skipping stones. When we all had 7-8 rocks we went to the edge of the water for the demonstration "OK boys are we ready?"

"OK skipping rocks is very similar to the second way I showed you how to throw the Frisbee. 1st we stand at attention facing the water. GOOD, now I want you to take your right hand make a finger gun and point it straight right. Like this. OK very nice." "NOW turn your hand so your palm is facing down and take your finger gun and turn it into a backward "C" just like this."

EXCELLENT now take your rock place it between your finger and thumb and hold it tight." "NICE. Now, let's turn sideways with the left shoulder facing the water, lean a little bit forward and look at the water, I want you to look at the water and pretend it is a very large piece of glass and when you throw the rock your task is NOT TO BREAK THE GLASS. BUT SKIM IT ACROSS THE TOP. GOT IT?"

Aspen said; "I got it, grandpa."

"Yeah me too." Replied Effers.

"OK watch. I bent over a bit... look at my target... bring my arm back and with a hard sidearm motion and a FLICK of my wrist", SKIP, SKIP, SKIP, SKIP, skip, skip, (plunk), "6 jumps. Your turn Aspen" and with the most intense look in his eye that I have ever seen and that determined look on his face, he repeated out loud... "BEND OVER A BIT, LOOK AT MY TARGET, ARM BACK AND THROW."

PLUNK. That poor boy submarined his first attempt but no tears, and no shouting just a very shocked look on his face.

"Looks like you would have SMASHED the glass Huh, buddy?"

"Yeah. That is way harder than it looks."

"You ready Effers?"

"I think so."

"Okay." then he said aloud; "BEND OVER A BIT, LOOK AT MY TARGET...ARM BACK AND THROW"

"Well buddy at least you didn't smash the glass you flung the rock WAY over it."

We stayed at the lake that day for hours. Both boys tossed 100s of rocks and COULD BARELY lift their arms by the time we left but now they both skip rocks with no trouble.

That day was a turning point in our relationship and also a turning point for them. What life lessons were taught that day? In my opinion two of the most important, as young men and future martial artists.

THEY BOTH LEARNED THAT PRACTICE MAKES PERFECT THEY BOTH LEARNED TO RESPECT THEIR ELDERS MORE THAN THEY ALREADY DID CAUSE

SOMETIMES YOUR ELDERS CAN TEACH YOU SOME COOL STUFF.

The day we spent at the lake was almost 3 years ago from the date of writing this paragraph. Since that day we have been to no less than 20 different lakes, ponds, or some other body of water either fishing, swimming, or perhaps just a nature hike, and every single time WITHOUT EXCEPTION they run to the water grab a few rocks, and skip them before we do anything else. If there happens to be someone else at the lake and say "HEY, YOU WANNA SEE US SKIP A ROCK?. GRANDPA TAUGHT US."

YES IT MAKES ME SMILE WITH PRIDE EACH AND EVERY TIME KNOWING THAT THEY FIND IT NECESSARY TO SHOW THEIR SKILL AND TO MAKE SURE THEY KNOW THAT GRANDPA TAUGHT ME

May 16th, 2019; Today is Auntie Da's birthday and 2 days before Aspens 8 birthday so we were out looking for presents for both of them. I knew Amanda wanted a tattoo so we were going to several shops getting price quotes.

Aspen on the other hand has been asking for a pair of Jordan basketball shoes so we were stopping and shopping at many different department stores looking for Jordan's. Nothing available in the shoe departments of department stores but one salesgirl said her younger brother got lucky and found a pair at a second-hand sporting goods store. That indeed sounded like a great idea so we headed over to a PLAY IT AGAIN SPORTS shop that was very nearby. The salesman said they rarely if ever got used basketball shoes in this location but if we ever needed baseball cleats or golf shoes this is the place. But he did tell us that there was a Rogan's shoe store just down the road and knew for a fact they had a very nice selection of boys and men's basketball shoes including Jordan's. We went down to the store and they indeed had a great selection which included AND 1, Nike, and some other brands I never heard of but we did not see the Jordan's. As we looked around we found a pair of AND 1s that he liked and they were $45. On the way to the register just for giggles, I asked the sales guy why the did not carry Jordan basketball shoes. "YES sir we do. We have a section of just Jordan b-ball shoes up in the front corner of the store." Needless to say, Aspen was extremely excited, so we put the AND 1s back and started looking through the Jordan's. To be completely honest I almost pissed myself when I saw how much kids shoes cost. Anywhere between $90-$300 at this store for shoes that he would outgrow or wear out in a couple of months. I don't spend anywhere close to that much for MY shoes so spending a minimum of 90 bucks for a pair of kid's shoes was TOTALLY out of the question. We looked again and just to be sure we looked one more time and even on sale the least expensive pair was 90 bucks plus tax.

That was not happening so I told him I would be willing to buy him the other shoes even though I still wouldn't pay that much for my shoes. To my surprise and disappointment, Aspen uncharacteristically pitched a fit. I don't mean he whined because he was disappointed I mean he SCREAMED he wanted Jordan's that AND1 were garbage and would not wear them.

So with no yelling no discussion I just put the shoes back on the shelf and walked out. As he watched me walkout, the screaming stopped and he quietly followed behind me and got in the back seat not saying a word. He knew I was pissed and it would be very beneficial for him to get in the car, keep his mouth shut and just let me take him home. Nothing was said the entire ride home and when we pulled up in front of his house I simply said, "see you tomorrow." I watched him walk in to make sure he was OK as I always do and took off.

As I drove home, I started to think about things and realized he normally does not have a hissy fit like that, but he is only a kid. I thought and pondered and then thought some more to my surprise came up with an explanation and a solution while remaining calm. I thought I do a lot of business on eBay and sell quite a bit online so what if I looked on Craig's list, Market place, and eBay to see if any local sellers had Jordan shoes for sale. He knew about market place and we looked once or twice on eBay for Pokémon cards but I rally never explained the full power and potential of online shopping. I looked myself that evening and YES there are many pairs of boys shoes so tomorrow he learns how to bargain hunt. We had some time between after school and TKD class so we went to Whitnall Park as we often do before class but today instead of practice and play we sat at the picnic table and I showed him how to search Market place. Our first search was - boys gym shoes size 2 - there were too many ads so we narrowed it down to -Jordan's size 2 - A much more manageable search. We read several entries and narrowed it down to "JORDAN HIGH TOP BASKETBALL SHOES. WORN TWICE AND OUTGROWN. EXCELLENT CONDITION $20" we immediately text to see if available and yes they were. We took a 7-minute ride out to the burbs to take a look. She had a very nice pair of size 2, Jordan's but the younger grandson felt a little left out so this nice lady found another pair of size 1 shoes that were in VERY GOOD shape so they both had "NEW" shoes. I was happy, the boys were happy and this generous lady was happy. A WIN-WIN-WIN situation.

She sold her shoes and we were able to get $210 worth of shoes for 20 bucks. A few days later this same lady had reached out to me saying they had a rummage sale over the weekend and nothing sold. Her husband just wanted everything gone and if we didn't mind gently used clothes we could have anything we could use. Neither one of the boys cared so we took a ride back out there and left with 7 trash bags of very nice well-fitting clothes. Again

I was thankful, the kids were all happy because we found clothes that the girls liked also, mom was happy because we saved no less than $1000 on store-bought clothes and the lady was VERY happy because she did us a huge solid and at the same time getting rid of a large portion of things they wanted gone. Another WIN-WIN-WIN-WIN situation.

Since that day Aspen uses market place quite often. He goes online for things he wants and he also goes looking for products for me. He has also become very efficient at posting ads for things we are selling.

I FEEL LIKE I TAUGHT HIM THERE ARE OPTIONS. YOU WANT MONEY YOU DO NOT NEED TO WORK FOR SOMEONE ELSE. FIND A WAY AND EARN IT YOURSELF!

JUNE 6, 2020; Sometimes teaching/learning opportunities come at the strangest times. It has been part of my morning ritual for weeks now to go downstairs stand by the gate and let the baby see or hear me and she will come running hands up yelling "GAM PA... GAM PA" both of us well aware she wants breakfast. Today was different. She did see me...she did a come running and she did want breakfast but the difference today was the other young ones. The family has been planning a WATER BALLOON fight for days now but for one reason or another were not able to get outside. So as I am sitting there with the baby while she eats one by one the other young ones were coming to me to blow up their balloons because apparently, 69 is too cold to have a water balloon fight so they just wanted to play inside with balloons. After the second one was blown up and tied I heard those magic words: "WOW GRANDPA THAT IS COOL! HOW DO YOU DO THAT?"

As I said teaching chances come out of the blue. I would have never imagined that 4 young ones would have been so mesmerized and intrigued on how to inflate and tie a simple balloon

SIMPLE EVERYDAY THINGS YOU HAVE DONE A 1000xs COULD BE AN AMAZING TASK FOR A CHILD SO ALWAYS TAKE THEIR INQUIRIES SERIOUSLY AND WITH RESPECT.

June 10 2016; Today was a learning experience for me. It was a perfect late spring day. The temperature was in the mid-70s, very sunny, and no wind. I had just made quite a bit of money on a house sale I just closed so I suggested to the girls we go to have a fancy lunch then take the young one's fishing. The kids all like pancakes and there is a very nice little mexican cafe near my house that has very good food that offers a nice lunch special as well as sells breakfast all day. 3 orders of steak enchiladas and 3 orders of MICKEY MOUSE pancakes later we are on our way to the store for fishing equipment. 2 kiddy poles 1 full-size pole, a combo pack of hooks, bobbers, and sinkers. Finally a cartoon of night crawlers and off to the park we went.

Mama and her sister in other words both my daughters have enjoyed fishing since they have been young girls so when her boys were old enough to hold a fishing pole we were excited to get them on the water. BUT when we did get there we had two boys age 4 and 2 the baby was only a few months old and stayed in her stroller. We set up the full-size pull and 1 of the kiddy poles and tried to have either one of the boys hold it. The 3 adults were taking turns fishing with the adult pull while the other one kept trying to keep the two-year-old from either falling or jumping off the pier into the water. And finally, the last person trying to convince the 4-year old that fishing is fun. We tried for about 45 minutes chasing one then the other one decided that running from end to end of the pier was more fun than fishing.

THE LESSON TO BE LEARNED HERE IS EVEN THOUGH YOU MAY LIKE SOMETHING KIDS ARE PEOPLE AND HAVE THEIR IDEA OF WHAT IS FUN AND CERTAINLY KNOW WHAT THEY LIKE SO DON'T FORCE THEM TO DO THINGS THINKING BECAUSE YOU LIKE SOMETHING THEY WILL TOO.

SEPTEMBER 2, 2019; For a month now I have listened to nothing but "THE SECRET" while driving in my car. I believe in the law of attraction and the power of the human mind to create a life that you want. In my car, it doesn't matter who is with me or if I am driving alone the CDs are always playing. Some people think I waste my time and some are skeptical and listen with some interest but that is as far as it goes. But the boys, the boys are true believers. Now while playing cards they ask the universe for the cards they need or if we are doing something and some bad or negative words are said I am reminded to be careful because the universe may give me what I am asking for. Here is the story that made both boys TRUE BELIEVERS IN THE LAW OF ATTRACTION On this day it was raining and nasty outside so we could not go to the park after class for we decided to go play at the mall before taking them home today. When we got to the mall before we even parked Aspen asked if we could go play some games at the new arcade. (this was time 1 the idea of the arcade was released to the universe) Unfortunately, I had very little cash and the arcade was somewhat pricey, so I had to say no maybe later. On the way to the play area, we stopped at the toy store for exactly 18 minutes and continued to the play area. On route, we were distracted by a man standing in the doorway of a cookie dough store asking if we cared for a free sample so naturally, we all tried a free sample of cookie dough which only took a few minutes. The quest continued. A few stores down there was a new TEA store so another salesperson standing out in the hall offering free samples of hot or iced tea. We stopped tried a couple of sips of hot tea but Before we left heading to the play area Aspen was like "grandpa, can we check the arcade before we go to the play area?", "not right now buddy we will stop before we head out" (This was the 2nd time the idea of going to the arcade was released to the universe.) The play area was not quite as fun as usual with the thought of playing in the arcade looming in their heads. We normally spend a minimum of 2 hours in the play area but today we stayed less than 1 hour "Grandpa, can we go now?" (time number 3 this time with excitement and high energy emotions) "sure guys just keep in mind I don't have much cash so we can go and see if they are running any specials" (time number 4 the arcade was mentioned) "that's ok grandpa we just want to look and see what games they have" (time 5), On the way to the arcade we passed by a frozen yogurt stand and again they were offering free samples so yes we stopped for a few minutes trying frozen yogurt.

Now, what happened next NON-BELIEVERS call it a happy coincidence for me and my grandsons it is the universe and the power of attraction working in all its glory. Let us review the chain of events that got us here. It started with the weather normally we would have been playing in the park. 2nd The idea of playing in the arcade was released 5xs next we did not go directly to the arcade from the car. We did a specific chain of events that took a specific amount of time that brought us to the front door of the arcade AT THIS SPECIFIC MOMENT. The arcade was packed. We walked around looking at games for about 10 minutes then decided to go to the counter and see if there were any current gaming specials. There was not but instead of being sad and disappointed both of them were excited that I at least brought them in to look. I was very happy and proud but with no money staying there was silly. "Come on fellas We have to go", As I touched both of their shoulders and started walking out I just happened to look down and on the floor there right on the floor in front of us was an arcade card. I picked it up and was going to toss it in the trash on the way out but Aspen was like; "maybe there's money on it grandpa."

"I doubt it buddy but we can certainly check."As I said the chain of events that brought us to that spot at that time were specific and THE UNIVERSE responded to the emotional requests of two young boys; *THERE were 67 MINUTES OF GAME TIME ON THAT CARD. THE BOYS WERE ECSTATIC & BOTH PLAYED 2 PLAYER GAMES AND SHARED THE CARD. WHAT I TAUGHT THEM THAT DAY WAS TO HAVE FAITH. BELIEVE IN THE UNSEEN AND THE POWER OF THE LAW OF ATTRACTION. BELIEVE AND ACHIEVE.*

ROLE MODEL(s)

I knew for a very long time how important being a GREAT GRANDPA was going be. I studied and prepared for it but I never thought about how important being a good ROLE MODEL was going to be. From the first time they hear your voice they hear the voice of a strong, caring, and gentle man, they hear the voice of grandpa. From the very first time they see your face, they may see whiskers, They may glance at your nose for a second. they may even see a wrinkle or two but what they will see for sure is warm and gentle eyes looking down at them with a happy tear or two. They see the face of grandpa. From the first time you hold them, they can feel the strong secure safety of your arms. As you hand them back to Mama for the first time and he feels the skin on skin contact for the first time he knows he felt the hands of grandpa. From the second they are born you are no longer just YOU, you are grandpa and more importantly, you are their life-long ROLE MODEL.

What is a role model? When asked I answered; "someone to look up to."

While thinking about it and writing this chapter I asked the grand babies "What is a role model", Aspen answered "MICHAEL JORDAN." Ethen answered, "MY TEACHER.", I didn't even have to ask and Harlow yelled "QUEEN ELSA." Obviously, they didn't understand my question but their answers gave me the info I wanted. From the instant they are brought into this world they are seeing, smelling, touching, feeling, hearing. tasting and experiencing life all around them. From birth to approximately 5-6 years old a child's conscience and subconscious mind is like a memory sponge soaking up all the knowledge their little brain can hold. At some level, kids remember everything they are exposed to. So in reality you are helping form their future relationships, you are forming their taste in food, their taste in music, their relationship with money you are building their life long foundations.

Let me give you a simple but powerful example, You have a beautiful baby girl that just turned 6 months old and for some unknown reason is having trouble falling asleep at a reasonable hour so you try all kinds of different things and nothing works. Then one night you are completely exhausted and watching "WILLIE WONKA AND THE CHOCOLATE FACTORY." All of a sudden you noticed she yawned less than a minute later SOUND ASLEEP. So you gently and very, very carefully carry your bundle of joy to her crib. Like a gift from God, she slept through the night and for the first time in weeks...SO DID YOU. The next night you are getting ready for nye-nye and the fussing begins. The fussing soon turns into crying which escalates into full-blown screaming. Not wanting to deal with a screaming baby you decide to bring her out to the rocking chair to try and calm her. After a few minutes, you suddenly remember last night and think "HMMM I WONDER" and promptly put in WILLIE WONKA in the DVD player. As the movie plays she instantly calms down and intensely listens. The movie has been playing for exactly 13.8 minutes and YAWWWWN... by the time the movie clock shows 15 minutes she is sound asleep. Not being completely sure if this is a happy coincidence she fell asleep at the exact same place as yesterday you simply put her to bed and enjoy another good night's sleep. Tomorrow night bedtime. No bed no crying no fussing you decide to try an experiment. Sitting in the rocker, the movie in the DVD player remote in hand with your granddaughter on your lap. Again, the movie starts at the 13.8-minute mark the yawns start and by minute 15 she is sound asleep. For the next few nights, this is your routine. Then you decide to be somewhat creative and put the DVD player where she can hear it while laying in her crib. HALLELUJAH it works 13.8 minutes to get drowsy and sound asleep by 15 minutes.

MY FRIEND, YOU HAVE JUST CREATED A LIFELONG ANCHOR. YOU ARE ALSO A ROLE MODEL. WHY? BECAUSE FOR THE REST OF HER LIFE SHE IS GOING TO ASSOCIATE YOU TO SAFE & SOUND SLEEP.

Being a great grandpa means that kids will look to you for a number of different reasons but after years of spending time with Aspen day after day then night after night it became VERY clear I am his main male role model. As he gets older and spends more time at school in Taekwondo and at home, he is starting to mature and spread his wings making his own decisions plus getting more and more responsibility on the home front. Yes, he still looks to me for guidance and advice but not like when he was little. As he gets older I can see more and more of me in his actions, his vocabulary. The things he wants to do, The way he wants to do them. It was a very eye-opening experience the first time Aspen answered "YES I'M AWARE", That is a phrase I have been using sarcastically for years. For example, 98 degrees and 100% humidity and someone says "IT IS REALLY HOT OUT HERE",

"WOW aren't you miss obvious." That's the same place I would say, "Yes I am aware."

March 23, 2019; The title of GREAT GRANDPA & ROLE MODEL carry a lot of weight and responsibility not only do you need to continually watch what you do and think before you speak. YOU MUST ALWAYS KEEP YOUR WORD & DO WHAT YOU SAY YOU'LL DO.

Today was finally the day THE BEST OF THE BEST CHO'S TAEKWONDO TOURNAMENT. Ethen had just recently signed up for classes and at the time was a brand new white belt so I decided to allow him to compete but only to compete in the board break event. However, Aspen, on the other hand, has been in TKD for months and in my opinion, is a natural. For his age bracket and belt rank he could compete in the 3 different events BOARD BREAK, FORM, and SPARRING.

We talked it over and decided that board break & forms would be his best chance to win first place trophies. We knew about this competition and prepared for this day for months. In class, after class, asking the instructors for extra time and advice. We practiced in the park, at the house, watched videos, watched, and copied other black belts to see what a good crisp form was supposed to look like.

HE WAS STOKED...HE WAS READY...BUT MOST IMPORTANTLY HE WAS CONFIDENT.

Let me back up here, Aspen has been asking his mom for MONTHS to get his ears pierced and she kept saying he was not old enough. At the time he was 7 about to turn 8 in May and 8 years old was the age he could get his ears pierced. Hmmm, getting his ears pierced... sounded like an excellent way to keep him motivated to do well and practice. As his grandpa, I watch him practice and keep a very close eye on how the other students in his class/age group looked and practiced I was very confident he would EASILY walk away with two first-place trophies. For weeks I talked to him as if he had already won. The prize at the end of this rainbow was simply HE WINS 2 FIRST PLACE TROPHIES HE GETS HIS EARS PIERCED. I wanted to use this as motivation and it NEVER once crossed my mind HE MAY LOOSE. He was confident, I was confident and the moment of truth was upon us. The first event was FORMS and he did his so many times he probably did it in his sleep. Aspen was the first competitor of the 4 in his group. Flawless...he did an excellent job...snap on his punches...very high & good technique on his kicks then a very confident Ki-op at the end.

He definitely set the bar high and was the one to beat. Competitors 2 & 3 were OK but Aspen was still in the lead. Competitor number 4 was a young lady from a different branch and she was VERY good however

I felt Aspen had higher kicks, crisper punches, and an overall better form. Unfortunately, the judging master instructor did not see the same thing I did(I was watching through rose-colored grandpa glasses) She saw them as even. They did not have two first-place trophies so the battle for first came down to a HEAD to HEAD SIDE by SIDE FORM. They both did EXCELLENT. It was so close that the master instructor had to consult with the floor judge and together could not pick a winner so they had to bring it to the Grand Master.

After about a 15 minute discussion they awarded the trophy to competitor number 4. when I asked why I was told it came down the kicks...Aspen had very high and powerful kicks but competitor 4 had a slight edge on technique and in scoring forms technique scores higher than height & power. When it was all said and done and the dust finally settled Aspen was awarded a 2nd place trophy. I was VERY proud he did his best and they needed the Grand Master to make the final decision. I was PROUD but after he received the award Aspen can sulking off the mat head down and in tears. "BUDDY, ARE YOU KIDDING ME? TEARS? Your crying cause you didn't win? You did fantastic little man. What's the problem?"

At this point, I may have been a tad sarcastic with a bit of anger in my voice. In my world and the way I grow up he was acting like a spoiled little sore loser but thankfully it is not back in the day it was today and I knew he understood the possibility of maybe loosing usually he just gets mad and tries harder next time. Something was different today, he is not a sore loser nor does he cry because he lost "Ok dude what's the issue" he turned and planted his head in my shoulder "grandpa I lost and came in 2nd", "yeah I know you did fantastic." "BUT NOW YOU'RE MAD AT ME AND I CAN'T GET MY EARS PIERCED."

My heart shattered into 1000s of pieces and my stomach sank into my knees. So what started as a motivational tool, a way to keep him focused and motivated in reality turned out to backfire on me in the worst possible way. Not only did he crash and burn from thinking I was mad at him for not winning I was worried that he would be crushed and not give his all in the board break event.

"OH GOD NO BUDDY I AM NOT AT ALL MAD AT YOU I am extremely PROUD of you. And no matter how you do in the board break I will get your ears pierced for your birthday."

It took a while but he finally calmed down and did his board breaks the way we practiced and came away with the first-place trophy The moral of this story is as a grandpa and role model kids believe EVERYTHING you say so be careful what you promise. They also have this idea that disappointment equals anger, so they try hard not to disappoint and get you mad at them.

THE LESSON HERE WAS LEARNED BY ME. INSTEAD OF PROMISING EAR PIERCINGS FOR TWO FIRST PLACE FINISHES AND PUTTING A TON OF UNNECESSARY PRESSURE ON THE BOY TO WIN. I SIMPLY SHOULD HAVE MADE SURE HE DID HIS BEST THEN REGARDLESS OF THE RESULTS TAKE HIM TO GET HIS EARS PIERCED AS A REWARD FOR A JOB WELL DONE!

March 30, 2019; only 1 week after the tournament I have been noticing more and more the impact and influence I have on the boys when it comes to TKD. They know that I consider it very important and that I pay a lot of money for them to attend class. Today as well as most Saturdays before class they are asked to practice forms or techniques and during class, they could work on whatever they needed to have a chance to earn a stripe. Today the boys got to class and there were a few other boys already playing a game of tag. 98% of the students on the floor were doing what they were supposed to be doing but Aspen, Ethen, and 4 or 5 other students found it acceptable in their minds to play tag. I understand that boys will be boys but we have had this conversation more than once" FELLAS WHEN YOU WALK THROUGH THE DOOR YOU ARE COMMITTING TO 50 MINUTES OF SERIOUS TRAINING. YOU AGREE TO LEAVE THE FUN GAMES AND CLOWNING OUTSIDE."

When they bow in they are supposed to show respect to the flags, to the school, and their instructors. So when they bowed in and within a blink of the eye were playing tag I was a tad upset. Partially because they were playing tag but to me, more importantly, they were two of the highest belt ranks on the floor and the other boys in the game were the same rank or higher, High belts are the example students for the class.

"Guys, FELLAS, ASPEN, ETHEN, HOLD ON" they both stopped to hear me (yes the other kids kept running around) "GUYS YOU HAVING FUN? YEAH, IT LOOKS LIKE YOU'RE HAVING FUN. BUT DO ME A FAVOR CAN YOU TELL ME WHEN WAS THE LAST TIME EITHER OF YOU RECEIVED A STRIPE FOR PLAYING TAG. PLUS, YOU ARE THE HIGHEST BELTS ON THE FLOOR AND SHOULD BE SETTING AN EXAMPLE FOR THESE KIDS. HOW ABOUT YOUR PLAYMATES? HAVE ANY OF THEM EVER GOT A STRIPE FOR PLAYING TAG? I DOUBT IT BUT YOU GUYS ARE TELLING THESE YOUNGER NEWER LOWER BELT STUDENTS THAT TAG

AND NOT DOING WHAT YOUR ASKED IS ACCEPTABLE BEHAVIOR ONCE THEY GET TO A CERTAIN RANK...NICE JOB"

I was shocked I only raised my voice so I would be heard but I certainly was not shouting but all the other parents, most of the students on the floor and the two young instructors who were organizing the floor ALL STOPPED and listened as I scolded the boys.

Being a role model sometimes unintentionally extends to people and places it was never meant to but nevertheless finds its way in. Since that day I have heard both young instructors especially the young female teacher when she is trying to settle down a few rambunctious boys "what rank are you boys" or "you know you'll never get a stripe for _____." I have also brought the boys to class and kids will be in the all-purpose room clowning around unattended or even a time or two we walked in and other parents would stop their kids from clowning around.

Both boys now have a reputation for working hard and trying in class. They are both leaders and example students. It is even to a point that one father will pull Aspen off to the side and get a report on how his son did in class.

THEY ARE BOTH VERY PROUD OF THEIR SKILLS, PROUD TO HAVE OTHER STUDENTS LOOK UP TO THEM & PROUD TO KNOW THEY ARE AN INSPIRATION TO SOME BUT ARE BOTH ROLE MODELS IN THE SCHOOL

BUDDY DAY... Today was buddy day at TKD which means that any active student could invite and sponsor any person they felt might enjoy a free class then maybe sign up for lessons. Harlow had come to watch the class on several occasions and really enjoyed watching. She also practices along with them when they practice at home plus she is kind of the coach suggesting what and how many techniques or forms they should practice. She even understands that push-ups. Sit-ups and jumping jacks are an essential part of the practice and make the boys do those too. So when the choice of who to bring for buddy night the choice was east and they both said "HARLOW."

Harlow is truly a girly girl. Wears cute little dresses and has a good number of baby dolls and loves ponytails in her hair She was 4 years old at the time and had very few female role models(just her mother actually) so she identified with the females from the movie frozen walking around constantly saying "I AM QUEEN ELSA" so when they suggested bringing her I was somewhat tossed. She would either be a great choice and perfect student or the biggest pain in the butt telling the instructor, "YOU CAN'T TELL ME WHAT TO DO I AM

QUEEN ELSA."

Well, they brought her as a buddy and she was a model student. But the thing that pleasantly surprised me the most was during class Ethen was the one correcting her. He was very proud that his little sister was there trying and he knew what to do to show her the movements. HE WAS HER ROLE MODEL. As the class progressed, I was watching Harlow working & trying very hard. I saw madam Monique in the front of the class walking around showing students correct form and technique and when she got to Harlow she was standing directly in front of her and showing her the correct movement of a FRONT PUNCH. Both girls had a smile, both girls punched and ki-oped at the same time and as I watch them working together, I have seen Harlow's future.

I am hoping to get Harlow in TKD very soon because I believe all the instructors make wonderful teachers. I believe Monique would also be an outstanding role model for an active young girl.

May 15, 2020, If you are reading this book you will no doubt remember the quarantine that accompanied the corona-virus in the spring through the summer of 2020. on this particular day I have noticed a very big difference in the way both boys were talking, the tones they were using, vocabulary, EVERYTHING was different. I knew Effers was simply emulating Aspen but the question was where or more importantly who was he apeing. I know I don't talk or act like that. I know Tim certainly wouldn't and Aspen has not been to school or TKD for weeks so it definitely was not from there. Day to day I spend more time with Aspen then anyone else maybe not physically doing things but he is in my presents a large portion of his day and I had no ideas. It got to a point I asked mom and dad neither of them had a clue.

I was listening for days trying to pinpoint his new role model. At one point I asked him "DUDE WHY ARE YOU TALKING LIKE THAT? THAT IS NOT YOU. YOU SOUND LIKE A CLOWN TALKING LIKE SOMEONE ELSE."

"No I don't. I like making new voices and talking different sometimes"

I did notice however when he was playing his video game and had his headphones with mic his new persona came out more and more plus slang terms like "BRO" or "I'M OUT" were used more than when he's talking to someone in the house so the natural conclusion was one of his gaming buddies was the culprit. I was close but not quite there. The answer was revealed about a week later. Ethen was listening to a you tuber/gamer that had a channel dedicated to a game called MINE CRAFT.

I know they both play mind craft and I also knew they watched gaming videos and never thought anything of it until I heard his screechy laugh. I kind of stopped what I was doing to listen to this video. AN EXACT MATCH. If I did not know better I would have sworn I was listening to Aspen on my phone. The voice the tones the slang terms being used EVERYTHING.

So as a grandpa and finally figuring out who he was modeling his actions after, what should I do? Do I squash it? Do I let it play out and run it's course until the next hero comes along to worship? As I pondered the situation I realized that in today's unpredictable world A YOU TUBER that worked from home and has his own channel sells his own merchandise is not that bad of a role model. So here is what I said: "So you like listening to UNSPEAKABLE?"

"Yeah"

"Yeah, that guy is pretty cool. Do you think someday you will have a Youtube channel?

"I hope so grandpa."

"Yeah buddy, me too. So maybe we should start putting our coins away in the jar so you can save for some of the equipment you may need to start."

"OH YEAH THAT WOULD BE COOOOL."

"And how about this... we will practice with a mic and my laptop but instead of talking like someone else, you talk like you cause you have a nice voice."

"Sounds good to me! Can we practice NOW?"

"Sure buddy why not" and now we see what happens.

PLANT THE RIGHT SEEDS. The most important thing that I have learned in the many books I have read along with the videos I watch about the "secret" or the law of attraction is you become what you think about. It is also a proven fact that children follow closely in their parent's footsteps that is why it is said " the apple doesn't fall far from the tree" At a very very young age kids relate to and copy those adults they spend the most time with. So in most cases that is going to be mom and dad.

But what if as their grandpa you understood the law of attraction you truly believed and practiced the teachings of the "secret" and you have the privilege to see those grandkids as much or more than their parents. You are either a live-in baby while mom and dad work or you watch them at your house. In either case what if you made a conscious choice and decision to plant the seeds of success and greatness into the subconscious minds of your grandkids.

For example, every time you see your granddaughter you call her SMILEY GIRL and gently touch her face with the tips of your fingers. WHAT IF you did that EVERY TIME you see her be it once in a week or 10xs in a day? Do you think that after the weeks turned into months and the months turned into years do you think that it is embedded in her subconscious mind for the rest of her life that she is a kind and gentle soul?

As I have said before Aspen has been a leader in any group situation from a very young age and I believe that it is by design. He was my first born grandson and that fact alone promoted him to royalty status.   Long before he could walk and talk we were calling him sir and your majesty planting the seed of leadership in his head and subconscious mind. We did our best to also teach him bravery and self-confidence from a very early age. One time I can remember his auntie and I were in the living room playing catch (with him) he was maybe 5 or 6 months old. Now keep in mind this is my daughters first born son and here we are tossing him back and forth. Needless to say, she was going nuts "ARE YOU TWO F'ing CRAZY YOUR GONNA KILL MY BABY", "PLEASE STOP YOU'RE REALLY FREAKING ME OUT"

"R.E.L.A.X. Danielle, he's fine and he's loving it", and he was. He was laughing up a storm without a fear in the world. Granted he was only 6 months old and had no idea what being dropped would feel like... but whatever, "if you don't wanna watch go in the bedroom" so she did. We tossed him another time or two until she got through the door and shut it... then as hard as I could I stomped on the floor. Danielle came flying out of that bedroom so fast we barely seen her... "OH MY GOD... OH MY GOD... IS HE ALRIGHT? WHAT HAPPENED? WHERE IS HE? IS HE OK? I HEARD HIM DROP. WHAT HAPPENED?"

I laughed so hard I pissed myself (even as I write this that story still makes me laugh). Jennifer was laughing so hard she almost did drop the boy. But Aspen, Aspen was the best of all. He was laughing so hard, laughing as if he knew what just happened. We knew at that moment that this kid has guts and was fearless. We groomed him to be the leader of our pack so we knew that he would be able to and be confident enough to lead anywhere in his life. Before today Danielle NEVER dropped an "F" bomb around me but today twice in a matter of a few minutes.

To continue on the path of leadership and fearlessness when he was about 14 months old our living situation drastically changed. We found ourselves living with a friend for the summer who had a pool and a high flying kiddy swing. Her house was also directly across the street from a playground so he learned to like speed and heights by 15 months old. We spent a lot of time outdoors that summer. Both in the pool and at the playground.

To me the most important life lesson he learned that summer was to TRUST IN ME. He learned that I TRUSTED him. But I was there to make sure he did not fall and get hurt. Being just over a year he loved climbing up ladders then jumping off things. Although it was a backyard pool the water was still deep enough to be way over his head and he was fearless.

He would take a running start on the dock and jump off as far as he could. If I was there to catch him GREAT if not he did not care as long as he was wearing WATER WINGS he would jump on in and paddle his way back to the ladder, up to the deck and do it again.

At the playground, he would jump off the ladder into the sand "THAT DIDN'T HURT ME, GRANDPA", climb a bit higher the next time and jump again. The boy is both CRAZY & FEARLESS. I am not exactly sure of the date but I clearly remember one incident when he was just over 2 we were at the mall playing in the kiddy area and he was crawling up and over the wall of the plastic fort in the middle of the floor. After a couple times of up & over, he decides to balance walk to the middle of the wall and jump. It was only about a 2 ft jump and he landed flat on his butt. Up again he went but this time It was "GRANDPA WATCH THIS", he jumped and did a flat out belly flop on the solid carpeted floor. NO TEARS, NO FUSS, NO MUSS he just got up smiling and giggling "GRANDPA WASN'T THAT COOL?", and back into the play area.

At age 4 he had the uncanny ability to organize the entire play area either at the mall or a park and even the daycare at the gym. If there was 1 kid or a dozen it did not matter. The kids could be quiet normal all playing nice and calm then along comes Aspen and his little shadow (I mean brother) and within seconds EVERY KID IN THE AREA is running around playing tag or some other game.

When he turned 5 and started attending school he had the unfortunate misfortune of needing to attend 3 different schools in that year. Each and every time he emerges as a leader in the classroom and on the playground. As he got older he found himself interested in a good number of sports. At 7 we decided Tae Kwon do would be a good fit for him. In a relatively short amount of time, he became a role model in the school. WHY? Because he practices, works hard, is always there on time plus he never missed a testing cycle and passed each time he tested. A feat that is not easy to do and one that will get you noticed by the instructors, other students, and their parents.

AT THE TIME THIS PAGE WAS WRITTEN ASPEN WOULD BE 9 YEARS OLD AND HE IS A LEADER A ROLE MODEL AND ONE HECK OF A BIG BROTHER. WHY? BECAUSE BEFORE HE WAS 6 MONTHS OLD WE PLANTED THE SEEDS OF LEADERSHIP AND GREATNESS IN HIS MIND. THEN SHOWED HIM IT WAS TRULY POSSIBLE THEN CONTINUED TO ENCOURAGE HIM AS HE GOT OLDER. NOW AS HE MAKES IT TO MIDDLE SCHOOL, HIGH SCHOOL AND BEYOND HE WILL HAVE THE TOOLS NEEDED TO SUCCEED AT EVERYTHING HE PUTS HIS MIND TO.

June 13, 2020; Today I realized that role models come in all shapes and sizes they come in video game characters. They come as you tubers. They come as parents. They come as grandparents and they can come in the shape of either younger or older siblings. Who do they spend the most time with is who they will copy and emulate? Another thing I realized is that if you spend a great deal of time together the coping of actions becomes a circle of activity. Let me clarify now that the quarantine is in full effect all the young ones have been playing a lot of video games but even more than that they have been watching HOW TO PLAY videos on YouTube. So Aspen has not only been acting like but trying to sound like a very popular you tuber he watches.

So as his brother idolizes him and his ability to play their favorite game he watches and listens as Aspen talks to his friends in the same voice, the same inflections, and the same terminology as "unspeakable" Ethen also watches his videos so not only does he want to copy his big brother he wants to copy the guy his brother thinks is cool enough to copy so now we got two boys playing video games, not as ASPEN or ETHEN but the are want-a-be "unspeakable" Harlow also gets to watch the videos but she does not at like him because she is a GIRLY-GIRL and he is a boy. But what she does do is act like her big brothers which at times is the funniest thing ever. The other day both boys were grounded from games so Harlow was playing on one of their accounts by herself and as she played was on a headset talking to her teammates "CAN SOMEONE GET ME AMMO", "DUDE COME ON DUDE YOUR

CHEATING" and my personal favorite "BRO ARE YOU FOR SERIOUS." She tries very hard to copy her brothers while playing her game. Which shows the boys how important being a big brother/role model can be.

On the other side of that coin, Harlow is a very spirited girl who has her little hissy fits and acts of defiance. If she does not want to do something she doesn't. She plants herself and very rarely if EVER gets disciplined let alone spanked. The boys on the other hand are watching and learning from their little sister and the way their mom treats her. In the family dynamic, Harlow and Mama are the role models be it good or bad, intentional or not. They see what they see and learn what they learn. There have been times in the recent past that if I closed my eyes I would swear I was dealing with Harlow because her brother sees what she gets away with and copies her screaming and actions. The difference is he will and does get spankings for acting that way. I have talked with both parents about the fairness of what they do. Why does Ethen get disciplined for the exact same thing Harlow does but she continues to do it and NOTHING?

SOMETIMES BEING A GREAT ROLE MODEL MEANS YOU ALSO HAVE TO BE A GOOD DAD AND SOMETIMES POINT THINGS OUT TO HELP IMPROVE THE LIVES OF EVERYONE YOU TOUCH.

AUGUST 21, 2018; Since the boys were young I have tried to point out people and situations that I would like them to use as a life example. Today was one of those days. I was invited to a friend's birthday party and was told to bring the boys with me. The boys were asked to come because there was going to be a good number of old school race cars they would enjoy looking at. I jumped at the chance for them to come along because the party was for NORVAL"RED" ADAMS who was turning 90 years old today. The reason I was happy to bring them is because Red has old school manners and integrity, he treats women like ladies, he has money from business he owned and still owns, and was a professional race car driver in his younger days. I learn something every time I see him so I was quite certain the boys could learn a life lesson or two from him. AND WAS NOT WRONG.

Today was the day that they met him and had a ton of questions about racing, about speed, and how he still drives so fast being so old. Even though he has not had to deal with young ones this young for a VERY long time he was somewhat annoyed but also very understanding and answered their questions then bought them both a hot dog and soda. Over the next 2 years, we had the opportunity to spend time with Red on a business level. He and his sons own a number of rental property so when they have a MOVE-OUT they call us to clean, take out the trash and sometimes remove old carpet and paint. Although it is work they both enjoy it and they don't get paid unless they do a fair day's work for a fair days pay. Not only are they learning the value of the feeling of a job well done they are also learning the value of being a business owner they are also being taught fairness and being a good boss because not only do we get paid depending on how long the job takes we either get lunch or dinner paid by Red.

On one occasion we were doing some cleanup work at Red's lady friend's office and when we were finished we were all going out for dinner. I did not ask him to do this and that day I even learned something about OLD SCHOOL CHIVALRY. We left the office he stayed behind to hold the door for her. When we got to the car he made sure to open the door for her and something that even shocked me, but I guess was acceptable back in the day, he reached over and buckled her seat belt. After she was safe and secure he got in. Then at the restaurant, she undid her belt but he was at the car door to open it, I went first to hold the door for everyone but he would have also held the door for her there. In the restaurant, we usually order youngest to oldest because both boys usually know right away what they want but today we were at a Chinese buffet so meal choices were all the same however when our server asked for drink orders Ethen being the youngest blurted out "I wi..." and before he could finish Red interrupted him; "HOLD ON YOUNG MAN... ladies first, go ahead, my dear."

After dinner, there was no debate no arguing who was going to pay it was simply said "I invited you I got the bill" in my opinion, the boys witnessed more in those few hours we were at dinner about being a gentleman and how to treat a woman than they could learn from any men my age or younger. As of the time of this writing, we had the opportunity to work for and go out with Red and his lady friend. Nothing ever changes He is and always will be an old school gentlemen showing the boys.

CHIVALRY IS NOT DEAD & HE IS A GREAT CHOICE TO POINT OUT AND USE AS A ROLE MODEL.

NOVEMBER 27, 2014; Today was the day everything changed. Today is Thursday, November 27, 2014, THANKSGIVING DAY. This is the day the boys were introduced to their future long time role model, the man who would teach them how to be men and quite possibly their future stepfather, Today was the day that they met TIM. To this point the boys had no full time be around everyday male role model. They had their sperm donor but he is less of a male role model than if they lived with BOY GEORGE. At the time they were living with grandma so there was grandma's on again off again live-in boyfriend and he was not the most reliable of people.

So when Tim came on the scene he had a lot of work to do and a lot of resistance from the family. As I said Danielle and the boys were living with her mom. I believe Danielle was 19 and Tim was 35. As you can imagine with such a dramatic age difference we as the family fought them with everything we had. Two major events took place in a relatively short amount of time that for me anyway was enough to give him a shot.

First Danielle was 19 years old with two young sons but pregnant with her Exs' third baby. Tim knew and didn't seem to care. He was there for the boys every day and when Danielle went into labor with the 3rd baby instead of being all "F!#K THIS I HAD NOTHING TO DO WITH THIS I AM OUT OF HERE", in fact it was just the opposite he was there for Harlow's birth and even brought his guitar to sing happy birthday. Well in my world it takes either a real man or a very desperate man to stay in a relationship with a girl not even old enough to buy liquor and was about to embark on the responsibility of 3 non-school aged kids that none of were biologically his.

Secondly, it became clear to me what kind of manners and family values he brought with him. When they decided to move into their own apartment his mom and sister took Danielle out shopping for clothes for the boys and they had baby clothes for Harlow. At another time they took her for used furniture and finally they took her to help buy food at which point they were so pissed off they refused to take her anywhere and do anything for her. When I had a conversation with her she HATED THE MOM & SISTER because they expected a Thank you. In her mind, they offered to take her and when someone offers no thanks is necessary. Then she said she did not know them at all and felt very uncomfortable saying Thank you.

To be honest I couldn't believe that one of my kids was that disrespectful. I told her; "So if I invited you out for lunch and we stopped at the thrift store for clothes for the boys just because I invited you, you don't have to say Thank you as a common courtesy? But I know you and feel comfortable saying Thanks. "WOW ALL I CAN SAY IS WOW that is the biggest pile of a bullshit excuse I have ever heard. SO YOU ARE WALKING INTO A STORE PUSHING THE CART AND SOMEONE HOLDS THE DOOR... YOU DON'T SAY THANK YOU BECAUSE YOU DON'T KNOW THEM?"

"Yes I would say thank you but that's different."

"Different? HOW CAN YOU SAY IT'S DIFFERENT?"

"I don't know. It's just different."

"NO DANIELLE NO IT'S NOT. It is simply a matter of common courtesy. No wonder his family don't want to help you anymore."

I later found out that he felt the same way and I knew then and there he would be the one teaching the boys and eventually Danielle respect and manners.

Over the 5 years they have been together there have been times that I disagreed with discipline methods or punishments and groundings. The fact that for awhile he was the man of the house with no job did not sit well with me. A one-point Danielle was asked to leave her mom's house and she and the kids lived in a shelter for some time and in my opinion, if he was going to take on the responsibility of step dad he should have been able to provide a place to live. But that was then and this is now.

The old saying of opposites attract is very true where these two are concerned Danielle is very much the type of person who will go out of her to avoid speaking to people if there is a way to email or text instead of talking on the phone she is all over that. Tim on the other hand will chat with anyone, say good morning and play his guitar in public. THE role model story I would like to tell you is this, Last Halloween Tim and his friend wanted to go to a Halloween costume/ talent show party at a local bar dressed as a 3 piece zombie band with Danielle as the lead singer. She declined the invitation so instead of scrapping the idea he and his friend learned some jokes and went to the show as comedians. Both had been in a band playing in front of people but yet neither had ever done stand up and came home with the 2nd place trophy and prize money. Before he left they took pictures and at the show the bar owner took video and put it on their FB page. All the young ones thought his costume was cool and also thought winning 2nd was GREAT but the video on FB made him a KING in their eyes.

The second story I would like to tell you is related to the first but completely happened by accident. Both of the boys watch YouTube videos of players that play their games professionally guys like Mark Plier & Unspeakable. For months now they have been talking about being 18 and living together buying what they need to become professional you tubers. So one night they are watching YouTube and start talking about Tim and his Halloween video so they decided to jump on mama's FB page and look for the video because she no doubt had it saved. And correct they were. They found his video on FB but what they also found was a link. A link to what you may ask? GOOD QUESTION. It is a link to Tim's YouTube channel. YES, he has been recording and posting videos for months and none of his family members had a clue.

Once again he made KING status in their eyes. He had a channel with 45 followers and 10 subscribers next A friend for months has been talking about owning a large plot of land in Florida. The plan was Tim & Danielle would agree to move their family to Florida stay with this friend and build 2 brand new houses on the land they owned and start then run a business. THE plan seemed like a sound one. I was discussed and talked about on the phone, Emails were sent back and forth. More phone calls... more emails until the decision was made and bags were packed, noticed were given plane tickets were purchased and my daughter and her family were Florida bound. It was a bittersweet time for me because I spend a great deal of time with the young ones then one day they are gone and living in Florida. However, I did respect the fact He had the Balls to move the entire family to Florida to chase a dream.

The plan had been put in motion, but the circumstances were completely different when they got there than what they were told and what they expected. Tim's friend guaranteed he had a job for him paying 15-18 an hour and within a very short amount of time They would have an apartment of their own and then the building of the business could start. As exciting as it is and the adrenaline rush that comes from a move like this nothing worked out as planned. This so-called friend never had a job set up. They were expected to babysit while the two "FRIENDS" went to work. Finally, they could not take any more of the lies and bullshit and left. For 3 days they were homeless in Florida staying in someone's garage until they could find a way home. At the time I didn't have the money to buy them plane tickets myself and with his mom's opinion of Danielle, it seemed unlikely she would help. I was prepared to find a van or SUV and drive down to get them. Sometimes you have to bite the bullet and lie, beg or steal to do the best thing for your family. That is exactly what he did. He phoned his mom she bought plane tickets and I was able to pick them up from the airport. Within days of coming back to Milwaukee, they had an apartment, a job, and all the young ones signed up and enrolled in school. There are a lot of things in this story that makes him a great role model for the kids but the one that stands out as the most impressive for me was the fact he ended a 20-year friendship and stood by his family then swallowed his pride to call his mom to get them home.

Although he was never (as far as I know) an alcoholic he completely quit drinking and in today's world of CBD oil and legal marijuana in certain states, Tim smoked now and again but it bothered his lady a great deal so he quit. By quitting smoking dope that allowed him to get a nice paying job which is providing the necessary income for a house, to keep their bills paid and up to date, nice T.V.'s for all the kids in each bedroom, gaming systems for everyone clothes on their backs with good daily food on the table. There have been some VERY good changes in the actions and attitudes of both Danielle and the boys Since he came on the scene. As far as the girls He has been there for them since day one.

AS A ROLE MODEL HE IS TEACHING THE KIDS *NOT TO BE AFRAID TO SHOW OFF WHO YOU ARE BECAUSE EVERYONE IS UNIQUE AND DIFFERENT. BE WHO YOU ARE AND BE PROUD OF IT *MANNERS & RESPECT *FAIRNESS & DISCIPLINE.

Just the fact that he is still here after 5 years through some VERY hard times and some very intense moments that is a testament to his commitment as a father also treating the 3 that are not biologically his with no prejudice or bias and as equals says a lot about his character as a person. In the beginning, the age difference was a complete shocker for me, and the rest of the family. We did what we could to discourage Danielle but thankfully we did not push him away because he has turned out to be an OUTSTANDING ROLE MODEL and I am glad to put it in this book that I WAS WRONG.

At the begging of this chapter, I asked the young ones to describe a role model but they all gave me examples of who not what it meant. But as a true role model, it is my responsibility to encourage good role models and try to steer them away from negative ones. So for a young boy, a pro athlete can either be a great role model or completely wrong. Aspen liked Michael Jordan although he never saw him play and has no idea what kind of teammate he was. What kind of person he is. Aspen had no clue about Michael Jordan the athlete all he knew was the Jordan had a cool line of shoes, he liked the shoes he liked playing basketball so Michael Jordan MUST be a cool dude and he wants to be just like him.

Now as parents and grandparents we did not know much about Michael Jordan either so we did not encourage or discourage Aspen's admiration for the basketball player we simply let him talk to friends, read articles and watch videos of Michael Jordan the basketball star then make up his mind. However, we did encourage him to use Michael Jordan the business owner and entrepreneur as a role model. I don't know much about pro athletes as role models I don't watch many sports but over the years I have hears some very good things about Julius Erving "DR J" for his work ethic and ability on the basketball court so as a little push I asked Aspen to do a little research and write me a report about Dr. J. He was not interested because he did not have cool shoes to sell.

Ethen wanted to be like his teacher. Having a good teacher or in most cases, teacher(s) is very important in a young person's life. In most cases, the only adult's kids inner act with are family members mom during the day and mom and dad after work, and maybe they get to spend time with grandma & grandpa or aunts & uncles on the weekends or holidays so when your 5 year old likes his teacher enough to say he is his role model that is a good thing. When asked "why your teacher?", his answer was very impressive for a little boy "because he is very smart. I want to be very smart. Mr. Smith knows about math. He knows all the words in the stories we read. He is a good drawer and he plays with us at recess. But most of all he made leprechaun traps".

In my opinion, all very good reasons to like someone so we are encouraging him to follow the teacher's lead of being smart, kind & athletic and can build leprechaun traps all good qualities for a young man's role model.

Harlow is very difficult to guild her down the right path. She has a very vivid and active imagination. Having those qualities is a good thing if she had real female role models to copy and model herself after. She has only one and that is her mother. She and mom spent a great deal of time together but unfortunately, a lot of that was watching Disney movies. When asked what she wants to be when she grows up the answer is 1of 3. Either she is going to be Queen Elsa, Mulan, or Ariel. She never says any sort of profession or just like mommy. However, when she plays alone she does pretend to be the mother and is always talking very sweet to her dolls.

This year she was enrolled in K4 and rode the school bus with her brothers. We were hoping that her teacher who is a very sweet and caring woman would spark something in Harlow and give her some sort of vision or glimpse of a female role model other than her mom. At home, Harlow is very loud, very opinionated, and in all honesty very spoiled and for the most part, allowed to do and get away with anything she wants. In school, she is quite the opposite very shy, very reserved, and afraid to talk to her teacher to a point she has had 3 major POOPING incidents where she needed to be sent home. When asked what happened the first time she says she was having too much fun and did not want to stop playing. the next 2 times she says she had to go but was afraid to ask her teacher. As her family and permanent role models, we are hoping that next year she will find someone to look up too or I am hoping that if I enroll her in TKD class with her brothers the older kids and female instructors will show her options and showing her how to be a polite young lady and not a spoiled little demon.

ROLE MODELS ARE EVERYWHERE SOME ARE GOOD AND OTHERS NOT SO MUCH. I FEEL IT IS MY DUTY AS A GREAT GRANDPA TO EXPOSE THEM AS OFTEN AS POSSIBLE TO THE GOOD ONES AND KEEP THEM AWAY FROM THOSE NOT SO MUCH.

BEING YOUNG, FIT AND HEALTHY IS A BLESSING

Being a great grandpa starts with FIRST accepting the fact that you are GOING to be a grandpa and secondly make a choice you can either be an ASSHOLE and miss out on some of the most exciting moments of your life or you can decide to be a GREAT GRANDPA. I was one of those parents that my daughter was afraid to tell me she was pregnant. For a very long time, she was correct. When I first found out I was furious. My baby having a baby at 15 years old. They say hindsight is 20/20 so after self-reflection and deep thought I realized it wasn't the fact she was pregnant how could it be, that would make me a HUGE hypocrite. I was only 18 when my first kid was born the mom was only 16 and I became a grandpa for the first time at a ripe old age of 33 because our oldest daughter had a baby at 15.

So what was it about Danielle getting pregnant that bothered me so much? Then one day while having a heated ADULT conversation with Danielle's mother it hit me like a ton of bricks. The reasons were very real but unfair to Danielle. First, her mother blamed me 100% for the baby, and secondly, I HATED THE DADDY.

Even though I did not live with her mother Day after day all I heard was "if it wasn't for you this, you let them alone that" " how is she gonna live, she isn't living here with a baby" BLAH BLAH BLAH BLAH. I suppose at some point she wore me down and I snapped on Danielle because things I said to my daughter were VERY cold and cruel things no young girl in trouble should have heard from her father.

As I did some self-reflection it became very clear to me I did what I did and said what I said because I knew deep down I let her down. The verbal bashing and harsh words and actions were directed at me for not being there to protect her. I did not have any personal contact with her for months after the verbal bashing she took from me. To this day I have no idea what changed my mind and why I decided to become part of their life but believe me when I say I AM Remarkably HAPPY I DID. As I write this I will assume that there are 1000s of young girls scared and pregnant wishing they had someone to talk to. Girls that feel they can't talk to mom or dad. Girls that feel they are alone. Girls that feel their life should be over. If that is you and you suspect your daughter may be pregnant at the very least let her know she can come to you. Let her know she is not alone and for GOD sake let her know that you will always love her and the baby. I truly believe God looked down on me and opened my eyes to the true blessings of what being a grandpa especially a young healthy grandpa can be.

The stories you are about to enjoy were able to take place because of my age, health, and overall well being. I have done things that an older less active unhealthier man wishes he could do as a grandpa. I have looked through my Facebook posts & videos as well keeping a written journal that I have pulled times, dates and examples of why I feel truly GRATEFUL and feel it is a blessing and privilege to be able to be a young healthy grandpa.

May 18, 2011; Asleep, the phone rings, and its Amanda " She's in labor" If I would have stayed ignorant and cold I would have missed one of the most spectacular events of my life. THE BIRTH OF MY FIRST GRANDSON. Waking up, driving to the hospital, and staying up all night then remaining awake until 5:24 A.M. To be the 3rd person in this world to hold him. That is something a senior citizen may have trouble doing so from the very beginning.

BEING A YOUNG GRANDPA CAN DEFINITELY BE A BLESSING.

February 12, 2015; In my saved videos I was watching a clip on this day that we started our now infamous GRANDPA GAME. The game simply started with an innocent nap. At the time Ethen was about to turn 2 and Aspen would have been going on 4. Both boys were playing in the house boys just being boys. I believe the reason they were over was that I was babysitting while their mom was at school. well anyway as I said I was napping on the couch and they decided it would be funny to run by and slap me on the foot run away LAUGHING. Lap around the back of the couch and do it again.

After the 2nd or 3rd time they woke me up but I kept my eyes closed pretending to be asleep. As they made their way around I let them smack me one more time. Then like a cat waiting to pounce on a mouse I waited for them to come back around and SNATCH I grabbed Aspen by the arm dragged him next to me on the couch and the GRANDPA GAME was born(the amazing thing about the grandpa game is it withstanding the test of time. As I am sitting at my desk looking out the window trying to word this section correctly my grandson tapped me on the shoulder and asked if I wasn't busy if we could play the grandpa game) grabbing Aspen, Ethen kept running trying to escape and slapping my foot.

The weapons we use today were forged on the couch that day. I have the use of these few weapons. The dreaded right or left-handed one knuckle spike. Then we have the double finger right-handed knuckle spike. Or we have grabbed with the opposite hand to hold the thumb spike. And my personal favorite the 5 fingers grab and squeeze. this technique is very effective on either knee, either shoulder but is strongly encouraged as a stomach claw.

The young ones have an arsenal that consists of a few things. They are very very good at the PUNCH and RUN, Ethen and Harlow are extremely good at the SMACK the BACK DASH. But their favorite and most devastating move IS by far their patented BOOTY SLAM. So as the years passed the grandpa game has evolved but he rules on that first day were simple. The couch was my base and I could not get up. Harlow was not born yet but the boys had it down QUICK. Ethen run-up slapped me in the toe run while Aspen was crawling up on the back of the couch ...standing over my stomach...jump as high as he could sticking his legs straight out and WHAM... BOOTY SLAM. Ethen thought that was the funniest thing ever so up he went. WEEEeeeee up then down on my stomach with a continuous circle of BOOTY SLAMS. You would not think that small kids would carry enough weight to do any damage to a full-grown man that has been going to the gym for years. At least that is what I thought, but I thought wrong. Imagine if you will laying flat on your back with no protection over your midsection then out of nowhere someone drops a 30lb weight from about 3 feet in the air directly on your gut and before you have a chance to recover or tighten your stomach muscles another 20lb weight drops Then a few seconds (not minutes)later that 30lbs drops again and right behind that 20lbs more only this time in a slightly different place. That is their patented BOOTY SLAM. Aspen... back of the couch... JUMP... KICK... LAND... LAUGH OUT LOUD... RUN... REPEAT. Oh yeah, let us not forget his little brother is doing the same thing and is RIGHT BEHIND HIM.

As they got older the rules have changed slightly but the basic GRANDPA GAME has remained intact going on 5 years now. Some of the differences now are there are another couple of young ones who play. Now instead of jumping off the back of the couch we use the couch as a base I can't get up and they need to run by and try to smack me and I need to have fast reflexes to snatch their arms, hands, or any other body part I can grab a hold of to apply my dreaded RIGHT POINTER FINGER KNUCKLE SPIKE. Or the feared TWO HAND THUMB SPIKES. We also have an altered version of the GRANDPA GAME called the grandpa jail game.

During this version, I have to chase them around the attic and physically catch them and when caught they have to spend time in JAIL. (my bed) the only way to get out is by one of the other kids tag them out. They are all very quick so to make the game fair I am allowed to use a stuffed animal to tag them with. The rules are still the same they can sneak up hit, slap, or poke me then run away. The game ends when I throw all 3 young ones in jail at the same time.

As I said we have been playing the GRANDPA GAME for years but very recently the rules had to be changed, For the past year and a half both boys have been in tae kwon do and they are both very skilled. So as you can imagine an unprotected surprise roundhouse kick to the ribs from a 9-year-old BLACK BELT or EVEN worse an accidental flying sidekick to the "junk" from a 7-year-old HIGH RED BELT really hurts and is quite unpleasant, soooo they are no longer allowed to use any sort of kicking techniques and they must remain on the ground otherwise... GAME ON.

Besides the GRANDPA GAME, all the young ones enjoy watching pro wrestling and have their favorite wrestlers. So the obvious evolution of the grandpa game would be some intense wrestling matches. Most of the time I am the ref but every once in a while I shed my stripe shirt and jump in the action. **WRESTLING, REFFING OR JUST THROWING STUFFED ANIMALS AT THEM BEING A YOUNG GRANDPA IS MOST DEFINITELY A BLESSING.**

July 22, 2015; Today is a very hot very humid Milwaukee summer day I am spending the day with my two daughters my grandsons who would have been 4 and 2, and a very newborn baby girl 6 weeks or so. We were driving around from park to park looking for a public pool that was not packed. Full-size pools... kiddy pools and even the beaches along Lake Michigan were swarming with people(no threat of the corona-virus back in 2015) so we decided to take a drive about 15 minutes or so out of town to see if we could find a public lake clean enough to swim but with a small enough crowd to have fun. I was not completely sure but thought I knew of a lake just a bit out of town. We did find a small lake that had a small beach, a playground area, a fishing pier, and a docking pier that extended 30' or so into the lake.

The water at the very end of this pier was about 3 ½ feet deep or about shoulder high to me and just a tad deeper on my daughter. When we arrived at the lake there were only 3 other cars in the parking lot that all belonged to the same family who was there for a BBQ. The time was somewhere around 3 o'clock and hot as HELL. The water was clean and clear calling out to us. So as the adults Amanda and I took off to the water ran in up to our knees and finished with a headfirst dive. THE WATER WAS PHENOMENAL, and we were the only two people in the water.

The boys were right behind us and the frolicking began. This was a great idea a small beach, clean cool water, and no one else. The boys wanted to jump off the pier but the water would be over their heads and neither could swim at the time. I went to the end of the pier so the boys could get a running start. Like a shot, Aspen took off and ran to the end of the dock jumping as far as he could. SPLASH he hit the water and dunked under the water bouncing his feet on the bottom and working his way back to the pier where I was waiting to lift him back up. Wearing his water wings and jumping off the dock reminded me a lot of when he was younger jumping off the dock of the pool. Then a second later Ethen came running down the pier and feet first jump and SPLASH. He did bob up and down...under than above the water he did freak out a bit but he too was wearing water wings and calmed down quickly DOGGY PADDLED to me and up he went back to the end of the pier for another running start. Here comes Aspen... then Effers... Aspen... Effers... Briana?

"UM BRIANA WHERE DID YOU COME FROM?"

"She is our friend grandpa and she wants to splash."

Alrighty then. Here comes Aspen... Ethen... Briana... Aspen... Ethen... Briana in and out jumping splashing having a great time while grandpa was at the end of the pier lifting them out. 10 minutes or so later here comes Aspen again followed by Ethen... Briana... Asp... BRIAN?

"ANYONE CARE TO TELL ME WHO THIS KID IS?"

"He is my brother SIR."

"Yeah GRANDPA another friend."

At this point, I was getting a bit winded so I sent one of the boys to ask Auntie Da to come down to the water and help lift these young ones out of the water. Okee Dokie now she is standing next to me so the young ones are taking turns running to me then Amanda, then me and back and forth back and forth.

The time now is approximately 4:15 P.M. we have been playing in the water for about 50 minutes or so and did not notice there were another 3 or 4 cars that parked in the lot and about 4:30 another 4 kids were running and jumping in two were old enough and tall enough to get out on their own but the other two were very young and needed our help. About 5:10 2 more cars parked. By the time everything was in full swing we had 3 adults in the water at the end of the pier and 11 young ones were jumping in having a blast.

TO THIS DAY THAT WAS ONE OF THE FUNNEST YET MOST EXHAUSTING DAYS I HAVE HAD SINCE BECOMING A GRANDPA. BEING A YOUNG GRANDPA IS DEFINITELY A BLESSING.

December 29, 2019; The best thing about being a young grandpa and an entrepreneur is the fact that I can take off and do things anytime I want. None of my grandkids have ever been sledding so when they were on Christmas break, I thought it would be fun to have their first sledding experience happen on one of the best hills in the county park system. The challenge was who to take.

Well in the spirit of being fair I asked who wanted to go... UMMM let me think, OOOOH YEAH, now I remember. ALL OF THEM. I debated going myself with the 4 young ones then I thought if Amanda & Warren wanted to go that would be 2 adults watching over 5 kids instead of me trying to keep track of 4. I liked those odds much better so I made the call. Amanda and I do make a good team when it comes to the young ones when they need to listen and stay close and in sight to have fun. She makes sure they stay in front of her and in sight AT ALL TIMES because she is very concerned about people in today's society and that somebody might try to snatch them and run.

We only had 1 old plastic sled so we had to stop and buy 2 more. The arrangement we had at the hill was Aspen & Ethen would always ride together and Amanda and I would take turns riding with Warren than the girls. When we got to the hill it was early afternoon, the very pleasant surprise was there was no one else on the hill. I was kind of surprised because I expected it to be packed. Winter break, a nice sunny mild winter day, and the hill had plenty of snow but yet not another soul to be seen.

Well, the boys being the boys they ran to the top of the hill and made their first run before anyone else even got to the top of the hill. The hill is long and steep so trying to run back up was a waste of valuable energy. Back at the top, they wanted to race. So Aspen & Ethen are prepared at the starting line. Next Amanda and Warren ready and waiting. Next Violet in front then Harlow and grandpa in the back with my legs wrapped around both girls... waiting in a straight line on the top of the hill "ON YOUR MARK, READY, SET... GOOOoooooo!" All 3 sleds took off like a shot and nobody could tell who won because it was so close but to be completely honest I don't think anyone cared. There were smiles laughs and giggles from EVERYONE. YES EVERYONE me included. We raced took turns and sledded that day for hours.

SO IF YOU WERE WONDERING... YES... BEING A YOUNG HEALTHY GRANDPA IS TRULY A BLESSING.

FEBRUARY 2, 2019; Today after class it was far too cold to do anything outside. The boys wanted to go sledding or have a snowball fight but it was far too cold and windy.

"What else would you guys want to do that doesn't involve being outside?"

"How about the water park?"

"How about we see if Mama wants to take the girls out and we go to grandpa's gym?"

"Yeah, the GYM..can we play basketball? And racketball? And then go to the pool?"

"Yes, indeed fellas that would be the plan."

So I made the call and their mom did not want to go so it was just the boys and I.

The gym is most definitely kid-friendly with 2 full-size basketball courts. It also has 3 racketball courts an under 10 basketball area. The pool area is like a small water park with high-velocity water guns, a mushroom, a nice size slide, a basketball hoop with 4 water balls to use and play with. They have a box of toys the young ones can borrow including googles and life vests. During family times they even offer oversized inner tubes the kids can ride in the current pool as long as they are accompanied by an adult. The only real restriction is they are not allowed in the HOT TUB.

The best part of all of this is we can stay as long as we care to stay my entry is free because I am a member but the boys are only 5 bucks each with no extra fees for equipment rental, pool area entry, or towels. So for a minimal cost of 10 dollars, we were about to have a phenomenal afternoon.

Aspen is a huge fan of playing basketball and when I was younger I had a pretty mean hook shot and also still have an accurate 3 point shot so the first activity was on the basketball court. Aspen wanted to challenge me to a game of H.O.R.S.E. He lost... then he lost again the third time he was like, "Grandpa I can't throw the ball as far as you and I don't think that's fair so I am going to play with those other boys. Is that ok?"

"Yeah, buddy that's fine. But you know the rule if you start on the basketball court but go somewhere else just come tell me so I know."

With that, he took off and got to play in a 2-on-2 game with boys his age. Ethen on the other hand is not a fan of basketball he is a very tiny kid and has trouble getting the ball even close to the rim so he gets frustrated. I do know he idolizes his big brother and tries to do everything he does so while Aspen was playing in his game I went into the kid's area to play HORSE with Ethen because it has much shorter rims and much smaller lighter balls. A much better area for a tiny toon.

We played for a good while and then decided to trade in our basketball for 3 rackets and a ball. My rule works both ways if Aspen needs to come to tell me when he moves areas it is only fair that if we are in the kid area and moving to play racketball that we go tell him so he doesn't panic if he can't find us. It was a good thing too because he left his Bball game to join us playing racketball. Now neither of the boys knows the rules of racketball and to be honest neither do I but we have fun just hitting the ball and running around. That game lasted for about 45 minutes so we decided to take a break get a drink, turn in our rackets and head down to the family locker room because it was 1:45 & the pool area family time starts at 2.

We were there ready and waiting. EXACTLY at 2 P.M. The mushroom started spraying water. Streams of water shot out of the floor, and all the water attractions were up and running. Aspen was first in line to go down the slide while Ethen and I got his life vest on then headed to the deepest water he was allowed. The boys LOVE the pool area. There are always other kids to play with even if not they play against each other. Now please keep in mind that we have been active and playing (exercising) for hours already so grandpa trying to keep up with two active and energetic boys was a bit of a challenge today but one I was most willing to accept. In my opinion, the gym has a very good family time policy. They allow playtime for 50 minutes out of every hour than everything shuts off and EVERYONE out of the water which gives the lifeguards a chance to rest and rest their eyes. Then after a 10-minute break, everything resumes and that continues for the entire time family time is active.

So, as I mentioned earlier they do have a current pool that is allowed huge oversized inner tubes. With all the other choices to play with for some reason, this is by far their favorite. So here is how we do it...BOTH boys drag the tube to the water and jump on. Aspen is tall enough to touch the bottom but Ethen cannot but with his vest on he is NO WAY going under so if or when he falls off the tube he can safely and confidentially ride the current until I can catch up to him. Away they go riding the tube which is riding the current and then there is grandpa following behind bouncing and rocking them trying my best to jump them off. 45 minutes and I was watching the clock to see how long before a break.

After the first break, we went back in and the boys being the boys found a friend or 3 to ride the tube along with them. Although I was in the water and COOL water at that I was bouncing an inner tube with 5 kids trying to dump them off each weighing at least 40lbs. I did not know it was possible to work up such a heavy sweat while physically submerged in water. I have to admit this 45 minutes was a better work out than anything I could do in the gym and lifting weights.

I was sore and tired and knew tomorrow was going to be rough but I also knew the laughs and smiles from my grandsons along with the laughs and smiles from 3 kids I had no clue who the heck they were made it all worthwhile.

I CAN NOT IMAGINE BEING TOO WEAK OR TOO OLD TO JUMP IN AND PLAY WITH THE BOYS AND THEIR NEW FRIENDS. YES, BEING A YOUNG HEALTHY GRANDPA IS DEFINITELY A BLESSING...

JUNE 8, 2017; Ever since my kids were little when they got tired from walking around be it at the park or in the mall they were lifted on my shoulders for the rest of the way. Over the years kids have ridden many many miles on dad's shoulders so when the grandkids came into the picture that tradition DID NOT CHANGE. Today we were enjoying a family day at the zoo. Both of my girls were about 7 months pregnant so walking around was slow but that was ok because the young ones could go at their own pace and watch the animals. Everything went as expected and pretty much according to plan. We walked around seen the animals we wanted to see, played in the family area for about an hour fed the domestic animals in the petting zoo, and had a great picnic lunch. After lunch, we tried to make our way to see the lions again but everyone was hot and getting tired so instead of seeing the lions we stopped by a free show of "THE BIRDS OF PREY THAT MADE WISCONSIN THEIR HOME." This show was truly outstanding and I learned a great deal about hawks and eagles and a few other birds of prey. The young ones on the other hand were fidgeting and restless wanting to just go home. On the way to the car, Harlow and Violet shared space in the stroller but Aspen and Ethen were exhausted so instead of walking at a snail's pace to get to my car Aspen went on my shoulders and Ethen in my arms and I carried them out to the car. There are a great deal of younger men and quite a few right here walking around the zoo that looked to be so far out of shape they can barely get their fat ass out to the car let alone boost two kids up and carry them out so yes *BEING A YOUNG HEALTHY GRANDPA IS DEFINITELY A BLESSING...*

AUGUST 22, 2019; Today was great-grandmas birthday and she was having her party in the Hall of a church. The good news was there is a VERY nice playground connected to the church the bad news was that there was a cold front that quickly made her way into the area and it is extremely cold for a late August day. We went out and tried to play basketball but because it WAS August and warm when we left no one thought to bring jackets or even long pants so the outside attempt didn't last long. We, however, were allowed into the gym of the school which meant access to a basketball court, a basketball, and a couple of soccer and volleyballs. As messed up as this is going to sound I would much rather spend time with the young ones in the family playing some silly made-up ball game than sitting in a room full of adults.

With that being said the young one and I played a game or two of HORSE and a few of the adults from out of town came in to say Hello and even shot a bucket or 2. Now seeing this was my mom's party and she had friends and family that came quite a distance to be there I felt I should try and make an appearance and not be completely antisocial so I went in chatted a bit had some snacks and then my brother came to tell me the young ones were not supposed to be in the gym unattended so I went back and played ball. Aspen and I made up a kickball game. There was only 1 rule I would roll pitch to him and he'd kick it depending on where on the wall it hit that's how many points he scored. Thee the same thing going the other way he'd role pitch to me and after a kick depending on where it hit the wall either zero, 1, or 2 points with the first one to 10 wins. During the 2 hours, we played there were another few adults that tried to join in but were too uncoordinated to kick the ball or were so far out of shape they tried for maybe a minute or two then quitting.

BY THE TIME THE PARTY ENDED MY SHIRT WAS SWEATY, MY LEGS HURT AND MY FEET WERE THROBBING BUT I DID MAKE IT FOR OVER TWO HOURS PLUS I WON A COUPLE GAMES. SO YES BEING A YOUNG HEALTHY GRANDPA IS DEFINITELY A BLESSING...

MAY 14, 2019; Today we are having a double birthday celebration at bounce Milwaukee. We are celebrating both Harlow & Aspen's birthday. Over the past few years, I have been taking the young ones out for their birthdays that are far too expensive for a party but fun enough that they will enjoy it just the family. Today it was Me, mama, Aspen, Ethen, Harlow, and 1-month-old Olenna who got to enjoy the other mom's coming up and doing the "OOOO my is she adorable bit". Everything was fabulous the young ones were all being well behaved. Danielle and I were taking turns walking around with the baby while the other watched the young ones play and have fun. As the Birthday girl, Harlow received a certificate for 30 minutes of free jump time for anyone who was there for her party. Jumping on a trampoline may not sound very difficult but believe me, if you are not used to doing it it can be one of the most intense cardio workouts you can imagine.

TRYING TO KEEP UP WITH 3 EXCITED SUGARED UP YOUNG ONES TURNED INTO A HECK OF A AEROBIC/CARDIO WORKOUT. AFTER 30 MINUTES OF CHASING, PLAYING, AND JUMPING THAT BOTTLE OF WATER TASTED GOOD. AND YES BEING A YOUNG HEALTHY GRANDPA IS DEFINITELY A BLESSING...

BIKE TRAILS. We all live in separate houses but we all live just a few blocks from one of the largest lakes in the world. We live close to Lake Michigan which in and of itself is a pretty cool thing but besides for the lake itself, Milwaukee county has 100s of miles of very nicely paved and groomed bicycle and walking trails. Thee only one of the young ones that can ride a bike is Aspen so before he joined TKD and started going to Saturday morning classes his family was living with his grandma and that house was a block and a half away from the lakefront I lived 7 minutes from him so Every Saturday morning I would head over there around 8:30 A.M. Then we would map out where we wanted to bike that day some days we would go to the lake and just throw rocks in the water. Some days we would ride an hour one way along the beach and map out a different route back. One day we didn't even know Summerfest was going on that Saturday and we happened to get there at a perfect time. If you were there between 9:30-10 you got a free admission ticket so being on bikes we were able to bypass the traffic jam and go right to the front of the line get our tickets and head over to chain our bikes. What an incredible day that was. We got into Summerfest on the last Saturday they were open and some of the best side stage acts played that day. Other days the other two young ones are awake and want to go with unfortunately they are too little and don't know how to ride bikes and even if they did we cross a couple of major streets to get to the lake so they couldn't come anyway. BUT we do own a bicycle trailer that can easily & comfortably carry both of them. Now and again we hook up the trailer then all spend time at the lake.

RIDING TO THEIR HOUSE, HOOKING UP A BIKE TRAILER TO PULL BEHIND ME SO THE OTHER YOUNG ONES CAN COME ALONG IS QUITE ALOT OF EXTRA WORK BUT WELL WORTH IT SO THEY DON'T FEEL LEFT OUT AND YES BEING A YOUNG HEALTHY GRANDPA IS DEFINITELY A BLESSING...

HIDE N SEEK. The boys are huge fans of the game hide n seek. They play at the house and being an expert hider, I sometimes help them hide in unfindable spots; sometimes we move couch cushions so they can hide as part of the couch. Most of the time beds are not made so we bunch up the blankets or pile them on the bed and the hider will mix him or herself in the pile and it is extremely hard to tell simply by looking at a pile of blankets that one of the young ones are hiding there. Using my imagination to help them hide is cool but what they like about the way I help them play hide n seek is my ability to lift them to otherwise ungettable places. When they are playing at the house and someone wants to hide in the loft attic or if they need to check if someone is in the loft attic I can physically lift them over my head so they can crawl into the loft to hide OR seek. Playing in the park there are 100s of places to hide Their favorite by far is being lifted in a tree so they can climb to the top and hide.

BEING ABLE TO LIFT THE BOYS OVER MY HEAD SO THEY CAN CLIMB UP A TREE PLAYING A SIMPLE GAME OF HIDE N SEEK SO YES BEING A YOUNG HEALTHY GRANDPA IS DEFINITELY A BLESSING.

DECEMBER 14, 2018; For the past few years my interaction with the young ones was primarily with Danielle's kids. But last September that all changed. Warren James was born and when the other young ones were in school he and I spent a lot of time together.

He enjoyed visiting MEE MA (great-grandma) while his mama was working. From the second he learned to talk he was a smiley, happy boy. Everywhere we went if we were walking or if he was riding in a cart or standing in the basket no matter who it was or where we were if we passed by another person Warren would shout out to them "HI" most of the time the person would smile back and say hi back, if not "HIIII" that made it almost certain he would get a chuckle and a response "hi" Warren is a very happy boy that puts anyone he meets in a better mood. A good boy yes but he is also a runner. That's why when we go shopping if you turn your head for a second... WHOOSH HE'S GONE! Most of the time he will stop at the first person he comes across and will stand there yanking on the clothes "HI", "HI",

"HI YOU" most of the time with smiles and laughs until someone realizes he took off and go get him. No one has ever said anything bad but we have gotten some pretty nasty looks. Other times he simply takes off running just to run. On this particular day, his mama was working and I thought a few hours at the mall would wear him down so after work she might just take him home and relax with needing to chase her son. As I said he is a runner so as soon as he feet touch the floor he is off. For 15 months old he is a very solid boy and I didn't bring a stroller so when we got to the mall I had to walk with him on my shoulders all the way into the play area.

We get to the playground I set him down for 3 seconds or have ever long it takes to take a jacket off... " WARREN...WARREN WHERE ARE YOU BUDDY" I didn't see him anywhere and in that split second my stomach sank and I felt sick.

WARREN WHERE ARE YOU!!!" I heard a giggle looked up and seen him sprinting down the mall laughing like he heard the funniest joke ever. I don't even remember what I had in my hands but I dropped everything and took off running full speed down the hall to catch that little escape artist. I did bring him back safe and sound.

I WAS WINDED AND COMPLETELY FREAKED OUT SO YES EVEN AT THE MALL BEING A YOUNG HEALTHY GRANDPA IS DEFINITELY A BLESSING...

NATURE WALKS. Time and time again we have played in the parks I have spent 100s of hours pushing swings and building sandcastles but the one thing we have not touched on yet is the miles and miles of trails we have hiked. 3 public parks have hiking trail through the park and around the lake. One of these parks is named SCOUT LAKE PARK. Trail markers posted at the entrance of the park say that 1 lap around the lake is 1.2 miles. This particular lake has a pier that stretches out maybe 15 yards offshore and is a favorite place of ours to go pan fishing. It is very easy access to the water and the county stocks the lake every spring so the fishing most times is fun not because fish are biting but quite the opposite. There are so many people that fish here the fish would be classified as intelligent. They will nibble the bait off your hook so if you are skilled enough to hook one you did very well. Some frogs and turtles call here home. We have caught and released a good number of frogs from here. The most unique and thrilling animal that lives here ais a snapping turtle. Now, this is no ordinary snapper this thing weighs 200 lbs if it weighs an ounce. A couple of summers ago I had the privilege of being there late one afternoon the young ones while he was on shore sunning himself. I have seen a lot of neat things in nature in my lifetime, but that turtle and its sheer size were very impressive and the young ones had an opportunity to see him too.

Another park we go to is GRANT PARK. The reason we enjoy it here is it is right on Lake Michigan. So being right on the lake there are miles of hiking trails that go through the woods then maybe lead you down a nice cliff bring you along the water for a bit then up another steep hill which at the top gives you the option of heading back the way you came or soldering on. This is a very nice walk for the older kids but a tad too much for the younger littles. During these walks, we have seen a good number of waterfowl and found some pretty flat and smooth rocks that we have used for painting projects.

Another favorite place to go is WHITNALL PARK. We spend more time here than all the other parks combined. There are 3 very nice play areas, a public golf course, 2 very nice hills to sled on in winter and the reason we go there for hikes is there is a nature center where you can park and there is an information center to show you what you may see on your hikes. When you leave the information center there are 4 possible paths to follow, red, yellow, green, and blue. The yellow trail takes you around the lake and is exactly 2.2 miles door to door. On this walk, you have a chance to view turtle sunny themselves on the logs, geese, and ducks. The blue trail starts out the door and goes down the hill walk along the west side of the lake then veers off and up the hill and follows the golf course and you have the choice of either come back through the woods on the course back to the start or you can continue around the outside of the golf course which turns into the green trail. If you continue the distance increases to a 4.5-mile hike if you choose to come through the woods it is 3.3 miles. Either way, you decide to go you will have a good chance of seeing golfers, a variety of birds and a good number of different plant life along with small animals like rabbits, squirrels and depending on the time of day and season of the year a groundhog or two.

The final trail choice is the RED trail. This trail starts out the back door of the info center. It is a trail for experienced hikers, not a trail that grandpa and young ones would want to tackle. This trail is listed as 10.6 miles and the pictures show some very rough terrain to try and get through and as I said nothing that I have tried(yet) but for those who do hike this trail there is a chance you will see all the same wildlife as all other trails with the addition of deer, foxes have been spotted and photographed and at one point hawks were nesting somewhere in this area.

Trail 1 and 2 are a very nice hike for a grandpa and 4 young ones. We have been there many times and have enjoyed every time. This past summer we have invited Amanda and Warren to hike with us and the summer of 2020 I will be bringing Olenna with us.

GOING ON NATURE WALKS, HIKES OR SIMPLY WALKING AROUND MY YARD PLAYING WITH THE YOUNG ONES BEING A YOUNG HEALTHY GRANDPA IS DEFINITELY A BLESSING...

BALL GAMES. Over the years I have not only taught the boys the rules strategies and techniques of games like football, baseball, fireball, dodgeball, and a few others but teaching them was not enough I had to play along. One on one football both boys wanted to play football and just learning to pass and throw a spiral was never just good enough.

They wanted to play and play against each other and grandpa was the all-time quarterback. I got to run and get tackled and from one on one, it was two on grandpa. Besides playing tackle football they both are proud of there arm and ability to throw a spiral pass. They both know I have a great arm so what we do is they go out for the pass and I throw the football as far as I can. Obviously, neither can throw it back in 1 shot but whichever gets it back to me in the least amount of throws WINS Their favorite warm-up for TKD class is a good-spirited game of dodgeball. Both boys love them some dodgeball and they know practice makes perfect so while at the park before class practicing forms and techniques, they feel that it is only fair if they have a chance to practice dodgeball. They both have a decent arm, but they throw mid to upper body that might make it an easy catch for the opponent. My suggestion is they aim for the knees and lower that is a much harder catch and they will probably knock more people out of the game than they do now. Also, they play against other kids so during practice I throw at them and if they can dodge me or better still catch me they have a better chance of staying longer in the game. Since we have made dodgeball part of their practice routine Aspen has won a couple of games and Ethen has made it deep into games.

Fireball is another game they play at TKD only this is an after the class material finishing the day game. Fireball is played with 2 or more black belts against the whole class only the students are not allowed to touch the fireball or they are out and eliminated. So to practice it is a running game of dodgeball because it is just me against them with no partner for me. Sometimes however we do our practicing in the yard at Cho's and not the park and when we do that there may be another parent or two that are interested in playing kids VS. adults and we end up with a very fun fast-paced game. More than once the kids were tired and sweaty before class even started but I have noticed at least with the boys they have a much more productive class when already warmed up and focused beforehand. Baseball in the park is just a game of catch. However, we do the same thing as with a football. Only I stand on top of a huge hill and heave the baseball as far as I can, and not only do they have to get it back to me in the least amount of throws they have to throw it up the hill. But when we get back to the house baseball takes on a new and exciting twist. We use our practice paddle as the bat and use a beach ball as the ball. That may sound somewhat boring to some but until you play ball with a beach ball and karate paddle and physically see how tiring it can be, it is kinda hard to imagine.

PLAYING THESE GAMES DOES TAKE A LOT OF ENERGY AND STAMINA SO YES BEING A YOUNG HEALTHY GRANDPA IS DEFINITELY A BLESSING...

DECEMBER 29, 2017; For weeks the boys have been asking to go play and eat at McDonalds. Today they were very well behaved and received an excellent report from school, so I thought why not. After they ate and played in the kiddy area for a bit another family came in a had a daughter about 6. I can handle almost anything kids can dish out vocally. They can yell, holler, fight most anything and I can continue to read or work on the computer, but a shrieking scream goes through my entire body and makes me shiver to the bone. For me, it's like someone scratching their fingernails down a chalkboard only 10xs louder. This kid was a SCREACHER. I tried I truly did but after the 3rd time I was so tense, I could barely stand. I felt bad because the boys earned a trip to McDonald's, but I could not deal with the screaming. So instead of going straight to the car and take them home, we went for a walk to try and relax. I am really glad we did because just down the street there was an arcade but to my surprise, it was an indoor go-cart track. This is another thing the boys have been asking to do for a long time. So I decided to make myself look like a hero. I took the boys in and fibbed and said I planned this all along.

I guess because or the time of year and being during Christmas break WE WERE THE ONLY CUSTOMERS IN THE PLACE. When we went to the counter to pay the owner was the counter person, not an employee or even a manager. She gave her staff the night off which was a true blessing for us.

"How you boys doing tonight? "What can I do for you fellas?"

"Well we are here as kind of a late Christmas gift and the boys would like to race."

"Just the boys? What about you grandpa?"

"NO MA'AM I THINK I WERE PREFER JUST TO WATCH"

"What if I was to say Merry Christmas grandpa (no charge) would you go then?"

OH MY GOD YOU WOULD HAVE THOUGHT WE JUST WON THE LOTTERY BECAUSE THE BOY WENT CRAZY "YEAH GRANDPA COME ON COME RACE US YOU KNOW WE'LL DESTROY YOU THAT'S WHY. CLUCK... CLUCK... CLUCK... chicken grandpa is a chicken." Guess who geared up and had to show them grandpa had some mad driving skills? ME THAT'S WHO.

Aspen and I made the height requirement easily but Ethen was a tad short to drive a large cart but they had kiddy carts that went as fast but smaller and easier to handle. We paid for one race for each boy and this OUTSTANDING generous lady let us race for over two hours. Each of us winning a couple of races. Each of us VERY HAPPY. This day could not have worked out any better if I would have planned the whole thing.

I COULD NOT IMAGINE HOW OTHER GRANDPA'S FEEL BECAUSE THEY ARE TOO OLD OR TOO WEAK TO JOIN IN THE FUN. SO YES EVEN GOING GO CARTING BEING A YOUNG HEALTHY GRANDPA IS DEFINITELY A BLESSING...

WATER RIDES & ROLLER COASTERS. I started an annual tradition when my daughter was 8 and it lasted 10 years until her 18th birthday. Every year on her birthday regardless of the weather we went to SIX FLAGS GREAT AMERICA. Some years the weather was very cooperative, and it would be a fantastic spring day. We went in rainstorms and the one year we almost canceled it was COLD but we toughed it out and went. So we have not been there in years but my grandson turned 8 and we rekindled a family tradition and he and I went last summer for the first of many trips to GREAT AMERICA.

Now for those of you who have never been to a SIX FLAGS theme park let me set the scene for you. Before you leave home there is the packing of lunch if you don't intend on spending an additional 200 bucks on food. So we pack a cooler with sandwiches, hotdogs, and a couple of patties along with drinks preferably water bottles, not soda because caffeine will dehydrate you faster than the heat of the sun. next, make sure your little gas grill is packed with a full bottle of propane. Then you need to double-check to see if you have cash or at least a few bucks in quarters for the toll booth.

Okay, now everything is packed and you are ready to go. For us, it is about a 45-minute drive that takes over 2 hours because of road construction. Here we are at the entrance to the parking lot which is a 20-minute line. Get to the front of the line pay for parking, find a spot and now you could be anywhere from a quarter to a half a mile away from the ticket booth depending on parking location. We got lucky and are relatively close and take the walk to the ticket counter pay and enter. At this point, we are almost 3 hours into our day already walked a half a mile and we just walked in. Needless to say, the most fun fastest rides are at the furthest possible point at the other end of the park. So far the boy has been a true soldier and is excited to be there and has not complained once so you treat him to a $5 cotton candy. We were in-route to the roller coasters but we walked by small kiddy rides a young man was too big to go on even though this was his first time here. We were about halfway to the coasters when we came upon the bumper car ride. With complete and total AWE he watched as the cars smashed into each other and it looked like fun.

"Grandpa, can we try these PLEASE?"

"I thought the first ride you wanted to go on was THE BATMAN."

"Can we go there next, this looks like fun and I already checked and I AM tall enough... PLEASE?"

That's how our day started.

We drove on the bumper cars 3 times in a row because of no one else in line. After that we found the TEACUPS then we tried a mid-range coaster called THE WIZARD and he loved it.

So from the wizard, we were off to find the BATMAN. I have been in six flags 100s of hours over the years and rode EVERY RIDE except one. "THE GIANT DROP." A ride that lifts you 100 ft straight up and as soon as you reach the top... WHAM - free fall at 80+ miles an hour and stop. I tried to keep Aspen from noticing it because I knew that crazy little daredevil would want to go. AND I was not wrong. HE STOPPED DEAD IN HIS TRACKS. As the car went up to the top his eyes never left it then at the top...WHOOOOOOSH straight down.

"WOOOOOW that was cool! Come grandpa lets go. Come on... come on!"

Do I tell him that I am slightly freaked out by this ride? Do I tell him I am afraid of heights? Do I shatter his vision of a fearless grandpa and not go? Or do I just bite the bullet and face my fear?

"I thought we were going to the BATMAN next? Let's head over there while the line is short" that was a good plan in theory but did not work, He insisted that we could do the coaster next and we were here and now and there was a very small line so let's do this. I DID...I LIVED and IT WAS AWESOME. That is now my 2nd favorite ride in the whole park and I was missing the thrill for years until my little DAREDEVIL grandson showed me the light. We finally found our way To the BIG roller coasters and they were great as well.

After several rides on the big coasters, we felt hungry so we started the hike out of the park and out to the car for our BBQ lunch. At this point, the day has been excellent and it was getting late in the afternoon and the temps were flirting around 90 so we were hot and tired but agreed to go on one water ride before heading home. The line for this ride was extremely long but well worth the wait. We rode on a giant round raft that when it hit the bottom of the hill sent a wave over the bridge soaking anyone standing there watching but more importantly SOAKED US.

Afterward, we were done. We again headed out and started the ½ mile hike back to the car. On the way home, he made it about 15 minutes out of the parking lot and fell sound asleep. His first birthday trip to great America was a huge success. As for me we walked for miles, drove even further, waited in lines, rode some of the fastest and highest roller coasters in the country, and more importantly faced my fear challenged and conquered the *"GIANT DROP" SO YES EVEN AT SIX FLAGS GREAT AMERICA BEING A YOUNG HEALTHY GRANDPA IS DEFINITELY A BLESSING.*

BOYS vs GIRLS

CAN YOU EVER BE COMPLETELY FAIR?

Being a GREAT GRANDPA means you have to be fair to all your young ones. If you are asked to pick them up after school and decide to go for ice cream before you bring them home make certain you stop at the house to pick up the younger non-school age kids before heading to the ice cream shop. BE FAIR. What if you are going to the mall to play in the play area, maybe you are stopping at the park to play on the swings or in the sandpit, perhaps you are just stopping to walk around the small lake to look for turtles or frogs stop at the house and at least ask who wants to go. Take everyone who wants to go. BE FAIR. Sometimes it is a matter of boys and girls and sometimes it is about age and who gets to go because they are old enough and sometimes it even may come down to money. But it should never be because you have a favorite, they all look at you as grandpa so you should look at them as grandkids boys or girls always do your best to BE FAIR.

Time after time I have seen the boys get punished and disciplined because their sister will start something, and they will finish it. Especially playing games. Harlow will want her turn and just try to take the controller or just go to the T.V. And change the channel. The boys get mad and will holler telling her to go away and she starts to hit or scream then they fight back. At that point, she runs downstairs saying her brothers hit her getting those boys in trouble every time just taking Harlow's word.

The problem is that Ethen still wants her to be involved with the things we do. He has been told numerous times not to ask her to join unless he asks the adult first. Sometimes I just want to play cards with the boys and leave her out of the game. If she is near us she will ask to play but if we are about to start Ethen will go downstairs to get her. Another huge example of this is both boys have been in Tae Kwon Do for a while now but every time they go to class Ethen finds it necessary to ask if she can join a class. I know Harlow would enjoy it and probably be good at it but it is a matter of grandpa time. The other thing is age and money. Both boys were old enough to go to class and I did have the funds to pay for them. Harlow at the time was still being potty trained and would no doubt had accidents in class so I did tell her when she was potty trained, I would consider signing her up. Now that she is potty trained, I am having issues with the cash flow but every time we go to class

Ethen makes it a point to say she is potty trained and should be signed up.

SOMETIMES YOU TRY TO BE FAIR TO EVERYONE BUT FINANCES MAKE THAT HARD SO YOU TRY YOUR BEST TO BE FAIR. IF IT WORKS LIKE CANDY AND TREATS IF I CAN'T BUY FOR ALL DO I NOT BUY FOR ANY. SO, IF I CAN'T AFFORD TO SIGN HARLOW UP. DO I TAKE THE BOYS OUT? AT WHAT POINT DO I DRAW THE LINE TO BE COMPLETELY FAIR?

MAY 25th, 2020; anyone that is old enough to remember will no doubt remember the quarantine pandemic that closed the world for months. So for the past two months, we have been stuck together trying to stay busy and trying to stay sane. For months now our morning routine has been the same. The boys and I will wake up around 8 A.M. Tim will be gone to work. I will make myself a cup of coffee and grab a cold soda then go work on my laptop while the boys watch videos and the girls stay asleep. 10:00 – 10:15. Harlow and Violet wake up wanting to eat. The boys and I go downstairs and I fix 4 bowls of cereal while one of the young ones find spoons. After the eat there is a 50/50 chance Danielle will be awake with the baby. If she is the girls stay down there with them if not they come up with us until mama gets up. Most of the time things upstairs run pretty smooth the boys watch their videos and Harlow will either sit and watch with them or she will go over in the corner to play with her kitchen set.

Today was different, after they ate breakfast instead of watching videos the boys wanted to play cards. Their game of choice today was Crazy 8s. The 3 card games the boys know are crazy 8s, garbage, and of course, go fish. Harlow knows how to play go fish and garbage. On this particular morning, we decided on crazy 8s. Both girls were playing nicely with their kitchen set until Harlow heard the cards shuffle... "I WANT TO PLAY" Now, this whole book is based on things I have done and suggested to others to be a GREAT GRANDPA so the fair thing would have been to re-deal a new and different game to allow Harlow to play along. RIGHT? So what about Violet? Harlow was over there playing nice with her little sister and now she is by herself. What about what I am teaching Harlow? She already feels she is the resident princess and does whatever she wants with no resistance from mama. What about the boys? They went away from doing what they enjoy which is watching videos of YouTubers that play the same games they do to ask me to play cards.

SO I HAD TO MAKE A DECISION THEN STAY WITH IT. SO CRAZY 8s IT IS. SOMETIMES BEING A GREAT GRANDPA REQUIRES YOU TO MAKE SOME

TUFF CHOICES. AS LONG AS YOU FEEL THOSE CHOICES ARE FAIR AND DON'T ALLOW WHINING OR HISSY FITS TO CHANGE YOUR MIND YOU WILL BE CONSIDERED FAIR & A GREAT GRANDPA.

JUNE 1, 2018; I have been taking the boys to the park for years now. I have been told it is not fair to Harlow because she keeps asking to go and I keep saying no. It is not that we don't want her along in fact it is quite the opposite. Every time we go Ethen is always begging for her to come along. The problem is she is 3 ½ years old and is nowhere near POTTY TRAINED. She should have been trained over a year already but unfortunately for her still in diapers. With 5 kids of my own and 8 grandkids, I have changed my share of diapers and if mom or auntie ain't there I REFUSE TO CHANGE HER DIAPER.

To be completely honest part of it is at over 3 years old she can LOAD a diaper and the sheer grossness of changing a poopy diaper was enough to keep her home. The other BIG factor was that we live in a sick and twisted world. I feared that we would be in some park or at a lake that did not have a public bathroom or private changing area and I would have to change her in a remote outdoor corner of the park or worse change her in my van. To some people, this may sound cold and unfair to Harlow but as a man and especially as a grandpa I didn't want some sick f@#k walking by or taking pictures that end up on the internet showing me as a pedophile for changing a diaper.

Her parents know and respect how I feel about this and they are trying very hard to get her potty trained. We go to fun places quite often and poor Harlow is missing out but as soon as she can use a bathroom she is more than welcome to come along. We go to places like parks, the lake, and maybe the mall once in a while but to be truly fair there are places I am waiting to go. For example, I have not taken the boys to any sort of pool or waterpark without her. If I know we are going to a place like that I make certain another female adult is along so Harlow doesn't miss out. Another place that is on my list now that she is potty trained and the boys and I have not been to 6 FLAGS GREAT AMERICA. That is a very fun place that everyone would enjoy so we waited.

For the past couple of weeks, she has been doing well on the potty. She knows when she has to go and can go on her own. She may have an accident every other day or so but is still having problems pooping on the BIG GIRL potty. So today we had plans to go to the mall then the park finally TKD class and dinner at Wendy's. As I said Harlow has been doing well so I decided to give her a chance maybe spending the day with us she would understand what we do and what she is missing out on and try a little harder. We packed a diaper and an extra pair of undies with clean pants. I was prepared to give her all the chances I could to let her stay with us ALL day. (I do try to be fair) Harlow was one happy and excited young lady she was spending the day with me and her brothers. We started at the mall in the kiddy play area. For the first 45 minutes or so everyone was having a blast. Then I saw the dreaded wetness on Harlows pants. I did expect this because she has never spent this much time with us and she was REALLY excited so I did expect an accident. See now in a mall there are family changing areas so I was a tad uncomfortable because of her age but I dealt with it. So off to the bathroom and she changed her pants and undies then back to the play area. We stayed there for another two hours. In that time she told me once she had to go and we did make it to the bathroom. On the way out she did have an accident but she did tell me she had to go but we didn't make it back in on time. So here is the challenge no more undies slightly damp pants and she is in a diaper with about 3 hours before heading back to the house. We were at the park for about an hour when she LOADED her diaper. I mean up her back down her leg with a FULL load in her diaper. Even if I was willing to change a soiled diaper I had nothing to change her into. I had no choice but to take her home. I told her mom she had a very good day had an accident in the mall but was not her fault on the way to the car but the loaded diaper was more than I was willing to deal with so we brought her back. Yes, she was upset that she couldn't come to watch her brothers do their TKD class but she did understand we do have fun and needs to try harder so she can join the fun.

SOMETIMES BEING A GREAT GRANDPA MEANS YOU HAVE TO USE TOUGH LOVE AT TIMES. SOMETIMES BEING A GREAT GRANDPA MEANS YOU HAVE TO BE FAIR TO YOURSELF FIRST. BUT NO MATTER WHAT TRY TO ALWAYS BE FAIR!

JUNE 10, 2020; Today I learned that being fair works both ways. I woke up with a headache and decided to take a couple of aspirin then lay back down until it went away. I knew all the kids were hungry so I told them I would feed them when my headache went away. I took the meds and laid back down falling asleep for two hours or so. When I did wake up I was walking down the stairs to hear Danielle complaining about this and that. Getting up to handle her kids is something she is not used to. So with me being incapacitated for a few hours one of the young ones decided to make cereal for everyone and again in a normal family mom would have been thankful her kids tried to take the incentive to make breakfast for his siblings. NOT HERE...she was pissed that the girls were out of their room, she was pissed about the cereal being left on the table and she was most pissed that they woke her up.

As I was walking down the stairs I was listening to Ethen trying to throw me under the bus - "grandpa did this and grandpa did that... grandpa was supposed to do this and didn't he said he needed to do that and is not doing it."

I know that Ethen has been doing this crap for weeks blaming me when I am not around but today I heard him and WENT OFF. His mom was standing right there and I came flying down the stairs and got right in his face...

"WHAT DID YOU SAY?? I DID WHAT? I TOLD YOU I WAS DOING WHAT? WHEN? WHAT I DID TELL YOU IS I HAD A HEADACHE AND WAS TAKING MEDICINE THEN LAYING BACK DOWN SO HOW WAS I SUPPOSE TO DO THAT WHILE SLEEPING?"

"DAD TAKE IT EASY HE'S ONLY A KID"

"YEAH, HE IS BUT YOUR NOT. I AM TIRED OF THIS BULLSHIT. GRANDPA DID THIS, YOUR DAD DID THAT. LIVING HERE IS LIKE LIVING WITH 3 PEOPLE EXACTLY LIKE YOUR MOTHER and I am sick of it."

Then I turned around and went back upstairs before things that were in my head came out of my mouth and yet another one of my daughters and her family would be on the SEE YOU AROUND LIST.

SO IF I AM EXPECTED TO TREAT THE YOUNG ONES WITH RESPECT I DO NOT THINK DEMANDING THE SAME CONSIDERATION IS AT ALL OUT OF LINE. EVERYONE SHOULD ALWAYS BE FAIR.

Later in the afternoon, I wanted to take a walk with Ethen and have a man to man chat with him to explain why I was so mad and try to give him some kind of explanation of why what he did was wrong. He did not catch me doing something wrong and threw me under the bus HE FLAT OUT LIED TO PURPOSEFULLY TRY TO GET ME IN TROUBLE. We were unable to go for a walk but later in the evening, we went for a ride. After we drove for a while he asked if we could stop at the dollar store for POKEMON cards. I had a taste for ice cream anyway so I was like sure why not. We went in and I bought ice cream for me POKEMON cards for the boy and not wanting to go back empty-handed for the other young ones I bought a box of cheesecake ice cream bars. HAPPY I didn't forget anyone when we got back Ethen was like; "look at my new POKEMON cards" and before I could even open my mouth... Aspen asked, "did I get a pack?" "Me too, I want POKEMON cards" exclaimed Harlow.

"Ethen was with me so he picked what he wanted but I got you guys ice cream bars." As you may have already guessed ice cream bars were not good enough. Aspen looked me dead in the eyes and said; *"OBVIOUSLY YOU DON'T READ WHAT YOU WRITE, HOW IS IT FAIR GETTING HIM WHAT HE WANTS AND NOT US?"*

I ALMOST PISSED MYSELF WHEN HE SAID THAT TO ME BUT HE IS CORRECT HOW DOES AN ICE CREAM BAR COMPARE TO POKEMON CARDS? IT DON'T SO REMEMBER ALWAYS BE FAIR

OCTOBER 24, 2019; On this day I picked up the young ones after school which is Harlow, Ethen, and Aspen. Violet is too young for school and I don't have enough car seats in the car to take her with. After school today we planned on taking a ride and check out a new Halloween store that just moved into the area and we did not stop for Violet because her mama thought she may be too young and life-like monsters may freak her out. On the way, we stopped at one of our favorite places and that would be a roadside fruit stand. It is a bit out of the way but sells the best fudge and honey suckers in the area. Each of the young ones got a small piece of fudge, a candy stick, and a honey sucker.

The Halloween store was amazing. As the customers first walk in they are greeted by an 8ft tall lifelike PENNYWISE with a motion sensor which made him bend down and reach out to you for a hug. The rest of the store has masks, haunted tunnels to walk through and several other very scary motion censored monsters. Aspen was loving it he thought this was one of the coolest places EVER. Ethen knew he was supposed to like it because his big brother did but Harlow, that poor girl was freaking out. Aspen put on a rubber mask and she thought he was eaten by a zombie and went screaming.

We left a lot sooner than I was hoping but I knew it was a 50/50 chance that all 3 young ones could handle it. I did feel bad about the girl so instead of just bringing her home in a panic I thought I would take them to the dollar store for some small trinkets to get her mind off ZOMBIES. Thankfully that worked. She walked around found herself a MINNIE MOUSE puzzle and a LITTLE PONY. Both boys wanted a pack of POKEMON cards and a BALL.

The boys did not have class today so we stopped at Wendy's had a quick bite to eat then back to their house. Dinner was pretty good and the kids ate theirs ALL GONE. So all in all this was a good day. A good day until I got them home. The door was locked and they were not knocking loud enough so I got out of the car to bang louder so they can get in. BANG...BANG...BANG. That did it we could hear someone coming. We were gone longer than I thought because Tim was home from work and the person that opened the door. All the young ones

"Hey, Tim... Look what we got from the dollar store."

"WOW very cool" time said. "Yeah the Halloween store freaked Harlow out so I stopped at the dollar store for some small prizes."

"Yeah that was pretty thoughtful but where is violets stuff?"

My first thought was WHAT ABOUT VIOLET, SHE WASN'T EVEN WITH US BESIDES THAT SHE IS YOUR KID. I thankfully did not say that out loud but simply said "CRAP we kind of rushed out and forgot to grab the girls a prize", then walked away. On the way back home I was upset thinking who the hell is he asking for stuff for HIS kids. Then I thought about why he would even bring it up. Putting yourself in other people's shoes and try to think as they may think helps to avoid unnecessary conflicts. So why would he ask me that? The answer was obviously yes the girls are HIS kids but they are ALL my grandkids. The baby is too young to care that she didn't get anything but Violet came running up to the kids with her hand out looking for her prize from GRANDPA. When I found that out I did feel bad but I was very happy that Aspen was quick enough to realize what happened and gave her his BALL. Although ALL the young ones may not be physically with you, so must remember that siblings are waiting at home and they have feelings.

FROM THAT DAY FORWARD IF I COULDN'T BRING SOMETHING FOR EVERYONE I DIDN'T BRING ANYTHING AT ALL. ALWAYS REMEMBER... BE FAIR.

SEPTEMBER 8, 2017; Today the landscape of fairness completely changed. Not because he was my first grandchild not because he was a boy or girl. It is simply because he was our family miracle baby. For a long time, his mom was depressed and spoke more than once about jumping off a bridge. She had issues as a girl and for a very long time, I feared when the phone rang I was going to get the call she was gone. Then she found out she was pregnant and things changed. She was very very happy she was going to have a baby. But getting into this world was no easy task for him. When she was very much pregnant not only should she have not been riding on a motorcycle but she was in a crash that send her to the hospital. and he survived. While she was in labor she made it to 7 centimeters and his head would have never made it and he was brought out through a C-section and he survived. When he was removed he had poop in his lungs and needed to be in intensive care with tubes and breathing apparatus FOR DAYS and he survived. So there are people who have said Warren is my favorite and I spoil him and treat him differently because of who his mom is and people feel that Amanda is my favorite so naturally Warren would be treated better than everyone else. That is not even close to the truth.

All the young ones have special qualities that at times make them my favorite. At other times they are loud and disrespectful making me want to walk away and not spend time with any of them. As far as a favorite Warren is our miracle child and the older he got the more time I got to spend with him it is as simple as that.

What people don't realize is that it is 5-1. When I am running errands with Amanda and the boy if I decide to stop for lunch, I am only paying for 1 other person because Warren is still free, and If I am running errands with Danielle and her kids if I stop for food I will be buying for 4 instead of 1. Also going out with all the young ones is a bit more of a challenge because if they are a bit feisty it makes for a very stressful lunch.

Also, one thing that is a complete pet peeve of mine is finishing food. The young ones will be whining and screaming they are hungry and if we stop to eat and everyone eats everything all gone I have no issues. My problem is when we order and they don't want what they ordered or eat a bite or two and suddenly become full. When I take people out please eat what you order and if you don't the next time I will seriously consider just going home and let you eat what you have there. I have tried to make sure that if there was snacks for one there would be snacks for all. This policy has been tested a few times with the different mamas but the same car and same family. Amanda has bought things with HER money and made sure everyone knew it was just for Warren. That is something that as a grandpa and in this instance as a parent I did not like. If there is a bag of candy in the car share with everyone or save it until you get home and don't wave it under their noses saying NO. As a parent I thought I taught her better than that. Warren would be more than happy to share but because of some nonsense jealousy, I think she feels that when she buys it for her son it is just for her son even though it is in my car and it should be my rules that don't matter but it goes unmentioned because of the potential backlash it could cause.

A day or two later there was a bag of candy left in the car. I had Amanda and Warren already with me and we were on our way to grab the boys for TKD class. When they got in the car Aspen seen the bag of candy and asked if he may have some and then added right away "unless you just bought it for

Warren." I think that made her feel a bit salty because she is most of the time very generous about sharing unless she does buy for him. She has said many times people can buy for their kids and if she spends her money on her son it is his and his alone. The issue is if I buy things for the other young ones I will never say "sorry buddy your mama can buy yours" or if Danielle is with us and buys snacks she would never exclude Warren.

THAT DAY THE POINT HIT HOME AND THAT POINT BEING IF THERE ARE YOUNG ONES IN THE CAR IT DOES NO MATTER WHO BOUGHT THE SNACKS EITHER THEY ALL HAVE SOME ON NO ONE HAS SOME, ALWAYS BE FAIR AND SHARE!

AGE MAKES A DIFFERENCE. Today Aspen was asked to go to his friend for a play date with a friend from school. He is getting to the point where he wants to make choices on his own but is still a kid that needs guidance. He and his friend made plans and arrangements on their own for Aspen to spend the night. They started this plan on the fourth of July when Aspen called over to his house asking if he could come over to play. Unfortunately for Aspen they already had family plans and Aspen would have to wait until tomorrow for a play date which was cool with them because while they were on the phone they hatched the plan to spend the night tomorrow night. Everything was discussed with Aspen's mom and she was OK with it and they hung up.

The next morning Sergio's mom called at 8:30 asking if Aspen could come now because they had a full day planned. So he got ready, his mom was still asleep, and being the considerate child he is he did not want to wake her so he asked me for a ride. I had no problem taking him over there but was that truly fair to Ethen? He was up and begging to go along to play. I know that 7 and 9 seem like a very close age gap but when you are brothers the things 7-year-old likes are childish to what his brother likes and especially when going by a friend. Ethen was begging to go but it was Aspens friend and Ethen was not invited so I could not just say go ahead so the poor little dude had to stay home. However, no one else was awake yet when we left so I did allow him to ride along to drop Aspen off. He completely understood that it was Aspen's friend and that is why he could not go. On the way back he asked if we could stop at a few places but it was Sunday and we were still following the rules of the virus and every place he asked about was still closed.

The day went like most others they were stuck in the house watching videos and playing games. Around 5 o'clock I got a call saying they were on the way home from the lake and could I meet them at the house around 5:30 to get Aspen. I was sitting there getting my shoes on and Danielle asked "where are you going?"

"To pick up the boy"

"Why...WHAT HAPPENED?"

As far as I knew nothing happened or nothing was wrong it was just time to come home but she thought he was spending the night. So I called to inquire and Sergio's mom knew nothing of him spending the night. These plans and arrangements were made without her knowledge or approval. I was also told that Sergio was misbehaving yesterday and he was going to be punished and the only reason Aspen was allowed over was that Aspen was also looking forward to a play day. Sergio's behavior was not fair to take something away from Aspen. I thought that was very nice and glad that Aspen had a friend with rules and values like that however he was not allowed to spend the night because she knew nothing about their plans and she already had plans for the evening so I went to get him.

THEIR FRIENDS ARE THEIR FRIENDS AND AS THEY GET OLDER THAT WILL BECOME EVEN CLEARER. MY EXPLANATION TO ETHEN WAS SIMPLE... "YOU HAVE AN INVITATION TO A BDAY PARTY FROM SOMEONE AT SCHOOL" YOUR NAME IS ON IT NOT YOU & YOUR BROTHER. SOMETIMES YOU HAVE TO EXPLAIN ALWAYS BEING FAIR!

JULY 8, 2020 For some reason Violet is always the one who is left out from doing things with me. Most of the time because she would rather just stay home with mama and watch her paw patrol videos. But the days she does want to come along there is no room left in the car so she is forced to stay home. Why? Because she is my least favorite? That would not even be close to the case, she is a very smart and independent little girl who is a knowledge sponge. She loves to learn and I would love to bring her to teach her about nature, go to the mall, play at the park, watch the boys take their TKD class, or do some of the things I do with the other littles. The real reason is age. She is simply the one that is too young to come. That would no doubt be different if I still had my van or if I drove a car that all the littles could comfortably and legally fit she would go everywhere I went as long as she wanted to go. I do not force the young ones to do anything or go anywhere they don't want to go.

Now today Ethen did not want to go to the grocery store with me so as I asked who wanted to get out of the house for a minute because we have all been stuck for months without parks, malls, or other fun places. I asked Aspen he said yes, which was strange he usually will ask what store and if it doesn't sell candy or pokemon cards he will usually decline but today he must have been extremely bored because he jumped at the offer with no clue where we were going. I didn't even have to ask Harlow she heard me ask and jumped right in "I want to go to the store grandpa!" So she was going, now I was all set to go with the two young ones and I would never skip Violet to take the baby but as we were leaving Violet said she wanted to go. Her mama started saying no but I thought why not so we took her along to get out. She was a big help in picking out some of the snacks and groceries I bought. She knows what she likes and she also knows what her baby sister likes so we used her as a grocery guild and bought things everyone enjoyed.

After shopping later that afternoon turned out to be a huge Violet/grandpa bonding time. When we got back there was a box of brand new pots and pans that were just unboxed and the inside packing was cardboard holders that were circles with flaps. Laying flat on the table it looked a lot like the sun or sunflower. Harlow has a watercolor paint set and she enjoys painting pictures on blank white sheets of paper but when I saw these inserts and thought they would make a pretty easy art project to sit and do with the young ones.

Harlow and Ethen both had inserts to paint so I took a paper plate and cut some slits and made Violet one also. She was very excited to paint. Both the other kids got bored and quit relatively quickly and went to watch videos. Violet sat with me for over an hour painting. We painted the paper plate and we work on the bigger pieces together. I believe it was the first time all the other kids were present and she and I were the only ones doing something together. I could see it in her face that she enjoyed just our time.

THE LITTLES ALL HAVE VERY UNIQUE AND VERY DIFFERENT PERSONALITIES SO TRYING TO BE FAIR BY BUYING THEM THE SAME THINGS OR TAKING THEM TO THE SAME PLACES DOES NOT ALWAYS WORK. SO SIMPLY DO YOUR BEST AT BEING FAIR!

LISTEN AND LEARN

THEY WILL TEACH YOU MORE THAN YOU CAN IMAGINE

Being a GREAT GRANDPA means you understand the fact that even though they are kids they are young people with brains, thoughts, and ideas of their own. Understand they have ways to communicate even before they are born. Understand that you are not only teaching them, they are also teaching you. They are teaching you to recognize when they are hungry. They teach you when there is a poopy diaper. They teach you how you can and will function on 3 hours of sleep. If you let them and keep an open mind they will teach you how to use the imagination you left behind and be a child again.

If you believe kids and animals (especially dogs)can sense the good in people or that kids are so innocent that they have a special aura. Maybe you believe that some people are more in tune and connected with the power of the unseen forces of the universe or have a frequency so in tune with supernatural forces that they can see ghosts or the imaginary friends kids are known to talk with from time to time.

Do you believe children have a special gift and they can communicate with us from the second they are born? Children have the ability to make us laugh and smile even in the darkest of times. They can show us the power of friendship. Kids have an uncanny way of making you look at yourself with honesty and self-awareness. If you are a grandpa looking at your grandbabies you are taking that awareness one step further you are not only seeing who you are as a person you are seeing how you did as a parent. Spending as much time as I do with my grandkids I often find myself on both sides of the fence telling myself "man you did a great job" and then the very next day "man you dropped the ball on that one." I am one person that believes in the power of the mind and the belief that there is more to this world than what we can physically see not simply because of what I have read or seen in the movies but what I have personally seen and experienced in my own life. I have felt for years that I have a special connection with the universe. My daughter also has very accurate visions that come to her in dreams. If we both have some sort of connection with the universe. But Aspen, Aspen is different that boy has a gift.

There have been things he has done and said that are unexplainable. There are also things as a family we are not supposed to talk about because it may freak them out as kids.

Since Aspen was very little way before he could talk and could barely stand on his own I believe he was able to see a little girl ghost. I also believe that this little girl has been following him from house to house when he moves. It takes a while but she always finds him. When he was 6 or 7 months old he was laying in his crib screaming not crying like he was hungry not even like he was hurt he was straight up screaming like something or someone was scaring him almost to a point of hysterical. I tried to calm him down... I could not. So I handed him to his auntie and she tried... she could not. She laid him down because we just about to call the doctor. After all, we could not stop the screaming and thought something was seriously wrong. As I was dialing the phone the screaming stopped as abruptly as it started and he stood up at the end of his crib looking up at the wall near the ceiling. He intensely stared at that spot for almost a minute then started to giggle and bounce up and down.

From a screaming baby about a minute ago to a laughing happy boy that was acting as if someone was telling the funniest joke ever. After almost 2 minutes he simply laid down grabbed his blanket, thumb in mouth, and fell sound asleep as if someone was cuddling him and he felt safe and secure.

Amanda and I watched this scenario unfold in complete and utter amazement. We watched the wall, watched the ceiling, watched the boy lay down, and fall into a deep peaceful sleep. There is absolutely no doubt in my mind that someone or something in the spirit world was freaking him out that day but I am equally certain that someone or something came and took it away so Aspen could feel safe and go to sleep. We were not sure who that someone was until a few years later. That screaming episode happened as a baby when there was only Danielle and Aspen before any other siblings were around and while they still lived with grandma and auntie at grandmas house. when he was about 2 and a half, I had a very large 3 bedroom apartment where it was we all lived. While we lived from time to time he would lay on the bed staring at one spot on the wall laughing, smiling, and as best he could talk. He would say things like "ya you pretty" "yellow you dress is yellow."

Ignoring everyone else trying to get his attention but as soon as he stopped talking to "THE WALL", he would stand up and say HI to whoever was standing closest "HI THERE GRANDPA"

"Hi?"

"Hey buddy who were you just talking to?"

"The little girl."

"The little girl asks if I like her dress?"

"Nice. Is she your friend?"

"YES."

"I would like to say Hi. Can you show me where she is?"

"NO, her gone."

"Where did she go?"

"Her live in the wall and say bye-bye."

Needless to say, that was a tad freaky but the real freaky part was it happened more than once and it never scared him. The little girl in the yellow dress was his friend. When Aspen was around 4 we were living in a different house and he was sharing a room with his mother and infant brother. His auntie and I believe that his little ghost friend followed him somehow because late at night a few times we heard a similar conversation. Thinking he may just be dreaming we peeked in one night to see him standing there talking to the wall. When asked, his explanation was almost identical to the last time only this time he could give a better description because he could speak better and understood our questions. She is a pretty little girl in a yellow dress. She is 7 years old but he doesn't know her name. She saw him playing one day and followed him home.

You may or may not be a believer in the supernatural or you may or may not believe in ghosts but after doing a bit of research there was a little girl who was hit by a car and was in critical condition for days. She was legally brain dead for at least a day and was surviving on life support. The very hard decision of pulling the plug had to be made. That is a decision no parent should ever have to make. When the doctor turned off the life support and she was declared dead, it was in the exact same room on the exact same date very close to the exact time Aspen was born.

According to the report in the newspaper, it was her 7 bday she was running across the street to meet a friend who had a younger brother about 2 ½ and she was wearing a yellow birthday dress. Aspen is now 9 years old and we have not heard him speak about any little girl ghosts since he has been 4. however he has lived in several different places over the past 5 years including a family shelter and the state of Florida. I feel that she simply has not found him again but when he is settled in one spot for a while and his cosmic energy is released back into the universe she will be back.

JUNE 15-20, 2020; *HE TALKED TO ME ABOUT SPIRITS For weeks now I have heard things in the corner of the room where I sleep and I had just attributed it to being able to hear the activity from downstairs there are also some bird families nesting around the house some of which found holes in the siding and built nests literally between the walls so I thought maybe I was hearing birds. That all changed when my daughter Amanda came over for a visit and asked if I was hearing any weird noises in that corner. I have not said anything to anybody thinking it may be a cause of embarrassment if my daughter was engaged in some adult activity and I could hear through the floor.

"UMMM yeah I do. Why would you even ask me that?

"Because as I was walking up I was gonna try to scare you and there was a white orb floating around in the corner, stopped as if it looked directly at me and vanished."

So I just thought I would ask." Now, most people in most families would probably think that to be very odd and be freaking out. Us we looked at it as a sign. It has been a while and we have been talking about her recently releasing energy into the universe letting her know where he lives now. During this week Aspen has asked me several different times if I knew how to or ever used an Ouiji board. It is a matter of fact that I have but I am not allowed to talk to him or his brother about my belief in the spirit world because his mom is a non-believer and feels that I would scare him to a point he would need professional help. Being the grandpa I am and don't want to freak them out I respect their request and just say I have used an ouija board but I am not allowed to tell about it. At dinner, one night during this week he and I were the only ones still eating and he says to me out of the blue –

"Grandpa I can feel a spirit."

"Really?"

I certainly didn't want to discourage him but I had to be very careful about what I said because his mom would flip if she knew we were talking about spirits and also knowing full well I believe he has a little ghost friend that follows him around. So I asked;

"Do you feel it or can you hear her?"

"I can feel it, grandpa, I think it is the spirit of my dead turtle."

"Your turtle why would you think a turtle? That turtle has been dead for a LONG time."

"I am not sure... it just felt like a turtle."

I am glad that he can feel spiritual presents and personally I have no doubt it is his little friend but unfortunately we can not talk about it. I have seen things in there new house that is unexplainable to the non-believers but it is very clear spirits are lingering here but by the request of the parents I don't talk about it with the kids but I am sure that one day soon something unexplainable is going to be seen by one of the kids and perhaps we can finally talk about his little friend.

On the last day of this stretch, I was sitting on the sofa writing and Aspen was laying on the floor watching T.V. And his mom came up from the side asking if I could come down and watch the girls so they could quickly run to store. I had headphones in my ears and did not hear her so when she touched my arm she jumped back a little and squeaked a bit "what the heck is wrong with you?"

"NOTHING" "can you come down for a few minutes to watch the girls while we run to the store?"

"Sure... but why did you jump back and screech? You scared the crap out of me."

"It looked like someone was sitting next to you on the couch and startled me. But it was just a reflection from the window" I had a chuckle a little "are you sure?"

She knows what I think and what I believe so I took that opportunity to plant a seed.

AUGUST 18, 2019; Today was kind of a double whammy in the life lessons taught than learned today. On this day both boys had a class together at 5:15 P.M. and the current time 2 P.M. The boy's mom was just about to leave for the bus because she had to be at work at 4 but was concerned because the weather forecast was calling for severe thunderstorms. My plan for the day was to pick up the boys after school head to the park. Play then practice like most other days. Because of the storm prediction, Danielle called to ask if I could drive her to work so she was not caught in the storm. I said sure I just needed to get gas and stop at the bank then I'm on my way "you're coming now WHY?

What am I going to do for an hour and a half?" As you may have imagined that response PISSED ME OFF. But thankfully I have learned to think and explain before I respond. I thought to myself "what if the boys were here in the car? How would I answer because I do make a very hard effort not to talk badly about other adults in their presents? Especially their mother. So after some thought and calming meditation, I Simply responded "Well, Danielle you are more than welcome to take the bus because that would get you to work around 3:45 and you could clock in right away. However, by the time I get gas go to the bank we get the boys and get you to work, it will be very close to 4. You know if I were somebody asking for a ride I would hope that I would be more thankful if that person was going to rearrange their schedule to get me to work. **BUT I SUPPOSE THAT'S JUST ME."**

On the way just to verify I asked the boys if they wanted to go to class after we dropped Mama off and they both still did. So Mama was dropped off at 3:45 and off to the park we went to. The play area near the beer garden we normally go to was packed because of a Friday night pig roast so we needed to go to a different playground. So we went to a much smaller playground but it is located right between picnic area 4 and just across the road next to the parking lot picnic area 7. we arrived at the parking lot just after 4 P.M. And there were quite a few cars in the lot but as we looked over hardly any kids in the playground. For some unknown reason the people were staying in their cars I later found out that picnic permits started at 4 P.M. On Fridays and the playground area was not part of the permit fee and stayed public for anyone to use and play on. I asked if they wanted to play here because of all the cars and the people in the picnic areas. That would have been a silly question because of course, they wanted to play and as for as the kids in the picnic areas they both didn't care as far as they are concerned THE MORE THE MERRIER. A little after 4 car doors were flying open, trunk lids were opening and the festivities were about to get rolling. THE party to our west was a Mexican family celebrating a wedding anniversary and the party next to the parking lot was a middle eastern family having a family reunion. Before 4:30 the play area was packed by watching the young ones there were not middle easterners, or Mexicans or towel heads or spics or any other negative and stereotypical slurs they may have heard at some point in their young lives. All they saw was a bunch of kids that wanted to play. Some boys came to ask if Aspen wanted to play soccer, he did. A little girl with her father by her side came up to Ethen and asked if he knew how to climb trees because she was never allowed by her grandfather to climb a tree.

Them boys had a blast Aspen played soccer and was shown moves that he had seen on T.V. But these kids along with older brothers and parents physically showed him how to execute. Ethen was intrigued by his new little friend he had no idea what hate and prejudice were he was curious. He asked questions. She gave answers. She asked questions. He gave answers. At some point, both boys were invited to eat and I did give them the choice to stay, eat, and mingle or go to class and out for a burger after class. Unfortunately, they both choose class, I would have liked for them to stay and be that submerged in another culture giving them yet another reason not to hate and be prejudice.

Kids are little people and have their ideas and sometimes when given the chance to explain GREAT IDEAS. From watching and observing other adults and parents they have this misconception they are always right and the child is always wrong. During class Aspen and Ethen are taught the proper way to kick, punch, and movements. Part of being a great martial artist is balance. One day we are in the front yard and the boys are practicing their form on the sidewalk doing very well. I was on the top step of the porch counting, watching, and advising how they could do better. Preparing for tournaments so practice and perfection were very important. I did not want to break their spirit so I was firm about errors but not harsh. After a few more forms on the sidewalk, I thought he was finished practicing but Aspen starting doing his form on the steps with his eyes closed. I thought he was goofing around and showing off so I asked him "what the heck are you doing buddy?" His response made more sense than anything I would have ever thought of "balance grandpa, when I close my eyes and try to stay on the steps I am improving my balance." That was GENIUS. He practiced his form a few times a day on the steps and for testing scored a perfect mark for balance and motion which is a huge accomplishment during form testing.

APRIL 7, 2019; This day was going to change me forever. Why? Yes, it is my birthday, but it was also the day my number 10 grand-baby was born. There is something special about sharing a birthday with a friend or even a relative. This was my cousin's husband's birthday. When I was in school my kindergarten teacher and I had the same birthday and believe it or not my very first job my manager and I shared a birthday. All of which is very cool but YOUR NUMBER 10 GRANDCHILD NOW THAT'S SOMETHING SPECIAL.

From the minute she was born I knew we were going to have a special connection not only did she share my birthday but hazel eyes are very unique I have them, Olenna also has them and so does her other grandpa. This chapter talks about what will they teach you? Well the very first thing she taught me is that I have pretty eyes. More importantly, is she taught me how to listen. I don't mean just the ability to hear I mean really listen. When she was just a couple of days old she had a couple of different cries. She would let you know if she was hungry like every baby will but she had a slightly different cry for her auntie Amanda and wanting to be held. She has a slightly different cry when she wants me and to be walked around and rocked. But the one she shared with me that no one else heard is the one where she was in pain. Not that I like seeing a baby suffering in pain or I certainly didn't want her mom panicking but something was wrong and no one else heard it in her screams. Her pediatrician found nothing. We did, however, notice she was quite a bit fussier with a dirty diaper so her baby doctor asked for a poop sample but every time we brought one it was not viable stool sample so one day we just said the hell with it and brought the shittiest diaper she could give us. After that we made an emergency appointment with a GI only to find out she had a milk allergy and if mama had milk product it was passed on through breastfeeding and the baby's intestines would swell and get tender which was causing pain and irritation. Mama went immediately on a dairy-free diet and baby has been happy and healthy ever since.

What else can they teach? At the time of writing this page, Olenna is only 14 months and her non-verbal communication with me is amazing. She tells me when she is hungry. When she is with anyone else she waits to be fed until they eat. But for me, if she sees me standing by the gate she will come a running, arms in the air hollering GAM-Pa. If she just wants up she stands there and grunts. If she wants to come through the gate just to play in the kitchen she will step up on the gate and bounce. However, if she wants breakfast or if she's hungry she will yell "GAM-PA! GAM-PA! GAM-PA! while she is standing on the bottom bar and shakes the gate like a madman. Lifted over the gate buckle in her high chair and she eats like a champ...EVERY TIME!

UNEXPECTED TEACHINGS. Sometimes things are shown and taught to you in the most unique and unexpected ways. Ethen has been feeling fine for with no symptoms of any kind. No cough, No sniffles, No stomach ache. As far as we could tell he was perfectly healthy. We however stopped at Wendy's for lunch and he ate well and had chocolate milk with his kid's meal. Later that night I received a call asking what he ate because he was vomiting up a storm for about 15 minutes and was fine again. He was fine the next day but was kept home from school just in case. FINE THAN POWER barfing for 15 minutes than fine as if nothing ever happened. We started to monitor what he ate to see if we could isolate the problem. About a week later he ate dinner at home that was pork chops, potatoes, corn, and a popsicle for dessert. But the same thing happened he was fine and later that night POWER PUKED for 15 minutes or so and nothing. He was fine the whole day with me beforehand and ate nothing, vomited, and afterward played as if nothing happened. Danielle called to ask what I fed him but he ate nothing the few hours he was with me. So we examined again what he ate at home. She told me everything he ate but not what he DRANK. Chocolate milk after he ate? So far this was the only common denominator in both cases. So she decided to monitor things without telling me and I took him out for a happy meal about a week later and BINGO. A few hours later he was home doing well and WHAM power heaves. Right away she called to ask if he had chocolate milk with his happy meal and he did. It seemed chocolate milk was the culprit.

On a very similar note, Ethen is a very good student and enjoys TKD class immensely. Most of the time he is bouncy with nervous excitement but on this particular day, he was jumping around as if someone plugged him into a wall socket. He was having problems listening and standing still for warm-ups. I knew he was not allowed soda after a certain hour because the caffeine got him jacked up and it was very hard for him to wind down and go to sleep but it never occurred to anyone that sugar or more accurately chocolate with lots of sugar gets him jacked just like caffeine. Before class that day we stopped at the store and had doughnuts for a snack and energy before class. I had a lemon filled Aspen went with a vanilla frosted long john and Ethen had a chocolate long john with chocolate frosting and I mise well have given him an energy drink because he was JACKED. It never dawned on me until after class when he came down from the sugar rush and crashed and burned. He did not want dinner and on the way home nodded off something which he never does. So after thinking about what could have caused that I started to monitor sugar consumption and it became very clear very quickly that sugar hit him hard. So there are no large amounts of sugar or chocolate before class and it is limited at home also.

***SOMETIMES LESSONS CAN BE TAUGHT IN THE MOST UNEXPECTED WAYS.
THIS TIME BEING BLAMED FOR BEING A NAUGHTY BOY AND DIDN'T LISTEN
CAN BE ATTRIBUTED A SUGAR RUSH.***

MARCH 27, 2015. Happy birthday Ethen...Today we are at Chuck E Cheese celebrating your 2nd birthday. Everything is going as planned friends and family are there having a fun time and enjoying the pizza. You and your guests are out enjoying the game tokens and riding on all the kiddy rides. After an hour and a half of playing and riding toys, the party is needing to wind down because we only have the tables for 2 hours and then we need to vacate so it is time for cake and presents. Wow-what some outstanding presents A kite, a box of crayons and a stack of coloring books, dinosaurs, a lighting McQueen race car, and lots more great stuff. Time for the cake, a marble cake with blackberry frosting, very tasty.

After the party and we said goodbye and thank you to his friends and family I decided to stay a bit longer to let them play in the ball area and I gave him a couple more dollars to ride a couple more rides. At the time Aspen was almost 4 and as stated Ethen is 2 today. Even at such a young age, Aspen was very adventurous and his brother was his shadow. The trouble was for his age Ethen did not speak well. He said very few words and the words he did speak were very hard to understand. So there we are talking and the boys were supposed to be playing in the ball pit and let me tell you when you go check on them and they're GONE you get a sinking feeling in your stomach and your head flashes all kinds of unpleasant thoughts. I walked around for a minute and couldn't find them. I calmed down after I realized that they could not have got out because we all had stamps on our hands and security checks before you leave. So I called out for aspen. He yelled back "UP HERE GRANDPA" 2 & 4 years old and somehow they made their way into the plastic tunnels. NOOOO not the tubes a couple of feet off the floor they were up in the high tubes and they were stuck.

"We can't climb out grandpa and Ethen is scared"

Now when my kids, THEIR MOTHER, was young we came to CHUCK E CHEESE regularly and I have been in those tunnels 100s of times but that was 10 years ago. As we were trying to figure out how to get them Aspen found his way down leaving his brother alone SCREAMING. Well, that kind of made the choice a little clearer a little quicker I HAD TO GO GET HIM. 10 years older and 30lbs heavier than the last time I crawled in these tunnels I made my way up and carried him out.

I was irritated at first but I had to ask Aspen how someone not tall enough to reach high enough got all the up in the tunnels. "I kneeled Ethen stood on my back got up then I got up & we did that all the way" There was no way I could be mad. Just the opposite I felt proud.

WHAT DID THEY TEACH ME THAT DAY? THEY TAUGHT ME TO ENCOURAGE FREE AND CREATIVE THINKING & ALSO EXPLAIN WHAT THEY DID WRONG WITHOUT SCREAMING. THIS DAY TAUGHT US ALL LIFE LESSONS WE USE EVERYDAY!

SMILE, IT IS CONTAGIOUS. My number 8 grandchild has taught us how to love thy neighbor and he is not even 3 but he has been doing it every second he has been on this earth. At this point, he is an only child and spends most of his days with mommy. He enjoys mommy time cause they watch movies and play games mostly learning games and fun movies. Sometimes he gets to go outside with daddy, sometimes he sits and watches his uncle play video games but what he likes to do is get out with people. When he comes over to visit his cousins he runs, jumps, plays, and laughs every second he is here. He brings smiles to everyone, auntie, grandpa, and ALL his cousins. Warren enjoys having fun and laughing but he equally enjoys it when he can make other people laugh and have fun. Before he could walk at the grocery stores especially he would be sitting in the cart not just saying nice things to everyone we passed but SHOUTING. Walking by a young mother with her son in the cart Warren Belts out "HI"... the little boy in the next cart(whispering) "mama that boy said HI", "well say hi back."

"HI LITTLE BOY."

With that they both busted out laughing and to be honest I chuckled myself. What was very cool about this is my daughter is a very withdrawn person and does not like to even make eye contact with strangers. She certainly would not go out of her way to speak to someone she did not know but as we passed by the other cart both of these young mothers looked at each other with a very large grin with a mutually nervous 'good morning' and both young ones with a look on their faces like they knew EXACTLY what was going on and they did what they did purposefully. As we kept shopping we had to go to produce and find some fresh fruit. Amanda and I were about a foot away from the cart checking out peaches and across the aisle was an older couple looking at grapes. Everyone doing their own thing minding their own business until "HI", I turned around and said hi apparently, it was not meant for me, he looked across the way and again "HI",

The lady realized he was talking to them at least that is what she assumed. Her husband kept looking for a bag of grapes and this nice old lady was like, "How are you, young man?"

"Noooo HI", she just smiled and tugged on her husband's shirt sleeve. "I think someone is talking to you" Warren looked straight at him and waved this time "HI", both of them smiled he waved back and said hi back but as they walked away you could see in their step and hear it in the tone of voice Warren without a doubt brightened their day. We finished our shopping and in the check line the girl bagging our stuff was doing her thing and getting our stuff loaded in the cart and our little man was like "HEEELLLO"

She didn't even have time to think she just cracked a smile and giggled "hi there young man" His smile makes people smile and when they smile back it just makes him smile harder.

THE LESSON LEARNED HERE IS SMILE AT EVERYONE YOU NEVER KNOW WHEN ONE RANDOM SMILE AT TH RIGHT TIME COULD COMPLETELY CHANGE SOMEONE'S LIFE BUT AT THE VERY LEAST MAKE THEIR DAY!

SEPTEMBER 2, 2019; I have a friend who owns a great deal of rental property and he and his bother do a lot of rehabbing. He will go up on ladders to work on ceilings he has been on airplanes and even roller coasters so when he called to ask if I would be interested in preparing the roof of his house with a pressurized sprayer and a cleaning chemical because he was afraid of heights I was shocked. Over the phone, he explained what needed to be done and I figured the sprayer would be powerful enough to stand on the pinnacle of the roof and simply spray until empty and do it again. Maybe 4-6 full containers and the roof would be finished.

Well, that was a great plan in theory but when I got up to the top the nozzle was clogged or broken because it only shot out in a mist not the spray like it was supposed to so instead of an extremely large area covered every bucket full a very minimal area was covered and I had to bring the sprayer to the edge of the roof Aspen would climb up to grab it then they would go into the garage mix another batch and he would have to try to get it up the ladder and then I would bring it to the rooftop and start spraying again.

This system was very dangerous and not working very well so I climbed down and we tried changing the nozzle then spraying from the ground. That indeed worked for the most part but the spray was not reaching the point of the roof where the tin cover was and the chemical needed to go so, either way, I had to go back up. Aspen at this point seen the way the sprayer was supposed to work and realized it was more or less a high-pressure squirt gun. So he suggested that we simply buy a $10 squirt gun riffle and try that.

That was an EXCELLENT idea not only because it worked but because I had a squirt gun in the trunk of my car we were bringing to the pool with us. So there we were standing on the ground with a super soaker squirt gun. We filled it up 8xs and we were able to get every square inch of the roof from the ground and a step or two up the ladder but did not go back on the roof.

NEVER UNDERESTIMATE THE CREATIVE MIND OF A CHILD. WHEN GIVEN THE CHANCE KIDS HAVE SOME AMAZING IDEAS. WE MADE MONEY, HAD A GOOD TIME AND HELPED A FRIEND WITH ONE GREAT IDEA.

JUNE 15, 2020; The fact of the matter is the kids today know much more about modern technology than I ever could or more than I want to know. They are allowed to watch certain videos and there is parental control for the parents to be able to try and monitor and police what the young ones watch. Yeah, good luck with that one. I was sitting here working and Ethen was next to me watching a video and when I caught a glimpse of what they were saying I stopped to listen for a second. I might not be an old prude and let the boys watch and listen to things they shouldn't like I will let them watch R rated movies or they watch the sopranos with me once in a while but what he was listening to that was aimed at a kids game was something I knew his mom would not want him watching or listening to because it was causing nightmares so I told him he could watch a certain YouTuber I knew he was allowed to watch. He got mad and went downstairs and I just thought he was going down to watch young kid videos with his sisters. Was I wrong, about 5 minutes later I went down to check on him and he was standing in the girl's bedroom watching the same videos I had just banned him from?

I had to tell his mom because there was something wrong with him just going downstairs and watching restricted Videos on the girls T.V. So Danielle checked and the PARENTAL CONTROLS were turned off. How that is done I have no idea so one of the young ones must have done it most likely Ethen simply by the process of elimination.

All the young ones know how to log on then navigate and watch videos they want to watch. Both boys want to be YouTubers as a career when they get older. Violet at 2 years old knows the different channels to get to certain videos. Even at 1, the baby knows visually when to start grunting loud when there is a video she wants to watch and the one at the moment would be baby shark. Closing out this particular story would be Harlow telling me "grandpa just give me the remote and I can find the paw patrol videos for them."

JUST BECAUSE THEY ARE KIDS DOESN'T MEAN THEY KNOW LESS THAN YOU. IF THEY ARE EXPOSED TO TECHNOLOGY DAILY AND YOU ARE NOT THE LOGICAL THING IS SIMPLY ASK!!

JULY 3, 2020; Today my belief in the power of non-verbal communication and gibberish or baby talk was confirmed 10 fold. If you think babies cannot communicate please think again. This morning the baby ate some breakfast or at least her mama thought she was done eating until I came down the stairs to use the bathroom. I said nothing and turned the corner and went right into the bathroom. Somehow she knew I was down there and came running to the gate calling me. I went to grab her after I was done and she was rocking the gate like she was starving I asked "are you hungry smiley girl?" I was informed she JUST ate and was not hungry. I put her in her chair anyway and she ate 4 strawberries, a handful of blueberries, and a hot dog so yeah she wasn't at all hungry.

While she ate we talked in baby talk and at the end of our conversation she bounced up and down and tried to undo her safety belt on her high chair and I knew without a doubt she wants to go play upstairs. How did I know? Somehow in our baby talk gibberish, she told me. I set her down and straight to the steps. She started crawling up one by one until she was about half way. She stopped completely turned around as if she was watching something float away, turned back around, and finished going up the stairs.

People that know me know I truly believe Aspen has a little ghost friend that follows him from house to house and today I truly believe Olenna has now seen her too. The question I have is why only those two? There are other brothers and sisters and none of them ever showed any kind of hint that they ever saw or talked to a little girl ghost.

WHAT SHE TAUGHT ME TODAY IS NO MATTER HOW THEY SPEAK THEY ARE SAYING SOMETHING. IF THEY ARE SAYING IT YOU CAN UNDERSTAND IT... YOU SIMPLY HAVE TO LISTEN!

SEPTEMBER 12, 2016, As a young mother my daughter was very concerned with the safety of her children(as any mother should be) but today she was especially concerned because at the time they lived in a predominately black neighborhood and although the school was an academy Aspen was the only Caucasian student there. He was in kindergarten at the time and the school was going to the museum on a field trip and he very much wanted to go. He did not care. "I am the only what? I can't go why? My whole class is going and there are only 14 kids. I will be good."

"Maybe grandpa can come and be a chaperon person." He had no clue he was the only white kid not just in his class but in the entire school. He didn't know and he didn't care all he knew was he like his school and he had a lot of good friends there. The school as well as the bus company that took him back and forth had a zero bullying policy so not only was he never touched he was never exposed to any verbal racial crap either.

Could you imagine if it was the other way around a 5-year-old black boy being the only black kid in an all-white school? Or what about this racial problem happening here in 2020 would they still allow him to go to an all-black school? Would I even have the guts to be a chaperone on their field trip?

HE WAS ONLY 5 AT THE TIME AND HE TAUGHT ME SOMETHING THAT DAY I TRY TO LIVE BY EVERYDAY. PEOPLE ARE PEOPLE SO SIMPLY TREAT THEM THE WAY YOU WANT THEM TO TREAT YOU!

LISTEN & LEARN. THEN LEARN & TEACH; For me I have their respect and cooperation because I listen to what they want and then allow them to feel like people and help me. Harlow is the worst of all she Will push and push but when you go after her she gives in and then will say how frustrated with you she is. But for her, this is no doubt a learned behavior because when she starts with me it happens, she is much better. What I mean is if she wakes up and mama is still sleeping, and Tim is gone to work, and she knows it's me she has to deal with we kind of compromise. She wants to get the little ones their cereal ready or pour the milk so instead of putting the complete cabash on her I will say" how about you get your cereal ready and let me take care of your sisters? That way if they spill or don't eat I will handle it not you. How does that sound?" - or something along those lines, and most of the time we are good and if she helps she is good. Helping me find diapers and wipes or showing me where the correct pans are. She has told me a couple of times how to correctly make macaroni and cheese how much milk to use the right spoon to stir with how much butter to use she is a very good little helper completely different little girl when she helps.

JULY 11,2020; Today I was taught by two of the younger young ones that just because they are only two years old don't discount what they know and /or how they can communicate and understand. Today my daughter called and wanted to come by her sister for a visit. When I pulled up my grandson came running up to the car yelling with excitement;

"Hi grandpa me and mama are going to visit auntie."

"Yeah buddy I know, that's why grandpa is here. I am driving you."

"OH, you are driving us grandpa? OK. We are going by auntie and I am going to play with..." and he went on to name them all in order pronouncing their names perfectly. He is an amazing little man and very smart but sometimes it completely amazes me how much they know and how clear it becomes on what they learn by watching and listening things you have no intention of teaching them they will watch and learn on their own.

Today as I was making lunch I was asking ALEXA to play certain songs as I worked in the kitchen. Warren. Violet and Olenna were in the bedroom playing. At least I thought they were playing but they may have been playing but they were also in there listening. After one of my songs ended and there was a very brief time of dead air Warren came out of the bedroom, followed by Violet. with Olenna right behind in a train. Warren stopped and as clear as a bell said to Alexa "ALEXA PLAY BABY SHARK", She listened and as the baby shark theme shark played all three of them in the line walked around the kitchen singing the baby shark song and clapping their hands like the baby shark dancers on T.V. I can only imagine the look on my face because I didn't bother to find a mirror but let me tell you I WAS IMPRESSED. Three young ones and I do mean young 2 of them are 2½ years old and the other is only 15 months they came out of the bedroom, instructed ALEXA to play a song, sand and danced to that song and went back into the bedroom and I was so shocked and impressed that I forgot to get a video but I did remember to write it down.

A few hours later the other adults asked I would be willing to watch all the young ones so they could go grocery shopping. I had no problems with that because I watch them anyway and Warren would be the only addition and he is a good boy that just wanted to play with his cousins. Besides that by them all going to the store there was a good chance there would be a combined effort for making dinner and would turn out better than normal so for personal and selfish reasons I said sure.

When we first go there I gave Amanda the keys to open the door because Warren had no shoes on and rode in on my shoulders. I always get the keys back and but them on the dresser upstairs unless Tim needs my car then I will put them by the dish rack so they will always be in one of those two places. Except for today. Today as we were getting ready to head out to the store the keys were in neither place. As we traced our steps through the house Amanda was certain she set them down where I told her to. We looked for a good 10 minutes then little sweety Violet went running in the kitchen, opened the junk drawer proudly declaring "I FIND THEM, THEY HERE, GRANDPAS KEYS."

Believe me when I say there is a time not so long ago I would have been furious. NOT THEN & NOT NOW I have no idea what changed in me but anger was the furthest emotion I was feeling. That little girl was laughing and smiling and proud she found grandpas keys there is no way that I could have ever squashed that spirit by being an asshole because she hid them. It ended up being quite the opposite everyone was praising and laughing saying what a smart and clever girl she is. This is one of those moments in life that stay with a child a lifetime and as a group of adults, parents, grandparents and role models I believe we handled it right and she will remember this as a very positive experience Later that evening after Amanda & Warren went home I was downstairs to grab a snack and Danielle and the baby were still awake in the living room. I stuck my head in to see if everything was okay. Okenna came flying to the gate, jumped on, and shook it like crazy, yelling for me. I leaned over the gate picked her up and strapped her in her high chair. Danielle came into the kitchen" what are you doing? She is just tired, not hungry."

I didn't say a word just went into the fridge and brought out the bowl of tuna salad and opened it so the baby could see it. She reached in grab a handful and straight in her mouth. I spooned 3 large spoonfuls on her tray along with a helping of peas & carrots which she sat and ate all gone.

I don't do things to show off or try to make the parents feel bad I simply learned to watch and listen. When Olenna comes running and yells for me while shaking the gate she is hungry for food, if she comes running and stands there and says eat she either wants a drink or a snack like fruit. When she comes running with her arms up screeching she is looking for a nap. I have been using these communications for weeks now and they are always the same. The baby has me trained well and I just hope her mama listened when I shared them with her.

THE LESSONS TAUGHT THAT DAY WERE CRYSTAL CLEAR. THE YOUNG ONES WATCH, LISTEN AND LEARN FROM EVERYTHING THAT IS SAID AND DONE AROUND THEM. THEY DO HAVE THEIR OWN FORM OF COMMUNICATION SO TRY HARD AND CRACK THE CODE!

REASONS

"IT'S OK CAUSE GRANDPA SAID SO"

Being a GREAT GRANDPA means you must be aware of when the young ones come and ask for things. Be aware of where mom is when they ask. Where is dad? Are they talking loud or sort of a sneaky whisper? Kids will be kids... let's ask dad...dad says NO...so they run to the kitchen and ask mom...mom says NO ...So they wait a couple of minutes mom and dad leave for the store and here they come...

LET'S ASK GRANDPA...

"MAY WE please have some chips? Mama said we can have a snack before dinner cause it is 2 hours away", "Aspen did she say it's OK?"

"Yeah she said we can have some chips before dinner as long as we still eat dinner" "Ok then go ahead."

So as far as they are concerned they are covered because they have grandpas permission. Ethen runs into the kitchen grabs the bag of ranch-flavored Doritos and runs back into the living room all excited that Mama says they can eat chips as long as they don't make a mess. So here we are, grandpa, feeling good that the kids are eating OK'd snacks watching an OK'd Disney movie while being OK'd to eat in the living room as long as they don't make a mess here is the reality of the situation... I was upstairs working in my area the kids were downstairs watching a movie eating snacks and the parents are out with the two young girls grocery shopping and grandpa is very calm and content assuming ALL IS WELL. What a wrong assumption that was.

The first thing was the young ones don't know how to eat chips by taking turns reaching into the bag they all must reach in and pull out at the same time creating quite the mess on the couch and floor. Secondly, the chips they decided to eat were hidden off to the side and were meant as a side dish for a certain meal. 3rd they DID NOT have permission to eat in the living room and yes they had permission to eat chips but each was supposed to take a small bag out of the snack drawer and finally, they were told to do an hour of school work and if they weren't home yet then the kids could watch T.V. Until dinner. It did not play out that way. Danielle came in caring a bag of groceries and before the front gate even opened "JESUS CHRIST ARE YOU F@#KING KIDDING ME? WHAT ARE YOU DOING?" She went on and on and on about no food in the living room and how the chips were not to be eaten how she had to clean this mess.

"Where the hell is your grandpa... blah blah blah."

The kids were completely prepared "BUT IT'S OK BECAUSE GRANDPA SAID SO"

Part of being a great grandpa is to be VERY aware of the consequences of your actions on the young ones. As I was writing this section, I was asked to help the boys take out the trash which is one of the daily chores to earn themselves good points. As I said I was writing but needed a break so I took a quick stroll to the corner store for an energy drink. Yes, the temp outside was cool but by no stretch of the imagination was it COLD. As I walked through the house to the back door to take the trash out, Aspen was coming down the stairs and was told to go get his jacket.

I just walked by and grabbed the garbage bag and shook my head. He continued to grab the recycle bin and started walking out the door again "I SAID HE NEEDS A JACKET." I said nothing shock my head and jerked my head a couple of times signaling him to just come on out.

"I AM THE PARENT AND HE NEEDS A JACKET." At that point, I knew it was nice enough for no coat because I had just come from outside but his mother was insisting on a jacket. We went out, dumped the trash and back in the house well inside of 2 minutes and the conversation went like this:

"I KNOW YOU HEARD ME... I TOLD YOU TO GET A JACKET."

"But GRANDPA SAID I didn't need one."

"DOE'S GRANDPA MAKE THE F*CKING RULES IN THIS HOUSE? THAT IS ONE BAD POINT AND NO VIDEO GAMES TOMORROW!"

Technically she had every right to do what she did but I thought it was complete BS, and yes I did keep my mouth shut and apologized to Aspen later because as silly as some rules are in my opinion the fact remains THEIR HOUSE THEIR RULES.

MAY 19, 2020, they have a new house rule that limits the playing of video games to one hour a day starting at noon. The rule is no YouTube videos before 8 AM and they can play games anytime afternoon for 1 hour and the ability to buy another ½ hour or even hour for points. Also, they are required to do at least an hour of schoolwork and chores which in most cases is just taking out the trash and cleaning their room once a week. That includes all video games. So, if they decide to play on their switch or X-box or the race games on my laptop they have one hour and can buy another hour giving them a total of two hours of game time per day. Those are the rules and those rules were explained to them a few times (NOT TO GRANDPA) on this particular evening Aspen was upstairs playing a game on my phone before bed which I thought was OK because the boys both told me that the hour limit was for the switch only. Which for whatever reason made perfect sense to me. On this particular night, they must have been being louder than normal because Tim came up and when asked what he was doing Aspen told him, "playing on grandpas phone."

"Playing what?"

"Red ball 4."

"You know your time is up playing games, right?"

"But you guys said that was only for the switch."

"NO, you were told multiple times ANY & ALL games are for 1 hour with the ability to buy another hour with points."

...and under the bus I went.

"BUT IT'S OK BECAUSE GRANDPA SAID SO."

JUNE 3, 2020, with the quarantine of 2020 in full effect the stress and pressure of cabin fever is starting to take its toll this morning was a challenge. The boys both woke up early and then woke me up to play cards. I was not in the slightest pissed, on the contrary, I was happy for weeks they were waking me up to use my phone or laptop to watch videos or play games. So to wake up to play cards was a step in the right direction in my opinion. After we played a few hands of crazy 8s then a few games of go fish they were both hungry. As I do most mornings I went downstairs and fed them. Today no one wanted cereal the simply wanted Nutella toast. If you are not familiar with Nutella it is hazelnut/chocolate spread.

After breakfast sometime around 10:20 A.M., I took a walk to the corner store for a drink and the boys went upstairs to watch videos. During this whole time, my daughter and her girls were still asleep. About an hour or so later when she finally got up the boys were called downstairs to eat. They both told her they had already eaten and Danielle flipped out; "NUTELLA BREAD IS NOT BREAKFAST" Aspen snapped back saying " YOU ALWAYS TOLD US ANYTHING IS BREAKFAST AS LONG AS WE EAT!" and...

"IT'S OK BECAUSE GRANDPA SAID SO."

JUNE 29, 2019; School has been out for a couple of weeks already and the boys have been practicing and preparing for marching with Cho's in the Greenfield 4th of July parade for weeks now. The day was very warm and I felt they needed a break so they got the OK to go to the lakefront to play and take a day off from practice. As always they had a list of rules they had to follow. As you will read in other chapters I DO NOT go out of my way to intentionally let the kids break the set rules to make me look good and the adult parents look like hard asses. However, as you will also read when they are in my care I feel that MY HOUSE MY RULES should apply.

So with that being said when they came out the rules of the day were: a limited amount of soda they should be drinking juice or water (fair enough) no chocolate or sweets after 6 P.M. If I keep them that late (fair enough) feed them (DUH).

Don't bring them home full of sand because it is a hassle to clean (we'll try) the lake water is too cold to stay out (yeah OK). So off to the beach we go. But before we went to play we decided everyone was hungry so pizza first then the dollar store for a couple of sand pales and plastic shovels. When we did finally arrive at South shore park beach it was relatively slow for such a nice day. Today there were two adults and 4 young ones. I was the person responsible for enforcing the rules to the three from Danielle but when Amanda is on the scene NOBODY and I mean NOBODY better ever presumes that they can instruct, or GOD forbid, correct or discipline her son although she can bark out orders to any of the young ones which at times can be very problematic. Today or an example none of Danielle's young ones were supposed to go in the water and she knew that and made sure that they knew she knew so whenever they would get close "YOU KNOW YOUR MOM TOLD YOU TO STAY OUT OF THE WATER." "Yeah we know."

She is there to let her boy go into the water but is also there to make sure the others don't. How is that fair? For some reason what is good for the many don't apply to the one as long as Mama is present. I MADE SURE SHE KNEW I appreciated her input but I will handle the three I am responsible for. Not a good or smart move because she did cop a pissy attitude and was like FINE...

SEPTEMBER 11, 2019, The very next class after high yellow belt testing students are required to start sparring once a week. They asked that students purchase and bring to class their sparring equipment. For the first few months, money was tight for me so Aspen had to borrow whatever equipment was available at the school. Unfortunately, there was never a full set of gear so he was allowed to spar and practice but only "body shots" scoring in sparring is a point for a hit between the waist and neck in the front of the body or on the sides. Punches or kicks to the back are not allowed. NO PUNCHING to the head and face but if you connect with a kick to the head that scores you two points.

Other parents as well as younger students enjoy watching him spar because as with all other areas of TKD he is VERY GOOD. After about 6 weeks there happened to be a mom watching him spar. She a current BLACK BELT at the school but her son is a former student who had sparring gear that she offered to Aspen FREE OF CHARGE. This was a very generous gesture and made sparring day much more interesting. For his age and belt rank, his sparring day is Wednesday. Now with a full set of gear and a new mouth guard he can go FULL OUT SPARRING.

During class for the next couple of classes, he sparred with a little bit of tentativeness not wanting to kick as hard as he could so he would not get in trouble. He did not realize that is why gear is worn so no injuries occur. He was still doing very well and winning his matches but he was just "TOUCHING" the head of his opponent not really "KICKING." I tried to explain he would not hurt anyone and kicking in the head is expected in sparring and he won't get in problems. Explanations did not seem to convince him because he was still just tapping not kicking. He was doing the punching and kicking the body the way he needed to scoring points.

What could I do to motivate him? MONEY! How could I use money as motivation? He was already winning... so winning a match NOPE. Winning matches was not the challenge using his skill, speed, and power to score head-shots was the challenge. So after a little thought I came up with this arrangement "for every head-shot he was able to score points I would pay him $2 and every time his opponent scored on him, he owed me $2" YES that worked and worked well. He was walking away with $10-12 every match. In a very short time, it was very clear to his instructors he needed stiffer competition, so he started sparring much higher belts and older bigger students. At the time of writing this story, HE HAS NOT HAD TO PAY ME A NICKLE.

When we got back to his house he was very excited that he not only won every sparring match in class today but he was $ 16 richer. When his mama asked how he made money at TKD class. After he explained the rules of our deal. She asked him; "Do you think it is a good idea to get paid to fight (before he could answer) yes, Aspen I know it's **OK BECAUSE GRANDPA SAID SO.**"

JANUARY 4, 2018; As young kids they are very active and enjoy new things as brothers they enjoy roughhousing and wrestling as grandpa I encourage both, and as their mother, she encourages neither. So far this Christmas break has been quite slow and boring for the young ones TKD class is also on winter break, so they have been stuck in the house for days and at this point going extremely stir crazy. Aspen has been blowing up my phone at first asking... then begging me to come to get them and go somewhere FUN. I asked where and he didn't know and he didn't care just to go have fun before school started. I had no idea where to go, the parks were too cold, the mall they have been to a few times and even for me the mall was old hat. I wanted to go somewhere different somewhere fun and because it was so close after Christmas somewhere cheap. I knew that some of the family attractions in the area had summer specials and I thought it was a long shot but I checked some of the trampoline parks in the area and BINGO. I found a place where it was buy 1 ticket get 1 free. Kids under 8 were ½ price kids under 3 and adult spectators were FREE.

I called to ask if Danielle wanted to go watch and get out of the house for a while she could even bring Harlow if she wanted. She jumped at the chance. So an hour later we were walking into a new experience, we were walking into HELIUM TRAMPOLINE PARK. This place has all the potential to be our new favorite place. IT IS HUGE, IT IS FUN, AND IT IS COOL. From the minute we walked in the kids LOVED it.

As you enter the trampoline floor it is broken up into 10x10 squares. It has rope and rock climbing, a dodge-ball area where the floor is a trampoline, an area where for the tiniest of tunes they could DUNK a basketball. You would get a running start jump as hard and high as you could off the trampoline and try to dunk a basketball and if you missed you were saved by a very well-padded wall and floor. There was also a small trampoline area with a ball pit where Danielle and Harlow spend the better part of the day.

The boys on the other hand spend the first-hour playing dodgeball and trying to dunk. After a while they got thirsty so while walking around looking for a bubbler we noticed a door and the sign said SIMULATED ARMY TRAINING. So you know I had to bring them in to check it out. NO OTHER PEOPLE were in here. There were 2 staff members dressed in army gear and there was a 10ft long padded balance beam about 5ft above a ball pit that had padded walls and thick pads under the balls. Both boys took off to try to cross this balance beam but NO, NO, NO, this was no simple balance beam as they approached the army guy was like "HALT" Scared the crap out of both of them.

"WHERE DO YOU THINK YOUR GOING SOLDIERS?"

"Um to go across the beam."

"IT DOES NOT WORK THAT WAY RECRUITS. ARE YOU BROTHERS? NEVER MIND YOU LOOK LIKE BOTHERS. I NEED THE OLDER BROTHER OVER HERE... RIGHT HERE... RIGHT NOW."

Aspen had no idea what was going on and neither did me or Ethen but we went along to see how this would play out. As Aspen made his way to the platform another army guy came up and handed Ethen a helmet and pugil stick and Aspen also got the same equipment.

"OK, SOLDIERS YOU WIN THIS CHALLENGE BY KNOCKING YOUR OPPONENT OFF THE BEAM AND MAKING IT TO HIS PLATFORM WITHOUT FALLING. NO HANDS, NO HITTING BELOW THE BELT NO FACE SHOTS AND NO POKING. DO YOU UNDERSTAND?"

By now both boys knew what was going on were chomping at the bit to get it on.

"YES SIR."

"Okay then... on your mark, get set, FIGHT!"

They went at it just like I knew they would. Aspen won the first couple rounds, but Ethen started coming on strong in rounds 4 and 5. What a battle They were having a blast. After a few more rounds they both noticed that there was a diving board looking object sticking out from a platform about 15ft above another padded pit.

Aspen simply being Aspen looked at the army guy and pointed to the board and yelled "SIR, WHAT IS THAT UP THERE SIR?" That kid working the platform had all he could do not to bust out laughing, but he did answer; "GOOD QUESTION SOLDIER, THAT IS A SKY DIVING PRACTICE PLATFORM DID YOU WANT TO TRY IT?"

"YES SIR I DO"

Up the stairs, he went to get measured and he made the height requirement by less than a half an inch.

Here are the rules:

1. YOU MUST JUMP FROM THE END OF THE BOARD
2. YOU MUST BE FACING FORWARD
3. NO LANDING FEET FIRST
4. NO RUNNING OFF THE BOARD

Now let's keep in mind Aspen is only 7 he is on a diving board with no water 15ft in the air expected to land on his back — So now you have that visual in your mind you can imagine why he was a bit nervous his first time. Yes, you read that right the first time.

"READY, SET, JUMP!"

"NOT QUITE READY?"

"OK LETS TRY THAT AGAIN."

"READY, SET, JUMP!"

This time he did make the jump but he went feet first and you only get one shot and if you do it again you are barred from the jump although the pit is heavily padded feet first is not allowed because you may arrow down and hit your feet on the floor under the pads.

I took the time to explain things to him and said if he was too scared to land on his back I would understand because I don't think I would jump either.

That conversation was meant to encourage him not to jump, that it was OK to be afraid. But it did not encourage him not to jump it pissed him off to a point he wanted to try again.

Up the ladder to the end of the board, briefly looked down and JUMPED. Feet straight out arms crossed and a perfect landing flat on his back. A proud, PROUD boy he was. He made another 6 or 7 perfect jumps then he wanted to go find mama and show her.

I didn't think that would be the greatest of ideas knowing mama would probably completely panic and not allow him to jump. We did go find her and Harlow and she came along to see not know what she was about to see but she came because He was VERY excited and she wanted to see what got him so stoked. We got to the room and Aspen told us to stay right here so you can see. He took off down the hall and from our vantage point could not see he was going up the stairs. Danielle saw the balance beam and we could see the pit Aspen would be jumping into but did not notice the board he would be jumping from.

"Where did he go?"

"NO CLUE DANIELLE I GUESS WE'LL JUST HAVE TO WAIT & SEE", about 15 seconds later "HI MAMA, UP HERE!"

"OH MY FREAKIN JESUS WHAT ARE YOU DOING? DON'T YOU EVEN THINK ABOUT THAT! GET YOUR LITTLE BUTT DOWN HERE NOW!"

He looked at her then looked at me I just smiled said nothing and nodded my head and he jumped screaming; "OK MAMA HERE I COOOOOME"

Poor Danielle her insane little daredevil just gave her a heart attack and had fun doing it. "Aspen are you trying to give me a heart attack"

"No mama I am not but it's **OK BECAUSE GRANDPA SAID SO.**"

WATER IS MY WEAKNESS. We spend a lot of time near water either by lake Michigan or some other small lake fishing. One hot July day I wanted to take the young one's fishing but I wanted to take them somewhere that we were almost guaranteed to catch something so living in the Milwaukee area there are a good number of choices but I decided to take a mini road trip to Kenosha county to a STATE park, not just a small local park. We packed up the van with the young ones and a small gas grill a cooler of food and fishing equipment. Destination BONG RECREATION STATE PARK. We decided to go there because it had a beach area for swimming, a very large hiking area, a decent size lake to hunt frogs and a nice pier for fishing. THE young ones were pretty stoked, to say the least, they have been fishing, they have been hiking, we have had BBQ's and they have swum in a lake but never have they done all of these things on the same day at the place. We arrived at BONG around 11A.M. And started the day with a nice frog hunt. We have caught and released many, many frogs since the boys have been old enough to walk around the lake and they think I am a frog catching expert because of how I grab them from behind and hardly ever miss. Today was a little different. I would see a little green hopper frog go over its head and snatch it up out of the water, show it to them that I caught it and let it go. Today in the lily pads there in hiding was one of the BIGest Bullfrogs I have ever seen. I don't frog hunt with a net because I do have skills with my hands but this big guy would easily slip through my fingers so I had them look in the trash and bring me an empty cup. So this big fella was only about 3 feet offshore but no way to get him from shore so I made my way through the muck and seaweed placed the cup in front of him and reach behind and splashed. That big old bullfrog hopped right in and the boys were in awe.

Now, how big was he you ask? Well, the cup I used was a 12 once plastic beer cup and the frog fit inside with his back legs hanging out. IT WAS HUGE. Next, we went to the pier to do some fishing for a couple of hours working our way out then back to the shore. Lots of nibbles but no fish so the boys and I decided to make lunch and fire up the grill because it was mid-afternoon no fish and hot as hell and everyone was getting hangry.

Danielle was a very good cook using a small grill even though hamburgers and hotdogs are not that much of a challenge. We were planning on eating then relaxing for a while because MOM always told us, "You must wait 45 minutes to an hour before getting in the water after you eat to avoid getting cramps"

So lunch was great and everyone was full but just lying in the sun we were still getting hot and sweaty the kids begged, "MAMA PLEASE CAN WE GET WET?"

"Not yet kids it has only been a few minutes and I don't want you cramping up" she answered.

As she laid back down on the blanket to enjoy the sunshine and catch those rays for a nice tan the young ones looked to me for an override on the lake rule and I said NOTHING. I simply closed my eyes and lifted my chin in the air permitting them to head in the water. Body-language, pssst, who knew

"UMMM where are my kids?", "we're out in the lake Mama but it's **OK CAUSE GRANDPA SAID SO.**"

RULEs? WHAT RULEs?... Sometimes being a GREAT GRANDPA means you have to play dumb and pretend you have no clue about what is going on even though you have been told by the young ones and by the parental units and you have even tried to play dumb beforehand and got busted for it. The kids and I enjoy playing the "JAIL" game. The rules are very simple the young ones run around the room and I have to catch and tag them. After they are tagged they must go to JAIL until a teammate tags them out once they are all captured I win and the game is over. What the problem is, is they are all way too quick and way too small so they can easily maneuver and get around the attic without being caught and getting me easily winded and wanting to quit. So to make it fair I am allowed to use things such as a rubber ball or huge stuffed animal. The rules are however no throwing things in the house. Understandably so, there are T.V.s that could be broken and windows that may be smashed so NO THROWING. We can follow that rule easily when everyone is home but when mom and dad are away Grandpa & the young ones will play. We do use things however that will not break a window and I am the only one who is allowed to throw so I am very careful to stay away from the T.V. And we only play upstairs so the chance of breaking the big living room television is 0%. Now we have been told more than once no throwing in the house but the game is no fun without a flying ball or sailing a large stuffed pelican at them running on the other side of the room. Very recently we were reprimanded again for throwing balls but we were not throwing the balls we were rolling them at their feet (wink wink).

I was out running errands a few days ago and mom decided to catch the kids in the act. As she listened for awhile she could hear them running around and could hear "that one hit you" so she decided to sneak up the stairs and watch undetected for a few minutes. She was not disappointed as she stood there and watched Ethen & Harlow were running around and Aspen was grandpa trying to get them to jail by flinging a huge stuffed dinosaur at them.

"AH HUM...I THOUGHT THERE WERE NO THROWING THINGS IN THE HOUSE?"

"BUT IT'S OK BECAUSE GRANDPA SAID SO"

THE LAW IS THE LAW. Seat belts I understand. They are tested, tested, and then tested again for the safety of the passengers. car seats for babies to make sure they have the best chance to survive in a crash and prevent them from flying around I understand. but when there are only two people in the car you are driving and your passenger is 9 years old why does he have to sit in the back seat? I have had more than one heated debate with my daughters about the fact that Aspen is old enough to sit in the front seat and he is plenty tall enough for the seat belt to hold him in.

The last time we went out alone he started in the back seat but as soon as we turned the corner he bounced upfront. He likes sitting up front to watch and learn about driving. He always has questions about the gears he tells me when I am speeding or when we need gas. In other words, he is a very good co-pilot. When we got back from running my errands he was buckled in the front and his Mama and auntie were both sitting on the porch neither looking all that happy.

"Aspen why are you sitting in the front seat?"

"It's ok mama grandpa says I can"

"WELL GRANDPA MAY THINK HE SAYS OK. BUT I SAY IT'S NOT AND YOU EITHER RIDE IN THE BACK FROM NOW ON OR YOU STAY HOME"

"DO YOU UNDERSTAND DAD?"

And I did the law is the law but when it comes to her child's safety mom's rules are GOSPEL and in the back seat he rides. Sitting forward and using a car seat if available, but at the very least always buckled up.

JULY 27, 2019; The one thing as a grandpa I have to remember to do is NOT LEAVE PHOTO OR VIDEO EVIDENCE OF DANGEROUS ACTIVITIES. On this day I took the boys to the park and we had a very interesting day.

We were out on logs in the water trying to catch frogs. We crossed ravines using fallen trees that were at least 10 ft off the ground. We waded in moving water that was very close to a very high waterfall but the most damning thing was I let them climb a tree and they both made it to the top. The day was great we all had a wonderful time a few bumps and bruises but no major issues. But not thinking I posted our days activities online blocking their mother so we wouldn't here about putting her young ones in harm's way. In theory, that plan was flawless but in reality not so much. It may have slipped my mind that she has friends and other family members that watch posts about her kids. Apparently, within a couple of minutes of posting, she was getting the reports. I brought them home and after a few minutes I received a message "ARE YOU INSANE?" letting my boys do what they did and they felt it was Okay,

'BECAUSE GRANDPA SAID SO'

JULY 4, 2020 - SOLID GOLD. When they are told something they know it is something they can take to the bank. ALL young ones have had disappointments in their young lives already Today would be a perfect example of this. The corona scare has canceled the firework shows for most of the area and as a family, the young ones look very forward to going to the park playing outside then settling into a spot and watch the fireworks while eating snacks and drinking juice boxes. The plan for the day was a tad different they were going to do a little road trip and stay over at a relative's house in a county the fireworks show was not canceled. However, things changed and the van they would have been using is no longer available so they are not going. I was not the person that made these promises because if I was they know somehow, someway, I would find a way to keep my promise. They only way I would not take them is if they did something disrespectful and even then I would probably take something else away.

THEY ALWAYS KNOW AND HAVE NO DOUBT THAT WHEN GRANDPA MAKES A PROMISE, WE WILL BE DOING THAT ACTIVITY. WHY? BECAUSE GRANDPA SAID SO.

UNBELIEVABLE. Yesterday was the holiday and Aspen called his school friend asking if he could come over for a visit. The boy's mother said not today because they were having people over and they were already to capacity. As far as I knew they had plans and arrangements for him to come for a visit on Sunday which would have been the day after the holiday. Now everything was in place as far as I was concerned Aspen already spoke to his mom and mom already spoke to the friend's mom and things were good to go. If they are not in the loop things change. This morning Aspen was up and ready to go by 9 A.M. And his friend's mom had already called and said to come on over. It is now 1 P.M. And Aspen has been gone over 3 hours but Danielle finds it necessary to come and question me if I drove him over there.

Now there are a couple of MAJOR problems here First; her ass just woke up and if Aspen would have gone to confirm he would have been deducted a bad point for going into her room and waking her up.

Second; As far as he was concerned he already had permission to go. And Third; 3rd I was told that we should have told Tim Aspen was leaving.

WHY? Just because it is a perfect time to make me look bad again and make it look like I overrode them again? Aspen did come to me asking for a ride, I did speak to his friend's mom and made the arrangements to get him there and yes he got to go at 8:45 in the morning instead of waiting for his mother to wake up.

WHY?

'BECAUSE GRANDPA SAID SO!'

FAMILY TRADITIONS. When my grandpa was alive I spend a good deal of time up north at his house and at a very young age was taught to shoot a gun. Not only was I allowed to shoot but it was encouraged. As I got older I got better and by the time I was a teenager I was a really good shot. From taking a can connect to a string hanging from a branch then swinging it back and forth a hit a moving target I was also very good at long-distance shots.

My grandpa passed away when I was 18 but we still had guns and a cabin up north so my skill stayed pretty good for quite a while. I had a couple of relationships over the years but with kids, the first 4 were girls, and when my son was born his mom and I split up when he was 6 months old so my dad never had a chance to teach a grandson how to shoot.

Me on the other hand I now have two grandsons that play video games and seem somewhat obsessed with guns. The bigger and more powerful the better. We still have a cabin up north but I have not been there in years so I don't see the boys going there either anytime soon. But my dad, their great grandpa has a good number of guns in his showcase upstairs at his house that the boys are always asking to see. They both know we have shot all of them so they are asking to try. Unfortunately, they are much too powerful for them and besides that, there are no shooting ranges in this area to accommodate high powered rifles and shotguns.

The good news for them is I have a friend who has a brother that owns a gun shop with a shooting range in the basement. The weapons are all up in the showroom so both boys already had the opportunity to handle and aim M16s, Ozzie machine guns, 45s, 9MM, and several other handguns and rifles. At this point, they have not been able to shoot anything because they are not old enough.

I know, I should get permission from their mom to shoot a live weapon but at the same time if I wait until Aspen turns 10 so he can shoot in the range, he will be able to and Ethen would not. So the other choice I have is to grab a small handgun and my .22 caliber rifle and head up north where live ammo is allowed and let them have at it. Now is simply shooting a couple of rounds going to be enough? For me, NO WAY.

When I first shot I seen I was close and wanted to practice until I at least hit it once. I don't know about Ethen the pop of the gun might freak him out but I would be willing to bet Aspen would want to continue shooting for two reasons. First to prove he can do it and second because I like to shoot. Now the million-dollar question, do we ask permission for them to learn how to shoot a gun with live ammo and not just a video game or do I take them, teach them until they are asked or come home so excited they spill the beans.

THEY GOT TO SHOOT REAL GUNS WITH REAL AMMO AND BOTH GOT REALLY EXCITED. WHY? CAUSE GRANDPA SAID SO!

PROBLEM KIDS, WHO'S TO BLAME?

Being a GREAT GRANDPA means you need to accept the fact that times have truly changed since we were kids and even since the time of us being parents. You must realize that kids are kids EVEN your perfect little angels. PLEASE don't misunderstand yes there have been times ALL my young ones have had screaming fits, temper tantrums or worse that deserved to get an OLD FASHION ass beating. In today's politically correct world full of parents that allow kids as young as 7 or 8 years old not only to disrespect their parents but these kids are allowed to disrespect other kids, siblings, adults, and worse of all authority figures. The SAD thing is that in some cases not only do the parents not discipline these little hellions but they encourage it.

I am not encouraging physical abuse however I am saying that common courtesy and respect are an art form that is sadly lacking in today's young people. I suppose I should have expected as much when the kids growing up in the late 80s and 90s had the attitude and nerve to tell their parents" if you hit me I will call the police and you will be in trouble for abuse."

Parents are not allowed to discipline problem children in public without criticism from other parents', teachers, and even the police. I could not imagine being 11 or 12 years old and threatening to call the police if my dad hit me. I am quite sure he would have the phone in one hand and a belt in the other and we would look like a couple of cowboys from the old west staring each down waiting to draw.

If I did have the balls to say anything let the party begin. He would no doubt tell me to dial quickly because he would bust me up before they got anywhere close to the house and when they did get there not open the door. Or if would scream and pitch a fit in the store if I didn't get the toy, cereal, or candy I wanted without getting a good hard smack across the face. When & How did it become politically incorrect for a parent to publicly discipline their child and at the same time become politically correct for society to dictate how parents can and should discipline their children.

Even back when I was first a parent and trying to figure things out there were people who found it necessary to stick their nose in my business as a parent.

I was probably in my early 20s I was with my daughter at a county park for an early afternoon Easter egg hunt. The hunt was scheduled from 2-4 but unfortunately for my daughter, we had to walk to the park and by the time we got there the line to get in was extremely long and we only made it ½ way before they were to capacity and people were being turned away.

I felt awful because this was an event we were looking forward to for weeks. I was very disappointed when we told to leave and my daughter did not make a move or take a step she simply went limp started screaming bloody murder that she wanted Easter prizes and wanted to see the Easter bunny. She was screaming, screeching, and kicking her arms and legs. I was not expecting this and I certainly didn't plan for it. She for the most part was a very calm and well-behaved child. Up until now I never even considered laying a hand on her.

At first, I tried talking to her explaining we had to leave. When the screaming didn't stop I had no choice but to get her out by any means necessary. Now please keep in mind this episode was taking place in the late 80s early 90s when the transition from strict discipline old school parenting was changing into don't touch these precious little angels cause they may break apart in your hands. I at the time was a believer in the old school method so I grabbed my daughter by the arms and flung her over my shoulder to carry out. She kicked and screamed and eventually I lost my grip and she fell.

At this point, I just wanted to slap the snot out of her but instead, I grab her by the ankle and started dragging her out. Back then cell phones were not a thing so no one was able to video this but there was a lady very close to my age that was screaming: "LEAVE THAT GIRL ALONE, LEAVE HER ALONE. POLICE, POLICE! HELP THIS GIRL"

"LADY SHE IS MY DAUGHTER AND NEEDS TO GO HOME, JUST MIND YOUR OWN F*CKING BUSINESS" I yelled!

This woman kept screaming and because we were in a county park there were sheriffs on me in a matter of seconds. This nosy bitch was right in my face screaming. I was able to explain to the cops what was going on so they handcuffed me and escorted us to the sidewalk outside the park and we were warned if we came back looking for trouble she would be taken to protective services and I'd be arrested. So the transition of the cultural shift started almost 30 years ago. The experts say that life happens on a 30-year cycle I just hope they are right to this day I wonder if that woman has any kids and am betting if she does they are the ones that helped turn the kids of the millennium into the lazy spoiled little demons we are dealing with today that are unsure of which bathroom to go in.

The rest of this chapter are stories about families I have seen in public places that some made me think that I wanted to go and bitch slap the parent's others made me proud to be a grandpa, yet others show me that old school discipline is still alive and well in some families, ENJOY...

MARCH 27, 2018. Today is my grandson's 5th birthday and we are celebrating at CHUCK E CHEESE. There are not a lot of people because his mom didn't have a lot of money at the time so we had his older brother and younger sister, me, his mom, great-grandma & grandpa, and a couple of friends from school. As I said mom didn't have much money so we had a couple of large pizzas and enough tokens for each kid to go on a couple of rides. They did have plastic tube tunnels as well as a ball pit with slides and some other free activities to hold their attention not making the whole party just a boring flop. We made it through the rides & pizza. Presents were opened but the party was winding down. His friends had already been picked up and great-grandpa and grandma were packing to go so that just left us. Ethen had a decent birthday not great but definitely decent so I had no problem staying a little longer, JUST US. We stayed for another hour or so and let him play. There were a couple of families that had one or two kids that would put tokens in a ride that had 3 or 4 seats and they allowed Ethen to fill a vacant seat cause he was the birthday boy.

The one thing I did not know about this CHUCK E CHEESE was after 4 P.M. They had an armed security guard on duty. I was conflicted about that on the one hand were should be safe and have fun without incident on the other hand we are in a part of town where CHUCK E CHEESE that required an armed security guard. He played as long as he had free rides than went to crawl through the tunnels got another ride but after a while, he must have got bored because he was crawling up on the top of rides whereby no stretch of his imagination should have been. The first time I walked by he was up on the top of the train. As I was walking toward him so was the guard, but he saw I was going so he veered off to let me handle it. I vocally told the boy to get down (and he did) so I just kept walking looking for the other young ones. On my way back to the table Ethen was back in the same place and it had only been like a minute or two. I walked up to him from behind and yelled "GET DOWN" that must have startled him because he scurried down and took off toward our table. He sat there for a few minutes and then asked to go play with his brother. After being gone only a minute I thought I should go see if he found his brother but to my disappointment, he was again up on top of the train. There must have been some kind of evil look in my eyes because again the security guard and I were about to collide at the train but he again slowed down this time to see what I would do. I said nothing however I walked up and smacked him on his backside so hard he almost fell off the train.

As I grabbed his arm to drag him to his mother until I could find his brother and sister to leave the security guard simply turned his head as to say, "I SEEN NOTHIN", I am quite sure if someone would have had time to video record that I certainly would have made it to social media as a child abuser.

SO, THE KID DON'T LISTEN NOT ONCE, NOT TWICE, BUT TREE TIME AND REQUIRES AN OLD SCHOOL SMACK ON THE ASS. WHO IS TO BLAME? HIS PARENTS? THE CHILD? OR THE GRANDPA? WHAT WOULD YOU HAVE DONE?

JULY 3, 2016, A day before a major holiday is generally very busy in the county park system but today we got lucky we were driving through one of my favorite parks and found a nice play area that only had a couple of families there. We pulled in and the kids made a beeline for the play area. Today with me I had Aspen who was 5years old, Ethen who was just over 3 and Harlow who was about 15 months. As I said very quiet so the young ones played amongst themselves for about 45 minutes then they all found other kids to play with. Harlow enjoys the sand so she made her way to the sandpit and found kids to build a castle with. Aspen naturally found a group of 3 or 4 kids and started a game of tag. Ethen found himself a little friend to play with. It was another little boy about the same age with his mom. Together they were climbing up then sliding down the slide. Uuuuuup then Ddddown they were having a blast and this little boy's mom was at the bottom catching them both. About the fourth or fifth time, Ethen went up and brought this boys plastic dinosaur with him and the mom asked very nice, "Please be careful with that little boy that is Marky's favorite toy and I would hate for it to break." Now it is very important to me that when I am with the kids they show respect to other adults and they treat other kid's toys with respect and care. I know that he heard her loud and clear because I heard her loud and clear, but he sends the dinosaur down the slide. NO DAMAGE again she pleaded "PLEASE BE CAREFUL LITTLE BOY" Now at 3 years old, I don't know if he was testing me or if he simply didn't understand but he grabbed the toy ran up the slide went to the edge of the platform, and intentionally chucked it as far as he could. Luckily for me and his backside, it landed in the sand with no damage, but the mom did grab it and put it away.

My first knee jerk reaction was to run up the slide take his pants down and tan his ass with my belt. But I have only ever spanked my kids once with a belt. Swung hard and heavy at my daughter and she ducked making me slapping her hard in the middle of her back leaving a mark that I will never forget. I have never laid a belt or even a hand on my kids before that and certainly not since. With Ethen, he was my grandson and it was certainly not my place to punish him with violence. At sat for a minute to think and calm myself down. I thought what would hurt more than a swat across his butt? Simply knowing I was upset and disappointed that his actions would also affect his brother and sister and we probably won't be going to the fireworks tomorrow because he doesn't know how to listen.

So here is how I handled this; "OK, GUYS IT'S TIME TO GO. ASPEN, HARLOW COME ON IT'S TIME TO LEAVE."

Harlow was too young to know what was going on so she just came when called. Aspen put up a bit of a fuss,

"BUT WHY GRANDPA? WE HAVEN'T BEEN HERE THAT LONG."

"ETHEN DECIDED HE WOULD RATHER GO HOME THAN PLAY LIKE A GOOD BOY, SO NOW WE ALL GOTTA GO."

Aspen and Harlow came running and Ethen was standing on the slide screaming his lungs out. He has had some temper tantrums before but this one was one of his worse. He was screaming, yelling he did not want to leave, screaming he is staying there and he was waiting for mama.

Again my first reaction was to go to the top of the slide and drag his butt to the car. I DID NOT. The other two kids and I just slowly walked toward the car and as long as the screaming stayed an equal distance I knew he was behind us. It took us about 3 minutes to walk to the car and he did calm down and came along quietly. Very uncharacteristically of myself I talked to him. My old self may not have hit him but I sure as hell would have screamed and hollered getting EVERYONE UPSET. This new approach was nice no screaming no yelling just calmly talking and moving on.

SO THE KID DIDN'T LISTEN NOT ONCE NOT TWICE BUT 3XS. WE ARE KEEPING TRACK OF A FEW THINGS WHEN HE ACTS LIKE THIS. DID HE EAT SUGAR OR CHOCOLATE TODAY? DOES HE NEED A NAP? SUGAR HAS A VERY STRANGE EFFECT ON HIM AS WELL AS BEING OVER TIRED. WHO IS TO BLAME? HIS PARENTS? THE CHILD? OR THE GRANDPA? WHAT WOULD YOU HAVE DONE?

JULY 19, 2018, This story actually occurred a few years ago but was added to this book on June 23, 2020, and with the politically and racially charged situation going on today I felt this was a must-add read. Summer break is in full swing and the young ones have asked me no less than 100xs if we could go swimming. The answer was YES but the question was where? THE outdoor pools and lakes are always packed with people and fighting a big crowd is never fun. So today we were on our way to the lakefront to check the crowd on the beach but luckily and quite unexpectedly we drove by a small park very close to my house that had a kiddy pool and only a couple people. PERFECT! Before the car was even turned off Aspen being Aspen was out of the car making a beeline for the pool. Now please keep in mind that a kiddy pool is about 15' across and maybe the entire circumference 150' with the deepest part being in the center about maybe 18" deep so these pools are only for children 8 and younger. It is very nice for young kids that just want to stay cool and play in the water but have no intention of swimming.

So Aspen was in the water playing tag before Harlow, Ethen and I even got to the pool. When we got there, there was a couple of young mother's one had her son about 6 the other had her daughter about 5 both women and kids were of Mexican descent. Then there were 3 young black kids. The oldest brother about 10 the younger brother 6ish and a little girl around 4. Off by herself, an overweight white lady was laying on a full-size lawn chair sunbathing. The lifeguard and in the center of the pool a huge rubber floaty that looked like it should be used for pulling people behind a speed boat not floating in a little kids pool taking up over half the pool and on this tube was a puggy kid. Also floating around the pool was a rubber ball and a few other water toys nobody was playing with. Now there were me and my 3 grandkids. As I said Aspen was there organizing a game of tag before we arrived. Beforehand we were at the dollar store and bought 3 water tubes which are a squirt gun only in the shape of a 2 ft tube that you pull the handle back and you pressurize the air in the tube pushing the water out in a 6-8 ft stream. Ethen grabbed his Harlow had hers and I kept Aspens because he was in the middle of a game of tag.

Ethen filled his and started chasing Harlow, Harlow grabbed hers and ran. Now Aspen and the kids he was playing with seen the water tag game that was starting and decided to play along. What a spectacle we had a little girly girl chasing a hand full of boys and the boys pretending they were scared of her running around like they were being chased by a flesh-eating zombie. OH YEAH, THAT IS WHAT SHOT OUT OF THE TUBE...FLESH EATING ZOMBIE JUICE.

Harlow quickly teamed up with the other two girls and they were the zombie sisters and chased the boys for a good long time After this game was going on for a while they decide to use other weapons and grabbed a rubber ball that has just been floating around and being used by anyone, so for a split second, it became a ZOMBIE BOMB but almost instantaneously...

"That's not yours and you need to ask if you can play with it."

"Can we play with it?"

"You need to ask little Jackie it's his ball."

"OK? Who's Jackie?"

Well all along I had a gut feeling this fat little kid was going to be a problem but not so far. There was just an unlikeable aura about this kid and his mother. I was not wrong.

"I AM JACK & NO YOU CAN NOT USE MY BALL."

Aspen was about to ask him why. I could see it in his face that he wanted the ball and maybe even invite this kid to play but something told me differently so I discouraged him as fast as possible.

"Aspers just let it go he said no and you guys have plenty of toys to play with JUST LEAVE HIM BE." So they did just that and left him alone.

You could just tell this kid was just a spoiled little fat boy and his mother was the cause. They were at a small neighborhood pool with enough expensive toys for a whole family to have fun at a lake and they had it here seemingly to show off. THE other kids played together and did a very good job of leaving him to float in his ½ of the pool and by himself.

To a degree, I kind of felt bad for this kid because I know parents like this they use their kids to make themselves feel better about life and the kids get fat, isolated, and alone. I did feel bad until he just got up and walked up to the oldest black kid. Now he was the big brother of two other young ones and when I say BIG brother I do mean big. This kid was about 12 years old and a very big boy. As I was starting to say this kid got off of his tube and just walked up to the group and said

"I WANT TO PLAY NOW!"

THE OTHER KIDS SIMPLY IGNORED HIM AND KEPT PLAYING. I really could not believe what happened next. This fat spoiled white boy stepped up to the older brother; "I SAID I WANT TO PLAY NOW!"

This boy was alone with his brother and sister with no adults to stand up for him. Obviously, he didn't want any trouble so he simply sidestepped and continued playing with the others.

Then the other boy spun him around yelled "DID YOU HEAR WHAT I SAID" AND SLAPPED HIM ACROSS THE FACE. This boy although did not want any trouble certainly was not going to take any crap from this kid so he nailed him with one hard straight punch to the nose and walked away. It was the best thing I have seen in years this kid started screaming bloody murder and ran to mama saying he was punched for no reason.

Now there were 3 adults and 5 kids that seen what actually happened but fat ass mama thought it necessary to stand up and call this little black boy names. At this point, I had to step in and stand up for this kid and in the process, I may or may not have threatened her but thankfully well before now the lifeguard had called and the police were on route. When the police did show up and 7or 8 people told the same story the spoiled little fat boy and his mom was asked to leave the pool and if they or anyone else returned to start trouble she would be sighted. As I said the politically and racially charged problems society is facing here in 2020 this story of racial diversity and involving the police had to be told.

SO, THIS KID WAS A SPOILED OVERWEIGHT SOCIAL OUTCAST THAT FOUND IT OK TO BULLY OTHERS AND RUN TO HIS MAMA WHEN SOMEONE FOUGHT BACK. WHO DO YOU BLAME? MOM? THE KID HIMSELF? SOCIETY? I WAS GLAD TO BE THERE TO STAND UP FOR WHAT I FELT WAS RIGHT. WHAT WOULD YOU HAVE DONE?

STARBUCKS. Over the past few years, I have spent a great deal of time at 3 different Starbucks because I enjoy to people watch also I get quite a lot of work done. For a very long time, I fought the idea of a Starbucks in Milwaukee. 5 bucks for a single cup of coffee, However after I started going and realized I could get a coffee for less than 3 bucks stay there a few hours with free WiFi, nice strong coffee, the ability to people watch and the barista's knowing my name and daily drink with at least 1 free refill $.75 an hour is a great price for coffee. Most of the time I get to my table to get some work done well before 7 A.M. Because each of the stores has a school very close and almost daily at least 6 students will make their way in before school for drinks and/or breakfast. Most of the time they will come in as a group order their things wait off to the side then leave quietly and make their way to school.

One morning I was watching and noticed to young girls working together on some sort of project. I don't know if they were thereafter school started because they had no class that morning or perhaps they were college kids but regardless they impressed me. As I watched them they were watching out the window and a mid 30ish woman was walking on crutches trying to open the outside doors. Without hesitation, one young lady got up to open the door and the other held the outside door. As the woman made her way to make her order the first girl waited knowing she would need assistance carrying her order to the table. This woman was VERY appreciative and thanked and thanked those girls. I was very impressed I was so impressed that when I left I asked them if they still lived at home or do they see their parents regularly. They both said yes so I told them "next time you see your folks give them a big hug and tell them they did a great job raising you" Pride... you could feel the pride that they both felt. It truly amazes me how one act of random kindness and then one kind word can do some much good in this world but yet people are afraid to let themselves be vulnerable and kind. Most people would rather be cold and mind their own business than help another person in need.

Those two girls at Starbucks were on one end of the kindness spectrum but here is the other side of that coin. A week or so later at a different Store there was a grandmother about my age with her granddaughter and from the conversation, I overheard the girl missed the school bus and grandma was driving her to school. Now, this kid looked to be about 12 or 13 years old and the disrespect she showed her grandma completely floored me. From what I could tell the parents had no way to get this girl to school and because she had an important test or some other reason she had to be at school that day her grandma out of kindness and the goodness of her heart was driving her. Not only was she driving her but thought it would be nice to stop at Starbucks for a hot chocolate before class. There were two other customers in front of grandma. Some average joe that looked like he was going to work and a 30ish woman dressed in a skirt and heels. This little princess was waiting by the counter ready to skip everyone to get hers first. This poor soul had every reason to leave her there but did Not... instead she asked;

"What would you like to drink sweetheart?"

"I TOLD YOU 4 TIMES ALREADY WHAT I WANT."

"What size dear?"

"GEEZ WOMAN, ARE YOU FREAKIN' SENILE? A LARGE DOUBLE CHOCOLATE FRAPPICCINO WITH WHIP CREAM!"

I felt bad for this woman she was just doing the family a favor by taking this kid to school and the disrespect was off the chart. When it was finally their turn grandma ordered a large double chocolate cocoa with whip cream when she set it down on the table this girl slapped it off the table ALL OVER THE FLOOR, YELLING "I WANTED A FRAPPICCINO!" Then storming out the door. Granny ordered a different drink, paid, and left. Every single person in the store was in complete shock and I felt bad for granny.

BECAUSE THIS KID WAS UNBELIEVABLY DISRESPECTFUL BUT WHO DO YOU BLAME? THE PARENTS? THE GRANNY FOR LETTING HER GET AWAY WITH IT? THE GIRL? OR EVEN SOCIETY AND THE OTHER ADULTS IN THE STORE? WHAT WOULD YOU HAVE DONE?

SUBWAY. I have been going to the same subway before work for over a year now so that calculates to 5xs a week so I would say I know the employees there fairly well and they know me. One day I had to work later than normal so instead of breakfast, I was there closer to noon or lunch. This particular Subway does not usually have a large lunch crowd so when I walked in and only seen a handful of people I was not at all surprised what did surprise me was the family there waiting in line. As I walked into the store I remember thinking to myself what a nice quiet family and how nice it must be to have two young kids being so well behaved. An assumption that was so far off I am still in shock when I think about it.

As I entered the restaurant a guy was ordering his food, a mom, dad, and son about 9 or so waiting behind him reading the menu and seated nice and quietly all by herself was their daughter about 11ish and she was reading a book. Behind this nice calm family was another woman than me. The first gentleman finished his transaction and left. Dad calmly looked over and asked the girl what kind of sandwich she would like. This precious little girl who was so quietly reading stood up a screamed at him; "I TOLD YOU I WANTED HAM!" So her dad ordered her a ham sub, gave his order the wife and son all ordered and that's when all hell broke loose.

This innocent young girl became the angriest violent child I have ever seen in a public place. "What kind of veggies would you like?", "I DON'T CARE!" Her brother simply asked if she wanted spinach and this girl reared back and kicked him in the leg screaming "YOU KNOW I HATE SPINACH." I mean she nailed him and continued kicking and yelling that she wanted lettuce and she hated spinach. Now with all this going on the Father simply continued to order.

The other woman and myself we stepped back to the tables and had a seat watching the show. The poor employee behind the counter was almost in tears because she didn't know what to do. And this abuse and screaming continued for at least 4 minutes. As I said the father did NOTHING but the mother completely blow me away instead of grabbing this kid and bringing her to the car while dad finished paying she said this "Honey can you please calm down, they have a camera here and we are being recorded."

I wanted to take the father outside and show him what actual discipline looked and felt like because it was clear neither one of those parents understood the meaning of discipline. Besides for me and the other woman in line being in complete and total shock the poor counter girl had no idea what to do she looked to us for advice and all we could do was shrug our shoulders and hope for the best. I know that these idiot parents probably were of the frame of mind that any spanking or disciplining this kid was considered physical abuse but what if a cop would have walked in? Or what if the police would have been called?

SHE WAS DISTURBING THE PEACE AND A PUBLIC NUISANCE WOW all I could say is WOW. THIS KID WAS PHYSICALLY ABUSING HER BROTHER IN A PUBLIC SETTING, SHE WAS SCREAMING AND CERTAINLY DISTURBING THE PEACE AND ALL MOM CARED ABOUT WAS BEING RECORDED. SO WHO DO YOU BLAME? THE PARENTS? THE KIDS? WHAT WOULD YOU HAVE DONE?

OLD SCHOOL. Many of these stories have been written because of the mass amount of time we spend at the park. One very hot summer day the playground was packed. Kids were playing in every area. The swings were full, there was a volleyball game going on and even the sandbox was full of young ones playing. There were a few different families that brought different toys and tools but the unique thing about today was every single kid was taking turns playing and working on the sandcastles with no fighting or bickering here were about 15 kids not related in any way playing nice together. At some point, this situation was too good to be true because after about 10 minutes or so some little kid decided that his idea of fun was to throw handfuls of sand in the air and let the wind take it landing all over the other kids. This little guy was in the park with his parents and grandparents both having a picnic lunch up on the hill and not seeing what this little guy was doing.

After 2 tosses a couple of the other kids asked him to stop. He did not.one more toss me and another parent insisted he stopped. He did not. He through sand in the air again and it sprayed Ethen square in the face. I wanted to go and scream at this kid, but instead of getting mad and starting something with this kid or his parents Ethen stepped in and handled it with a more adult approach. He walked up to the picnic table the parents were sitting and said this:

"Excuse me, sir, that little boy over there keeps throwing sand in my eyes and it hurts."

"We are so sorry young man. We did not see him but we will watch and if he does it again we will take care of it. Thank you for telling us"

Being a huge skeptic, I heard all this and thought to myself yeah okay, We'll see.

Ethen simply went back to the sandbox sat down with a shovel and within a couple of seconds this little boy didn't throw a handful in the air he intentionally hurled it at Ethen but thankfully he ducked out of the way and was not hit. This kid was reaching down for another handful but before his hand even toughed the sand his grandmother, yes you read that right, not DAD, not MOM, but grandma yelled; "PETER DON'T YOU EVEN THINK ABOUT IT!", grandpa and grandma both walked over to the edge of the sand. The other kids all scattered thinking they were about to witness an ass whooping and truthfully so did I, but, we were VERY wrong.

"GET YOUR LITTLE BUTT OVER HERE!"

With no physical abuse, no screaming nothing they just bend down and spoke in his ear pointed at Ethen, then did a circular motion pointing around the whole sandpit and then this little boy went to the center of the sandpit and did this;

"EXCUSE ME, EVERYONE. MY NAME IS PETER AND I AM VERY SORRY FOR THROWING SAND. I WILL NOT BE DOING IT AGAIN BECAUSE I KNOW BETTER AND IF I DO PLEASE GO TELL MY GRANDPARENTS BECAUSE MY PLAY TIME WILL BE OVER. THANK YOU"

Peter went back to playing, Ethen continued building sandcastles with the other kids. I sat there in shock and awe but not another grain of sand was thrown by anyone for the rest of the time we were there which was at least 2 hours.

In another example of old school parenting, I was shopping at a very large department store and we happened to come across the same family several different times in the store. There looked to be Dad, mom, and two kids the son about 11 and his sister about 8. Now I have no idea why I paid attention to them in the store I just thought it was odd we seen them in the different areas of the store because there was nothing special about them they were just an average family shopping together until they walked up behind us in the check outline. We were unloading the cart and the family behind us had a relatively full cart and the girl was holding the handle standing very nice but the boy, the boy started acting up a bit and tried climbing in the cart saying he was tired. Dad told him no because they had bread and other items he may squash in the cart and moved the cart away. The second time the boy made it into the cart and said he was tired. Dad lifted him out and again firmly said "I SAID NO, THERE ARE THINGS YOU COULD SQUASH" set him on the ground but this kid was like; "but I am tired."

This father said nothing he simply walked over to the cart handed his wife his wallet said that they'd be waiting outside and took the boy by the arms lifted him out of the cart and took him out of the store by one arm. Now in today's politically correct world and parents not allowed to "discipline" their children especially in public I thought for sure a security guard or some nosey parent would be sticking their noses in to explain why he had to leave his son alone. NOPE, he walked out the door with no resistance. I don't encourage physical abuse so I hope he did not beat the crap out of the kid but I am a VERY firm believer in respect and listening to your elders. It was very refreshing that there are other people not afraid to handle their own business by controlling their kids without fear of being on the 6 P.M. Facebook post.

VIDEO GAMES. There are skills in my life that I have been taught and are not allowed to be passed down to my grandsons. Skills like shooting and handling a real gun. They are allowed to use sniper rifles, handguns, and shotguns as long as they are electronic. We go to an arcade that has handguns that shoot and kill zombies, that same arcade has hunting games that you aim at, shoot, and kill animals. There is even a cops and robbers game where you can shoot the bad guys.

I have a very strong opinion about video games. Yes, I believe that in 1989 when the authorities took the right away from parents to discipline their kids was the start of the downturn of America that we knew and loved. For me, even more, responsible for the desensitization of our youth are the graphic and violent nature of some video games. It has been my opinion for years that as the graphics of video games become more lifelike the more gamers will be convinced that if you shoot someone they will simply come back to life in the next round.

My opinion of this strengthened just the other day when my 9 years old grandson asked me how long it would take to heal if he was shot with a bullet. Over the past few decades, there have been several mass school shootings. Why only in the last couple of decades? It is my opinion that as graphics get more violent and realistic kids have it in their minds that people will simply come back to life. I have been through school and my parents have also been through school and there has never been anything close to what happened in the last 20 years. School shootings were simply unheard of.

At some point, the writers of the T.V. Show criminal minds must have agreed with me to some degree suggesting the violence in games must be brought into the light. Here is a summary of an episode along with a few lines of dialog pulled directly from that episode: In the Washington DC area, a school bus transporting twenty-four high school students home after school is commandeered. The GPS on the bus is disabled, meaning that the bus disappears without a trace along with all its passengers, which not only includes the students, but also the driver, Roy Webster, and the bus monitor, Carol Roberts. Cell phone calls to the students are unanswered. The bus and the cell phones are eventually found, but the twenty-six are nowhere to be found. Initially, the B.A.U. (Behavioral Analyst Unit) believes the abduction has something to do with a previous altercation between Webster and the students, which resulted in the need for the bus monitor. However as the B.A.U. gathers evidence on the case, Rossi notices that much of that evidence is remarkably similar to a video game called Gods of Combat, pointing to the suspicion that the unsubs (unknown subject of an investigation) are extreme gamers who are turning their love of the game into reality. So the team delves into the psyche of gamers and the codes by which they live in the hope of finding the bus passengers still alive.

The conversation went like this:

David Rossi: "Abducting a bus, a form of transportation, gas masks, shock collars. Dividing people into teams. This sounds a lot like, Gods of Combat."

David Rossi: "This is a video game?"

Derek Morgan: "These guys are replicating a video game?"

David Rossi: "In the game, you take over a form of public transportation. Subway, train, bus. That's how you get your players."

I know Video games are a huge part of today's world and will probably never go away as a matter of fact they will most likely continue to get more violent and realistic. As I write this section my 5-year-old granddaughter is playing a video game trying to figure out a strategy to kill her opponent. In the game she can use shotguns, AR s, or several different handguns. My concern has always been how would she know at 5 that a gun in videos are not real and if somehow came across a real weapon would not shoot someone because the games taught her how to win by killing.

Now it may just be me but in my opinion, 5 years old is WAAAAAY too young to be killing people in games that are so graphic that blood splatters from the headshots you hit I do know that they span across all ages from old to young. Some teens as well as adults I know have no other social life other than video games.

Being an old school grandpa it truly disturbs me that I have watched some of these games being played for hours. I have seen games so graphic that made me queasy. There are shoot 'em up games, slasher games, and games where the hero is a movie killer and the object of the game is to hang your victims on a meat hook. I have seen war games that kill with a headshot from a long-range or you can walk up behind someone and blow their brains out.

I would only have 2 questions: First I would wonder if the parents that allow these younger kids to play some of these slasher games ever sat down to watch the game or if they feel it is only a game so it must be fine. I would be willing to bet that some of these parents have parental controls on the cable channels and the young ones are not allowed to access R or more adult content in movies because of graphic violence or sexual content when in reality some of the movies are a great deal less graphic than the games they are playing.

Second, how do they rate games? I know that some games in the store are rated PG13 and I have also been in the video stores looking with my grandsons when the clerk asked who they were with because of the adult content in the game or pictured on the case. So if they cannot but it or look at it in the store why are you letting them play it at home? For years people have been talking about the senseless but silly violence in Bugs Bunny cartoons. How Elmer Fudd blows Daffy's beak around the other side of his head or the Road Runner continually blows up the coyote. Yes, this is cartoon violence a cartoon person damaging a cartoon animal. How Porky Pig never wore pants and Bugs Bunny sometimes dressed like a female and how inappropriate that is for today's young people and want them banned or removed from television.

ALL I CAN SAY TO THAT IS ARE YOU FREAKING KIDDING ME? LOOK AT WHAT THESE KIDS ARE EXPOSED TO DAILY AND FOCUS ON FIXING THE PROBLEMS OF TODAY!

MY HOUSE, MY RULES

Being a GREAT GRANDPA means you must realize the kids have rules that they MUST follow both in and out of their house. They are expected to act a certain way in school, at home, restaurants, on field trips, and Tae Kwon Do class. Everywhere they go they are expected to act a certain way. Fortunately, in most cases, the actions required are the same. They are expected to be courteous to adults, show respect, and generally act like well-mannered kids.

When they are with me I certainly don't purposefully allow them to break rules. I know that ice cream, sugar, chocolate, and caffeine affect them in some strange ways sometime they may get hyper or super cranky or have a tough time winding down and getting ready to go to sleep so it is no sweets or soda after 7 P.M. No matter who they are with are where ever they happen to be.

There would be a few minor adjustments from home rules to being with me rules: For example, at home before they are allowed to have a beverage they must finish their entire plate and then get a drink to wash it down. Why? because they may get filled up on liquid not eating their meal. That is one rule I completely disagree with. When at my house or if we are eating at a restaurant especially a buffet-style restaurant they may not get 2 or 3 glasses of milk while eating because yes that may fill them up but they would get at least one with a meal and then as much as they wanted after. Another with dessert too if that's what they want.

However, there are different rules when they are with me than if they were with the family and they even have slightly different rules when their mom is with us. The basic difference is I let the boys be boys and when their sisters are running around trying to do what their brothers are doing I let the kids be kids.

This chapter is written from real-life experiences, future things to come, and maybe a what-if or two. I have a T-shirt that reads "A GRANDPA IS THE GUY WHO HELPS US GET INTO TROUBLE FOR THINGS WE HAVE NOT THOUGHT UP YET" An interesting MOTO to follow and live by.

Recently I had a couple of chances to cook dinner for the young ones and I also babysat the whole day a couple of times. The other day I made spaghetti and all the young ones sat nicely at the table and ate. After dinner, they all asked to be excused and we all had cotton candy pop cycles for desert then we calmly sat and watched a movie until Danielle and Tim got back. I did post this on my Facebook page and received many comments from other family members showing their approval for a good meal and how all the young ones were sitting like little angels at the table.

A day or two later I did not know Tim was home and not working and Ethen came up to ask me to fix them cereal but before I went downstairs the girls had woken up and were also hungry so I made all of them cereal and they all sat together eating and when finished they all rinsed bowls and went back to what they were doing. A few days later Danielle and Tim went running errands and were gone way longer than anticipated so I made the kids a late lunch. Only I did not make it alone, they all helped to make what they wanted. Aspen wanted Ramen noodles and PB&J sandwiches, Ethen & the baby wanted sandwiches on hamburger buns which Ethen made for me. Harlow and Violet went with hotdogs with catsup cut up on a plate and because the stove was involved I made those.

Again all the young ones were sitting nice and calm eating lunch when they did get home from running errands and it dawned on me...maybe they treat me like a second class guest because it may bother them that their kids are so disciplined and well behaved for me and not so much when Danielle is here alone with them but even when Tim is here the dictatorship is in place they whine and complain about the food. Violet will not stay still she runs around and eats when and if she wants so when they are all with me they have been sitting together and eating well making my authority and respect level way higher than it will ever be here without me.

The atmosphere is like that of the days of kings and queens. They run the house like a kingdom and being a royal does not make you special. That is why the kings and queens are no longer in power. The people (or young ones) will only be ruled by fear for so long. Even in their own house and me as a guest and certainly not someone who is allowed to make the rules of the house but I am surely expected to enforce them.

The problem is they change the rules to fit the situation at hand whereas I try to be as consistent as possible. An example of this would be the 4th of July 2020 because of the coronavirus all Milwaukee county firework shows were canceled. However, there were plenty of private people shooting off fireworks in the neighborhood, and the kids and I were out on the front porch watching when Danielle and Tim came back from driving Amanda and Warren home so they decided to take the young ones down the block for a better view. Now that is GREAT. Family time that showed them the chain of command and who is the boss. That was all fine and well until they came back to the house. It was 9;30 which is their bedtime on the weekend but Danielle found it Ok to allow them to stay up longer watching videos. WHY? Because I told them it was bedtime and Ethen ran downstairs to say I told them to go to bed. Now I thought I was being a good grandpa and helpful by enforcing the bedtime rule. But as it turned out I received a text that said: "YES I know what time it is and I also know they are waiting for me to put them in bed but I also said they could stay awake until then" Honestly, I just wanted to respond with a big F/U but did not I simply responded,

"OK."

It became very clear to me why they act the way they do around home when Danielle is here alone as the authority figure. Danielle as the authority will never work because first off she sleeps far too long in the morning allowing the kids to be alone and running the show. When she does finally get up she does not keep things consistent. If the rule is the rule be it no food in the living room or no jumping on her bed if the kids are whining she will give in to stop the whining or even worse she will break the house rules and allow them to do it because if she can they can.

AFTER STAYING THERE FOR MONTHS, I CERTAINLY SEE WHERE I FELL SHORT AS A DAD AND WHAT DANIELLE NEEDS TO DO AS A MOM. BUT AS FAR AS BEING THEIR GRANDPA THAT IS MUCH EASIER. MY HOUSE MY RULES SIMPLY MEANS CONSISTENCY!

FAMILY vs FAMILY. At times, the littles go visit other family members that have a completely different set of house rules. So how do you handle that without completely confusing the young ones? For example say we are over by great-grandma visiting and she offers everyone a cookie, just a cookie, and instead of a "thank you" one of the littles asks for more that is one thing great-grandma doe not tolerate. If she offers something take it if it is not good enough or you instantly ask for more you get nothing. It has been that way since I was a kid and although the young ones don't visit as much as they should that rule has never changed. Ethen is mostly the culprit for that one. He is used to his house where if offered something he immediately asks for more with no consequences either he gets more or he doesn't. Here again, the rule is completely different and something they need to remember. Another difference is toys even though there are not many toys to play with they are required to put back what they are playing with before taking out something else.

When they go visit Auntie Da they have different house rules to follow there also. The problem is who is home and who happens to be in charge at the moment. If grandma or Charlie are there the rules are different than if Amanda is there alone with Warren. Out by their other grandma's house the house rules, yard rules, and mealtime rules are all different.

SO I GUESS THE POINT I AM TRYING TO MAKE HERE IS YES MY HOUSE MY RULES BUT THE YOUNG ONES HAVE SO MANY DIFFERENT RULES EVERYWHERE THEY GO I TRY TO CUT THEM SOME SLACK!

PRACTICE BEFORE PLAYTIME. At home they are allowed to wake up and head right to the T.V. Not to watch any sort of shows which would be bad enough but they are allowed to watch videos on YouTube of the games they play. I don't mean a video or two I mean they are watching gaming videos for HOURS then they are supposed to get an hour of gaming time which never happens it is always 2 plus hours and when they are finally taken off the games they will all be fighting tooth and nail saying they have only been playing minutes not hours. That is how it works at their house for me at my house there is a very good chance there will be no video games but if there are there is no way they would just start watching YouTube or play games they would have to earn time.

I would take a page out of their playbook they use at home. At home, the young ones get a good point for eating all their food at mealtime and if they complain or don't finish they receive a bad point which is very effective but I would take it a step further. Instead of points, they would earn or lose time and there would be more than just finishing their meal for points. If they set the table 5 minutes, if they help prepare the meal 10 minutes, eat it all gone 10 minutes clean and rinse the dishes 5 minutes. So they would know right from the jump what they were earning. On the other side of the meal coin, they would not be required to help make food it would just be an incentive to earn more fun time. Not finishing – 10 minutes complaining about the food – 5 minutes not sitting nicely or running around at mealtime – 5 minutes.

Even if I do allow video time at my house there is absolutely no way they would be allowed to play video games for two or more hours. I feel that video games are a complete waste of time but they young ones enjoy them so I guess I would not take them completely away but in my house gaming time would be earned not just given.

How else could they earn time? Chores. My house has things for them that they can't or don't have at home. They all like fish, not to eat but to watch so a fish tank is a relatively easy way to teach the young ones responsibility to work their way up to bigger pets that require more responsibility. For the smaller young ones maybe not a fish tank but perhaps a fishbowl with a guppy or goldfish to start with. How do they earn time? 5 minutes if they feed them 5 minutes if they scoop them out and put them in the holding bowl 10 minutes for emptying then rinsing the home bowl and another 10 minutes for refilling it and putting their fish back home so the littlest of the littles can earn a half-hour changing the fishbowl water. The older kids can earn a half-hour simply by helping me clean the tanks but if they don't need cleaning the can feed them check the temperature and PH levels and add chemicals if needed. No time will ever be deducted for not helping this is a chore that offers extra time for helping but no consequences for not. But as they are getting older they are asking for different pets that will require more care and responsibility.

I am an animal lover so when the kids ask for pets I will be more than happy to take care of them when the young ones are not there but it is a perfect time to teach them self-confidence. I do have a cat and she is very friendly and playful. She loves the young ones and they love her but Ethen has been asking for a kitten to take care of by himself. Aspen, as well as myself, are huge fans of German Shepards so by the time this book is published and on the shelves, we will certainly have at least 1 male German Shepard puppy and depending on how quick this book sells a female Shepard to breed when they are old enough.

The girls are all fans of different animals, when we go to the pet stores they watch mice, rats, guinea pigs, and whatever other small animals I let them hold. Their grandma has a big ol' rabbit in her basement they can pet and play with when they go visit. Although years ago I used to breed rats and mice for pet stores those particular rodents did not seem appropriate for 3 young girly girls to take care of. So with a lot of thought and consideration, I went with an adult female ferret named yes you guessed it, Elsa. The deal we have is yes these pets are not just mine and they are not just theirs they are ours which means the priority when they come over is to make sure that all our pets are taken care of. So if they do the list of what needs to be done without me asking or telling them they earn 30 minutes of fun time. So the list would be this. First, they have to check all the food dishes to make sure they have food. If not they all know where the food is kept and they simply fill the bowls (when they are coming over I intensionally leave them only half full), after they fill the bowls the girls have to check the litter box to see if it needs to be cleaned.

Ethen does the same thing for the kitty box. I will not make them clean it out but they will tell me yes or no. Next, all the animals need to exercise and they all get along great so we grab the kitties and open Elsa's age and let them play awhile. Aspen will be taking the puppy out in the yard either playing ball or frisbee with him for a ½ hour or so then we put Elsa back and we all take the puppy for a nice long walk. When we get back everyone gets another 30 minutes added to their game time.

When I was staying there I have seen many many times the young ones would much prefer face time playing cards or board games with mom, Tim & grandpa than any video game. I think they play video games because they can compete and sort of bond as siblings also Tim is a huge video game fan so they try to be like "DAD" and want to play well.

However, the problem is they as parents don't make time to play games or make time to teach. They simply feel that providing them with a place to live with food and clothes makes a good parent which in my opinion does not. Anyone with any sort of decent job can provide the basics and set them in front of a T.V. Or game controller and say here ya go have at her. The kids crave face time and they also need to be taught not just punished lessons on what they do wrong but schoolwork and strategies for games like checkers or card games like garbage or crazy 8s. They will feel not only a sense of love but a huge sense of accomplishment if they happen to win.

When they are with me I try hard to discourage playing video games to a point where for fun I ask them if they would rather play cards if that doesn't work I will go to a board game. In most cases when given the choice between playing a video game and burning a ½ hour they both would rather play against me in Chinese checkers or regular checkers sometimes we compete in tic tac toe and have mini-tournaments. When they have been playing a while and I feel they need to take a break I offer to use fun time fishing or playing at the park. 9 times out of ten they will choose fishing over videos. The only time that I can remember them choosing games over park time is when there was cash involved. I am not a big fan of the bloody and gruesome shoot 'em up games they play I am more of a race guy when or if I play games. There is a traffic game preloaded on my laptop that does not compete head to head but it is a points and time game. For some unknown reason, they both feel that if they can beat grandpas high score it is worthy of compensation.

So to show them I was confident in my high score but believed they both had the skill to beat me over time so I offered a $ 20 reward for either of them if they could beat me in 10 tries or less if not the reward went down to $ 10 with no limits on how many tries it took. On try 12 I owed Aspen 10 bucks and on his try 14, I had to bust out another 10 to Ethen. Although it took me days to accumulate that high score and I thought the boys would get frustrated and quit never underestimate the power of a young mind to concentrate where money is involved or they have a chance to best their grandpa.

MY ROOM, MY STUFF, STAY OUT!   This whole chapter is written on comparisons from how they kids are allowed to live and rule the house when I was staying there as opposed to the way it should be in other people's homes but more specifically my house. The sleeping arrangements were very good. As far as space there is plenty of room, the boys have a bunk bed in the middle of the room, both girls have a single bed in their room and the baby has a crib butted up against Danielle's bed. I have a queen size mattress in the corner of the attic. Now the way things are set up I have a couple of boxes of leggings pushed up against the wall another 3 or 4 boxes of stuff up in the loft where none of the young ones can reach. I also have a couple of piles of things on the ledge going downstairs with my meds and office supplies in the second drawer of the boy's dresser. Most of this stuff is product that I have pictures and descriptions of online but the problem is most of it is on the floor in boxes or bags which makes it very accessible to the young ones. Now when I first started staying there Violet was a little demon child she would take everything from the leggings in the boxes to boxes I had on the ledge (I still wonder how she got those).

She was tall enough to get in the drawer where I kept my meds and I would find medicine bottles all over the house. Again it was THEIR HOUSE not mine so I was not supposed to discipline her for messing with my stuff. The mattress I get to sleep on is not even theirs it was giving to them by my other daughter to use until they bought beds for the boys. They did get beds and my mattress is a trampoline for all the young ones and is a complete rag. The padding is shredded with clothe covered springs making their way to the surface. Very uncomfortable to sleep on but do you think any of them care? Not for a second. As long as they have something to play on and jump be it someone else's or their stuff they don't care. For being part of my family it is very disheartening seeing what kind of disrespect they have for other people's things. Broken, lost, or destroyed they simply don't care. In my house, however, I have all my stuff that I don't want them to have access to in my room. Dresser drawers are locked as well as the bedroom door. At home, they are allowed to run across living room furniture as if it is playground equipment they run across my stuff they don't come in the front room. At home they jump on mamas bed and from the bed t the crib like trampolines at some point they will destroy her crib but at my house, they are no way allowed in my room. At home, they were allowed to grab anything they wanted and take off with it. At my house, they need to ask for permission to grab anything that they did not bring with them. Over their young lives, they have all had some very nice and expensive toys and video games that they have either lost or broke so when they visit if they did not bring it they do not play with it and if they find a way to break it we will find a way for them to pay for it.

MOVIES VS VIDEO GAMES. As I stated earlier I do not purposefully pick them up with the intension of allowing them to do things with me because they can't at their house. When I was staying there during the pandemic the boys were allowed to watch Youtube videos that were very adult orientated. These videos were about the game they play but some were dropping the F-bomb other times they were talking about other adult subject matter like how dogs made puppies and how people made babies. They watch the crap that talks about summoning demons at 3 A.M. I also heard something about kids being lost in or taken to a cemetery. The game itself has shotguns, automatic weapons, and pickaxes for killing. Now people can and o call me old fashion but these kinds of graphics and violent games should not be played by young kids especially boys that tend to get emotional and violent over a stupid video game. 9 and 7 are far too young for this game but a 5-year-old girl...come on how can you consider yourself a good and responsible parent when you allow your kids to play this crap and don't use their time or yours to take them outside to play, go to the park or even sit down daily and have family time playing cards or board games.

Day after day I was forced to watch them sit and fill their heads with this crap because sitting them in front of a T.V. Screen is much easier than walking to the park.

When they are with me I don't have a gaming system but I do have a DVD player and cable. One day before I had my house I was upstairs watching The Soprano's and one of the parents came up and said Aspen was not allowed to watch this series because it is not age-appropriate. The same thing happened when he wanted to watch 8 Mile again. We had already watched it once before a few days earlier and Aspen enjoyed it but this time around it was on a different network that required a parental password. I did not know it because it was not my account. Aspen went to get the code from his mom and when she asked for what? He told her he wanted to watch 8 mile again and she said no...it was too grown-up of a movie for him. Now as I said this would have been the second time in a few days we watched it and besides the fact that his mom and stepdad talk nasty crap around ALL the young ones as a common practice also allowing them to play violent video games or watch videos I thought she was a complete hypocrite but who am I to say I am only grandpa and she is mom and in this family, MOTHER DOES NOT KNOW BEST BUT SHE CERTAINLY KNOWS ALL.

So when the boys are allowed to come and visit they are not restricted to what they can watch I simply let them watch what I watch and I do know for a fact no movie I watch on cable or DVD will be anywhere close to the violence on their games or as vulgar as the language they hear every day. *SO, WHEN*

THEY COME FOR A VISIT AS LONG AS I WILL WATCH IT, THEY CAN WATCH IT, WHY MY HOUSE MY RULES!

JULY 18, 2020; At this point it is still unclear if the state will be opening up public schools. It looks unlikely so the boys need to read and practice math so they don't fall too far behind. Today Ethen demonstrated why things need to be consistent in the house for them. He woke me up asking if he could use my phone to compete with Aspen on a game that requires two phones. When he was done with the games he stood in front of me politely asking if he could watch videos on my phone. WHY? Because the last time he asked to play games and changed to videos without permission he got the phone taken away because I do not have parental controls on my phone and he has a habit of going to videos he is not allowed to watch.

After about 20 minutes of playing, they asked for breakfast. Both wanting a bowl of cereal. Every other time I make them cereal they happily eat whatever I serve them but not today. When Ethen came down for his he was having a fit about I poured the wrong stuff. Apparently, he wanted a specific flavor cereal today. He also saw I used chocolate almond milk in Aspen's cereal whining he also wanted chocolate milk for his cereal. He has never before asked for flavored milk in his cereal so the whining almost earned him a bad point but he did stop. After I explained that the ingredients in both kinds of cereal were the same it was just a different shape as what he wanted so again he could just stop crying and eat or get that bad point.

He had enough courage to tell me I could not give him a bad point because they didn't total yesterday's points. I made sure he knew as long as I was down there feeding them breakfast and I was the adult in charge being at my house or theirs if he acts up I will give him that bad point whenever I feel he deserves it and I don't care if they totaled yesterdays points yet or not.

Ethen is very smart and knows how to play the" it's our" house card so yes I agreed it is your house but I also explained you are watching my phone and you are also playing games on my phone so now if you want to use my phone you can earn time on my phone by doing some practice reading so Let's find a book you can read. You are more than welcome to still watch videos after we practice your reading for a few minutes.

IT MAY NOT BE AT MY HOUSE BUT IF I AM WATCHING THEM OR THEY USE MY STUFF AS LONG AS THEY REALIZE JUST BECAUSE WE ARE IN THEIR HOUSE IT IS STILL MY STUFF MY RULES!

THEIR HOUSE, THEIR RULES? They as parents obviously have rules that need to be followed but if they are at my house do those rules and punishments carry over or do I just simply live by the premise my house my rules? What about watching them while staying there? As far as I would be concerned the attic space should be looked at like a small apartment if I need to go to bed at an early hour so the kids get to bed at a reasonable hour or if the boys are punished or grounded from something I am supposed to watch and make sure they are abiding by the rules of the grounding so at that point I am the responsible adult and if I am not watching and they get caught playing games it is on me. So if it is n me anyway if the boys and I had plans to watch a movie on their weekend visit or what if I thought renting a video game for the weekend would be a nice surprise for them and when they get dropped off I would get informed no video games because they did "X" at home.

Now, this is where my problem comes in. First, I would be thinking the punishment would be for something dumb and secondly they did it at home and that should have nothing to do with my time. So do I monitor them while upstairs? It is their house and their rules so if I was not here someone would either have to monitor the boy's activity or they would have to keep them downstairs and watch them there. So with that being said do I allow their rules and punishments to leak into my domain?

I DO NOT THINK SO. WHY? BECAUSE MY HOUSE MEANS MY RULES!

My house is my space. Where I pay the bills and where I live so my castle is my kingdom so when there MY HOUSE MY RULES. But when staying there all those months what was considered my house, my space, or even my private area? Staying there in the beginning it was a give and take situation. I would take the young ones to school, work for a couple of hours and then go by Red work there for a bit then go back to take them to TKD. Buying food for dinners at least once a week letting them use my car when errands and chores had to be done.

For a long time, it felt equal. Then Tim's uncle gave them a van and I ran out of money, the quarantine of 2020 came into play the kids stopped going to school they no longer needed my car and no more TKD. My equal role was no more and I knew it. But being invited to stay to help me get on my feet so at what point do I consider it my house? The boys and I share the attic. Half of the area or even a quarter could easily be considered my space but it is not. I have no privacy I try to follow the rules to help the boys stay out of trouble simply biding my time until I can say THANK YOU. Walk out the door and get back to my house living my life, living by my rules.

THEIR HOUSE, THEIR RULES

Being a GREAT GRANDPA means that you have to bite your tongue a lot. Especially if you are a family that has control freaks in the position of authority. In a traditional family if you are the oldest male member of the family you are the matriarch of the family. Setting the family rules of who can go where for family gatherings, holidays, and the like. But if you find yourself in the situation where you live with family in the role of "house guest" you must realize you are no longer KING of the family. The challenge here is the young ones will still look at you as "GRANDPA" and look to you for the rules and regulations. However, I do have to keep in mind that there were house rules and regulations in place before I stayed there and those rules and regulations will be there long after I leave. As a grandpa, you may or may not agree with the rules but it is your duty, responsibility, and obligation to follow the house rules so the kids don't get confused also you don't want to disrespect the parents of the house.

RULE 1. MORNING ROUTINE

I wrote this book while staying with my daughter's family during the corona virus pandemic of the spring/summer of 2020. One of the reasons I agreed to stay here was that their stepdad had to get up early for work. I thought it would be much easier for me to get up with the kids to drive them to school It made more sense for me to take them then Tim maybe being late for work. Also so their mom wouldn't have to bring the younger girls to the bus stop in the brutal cold. If Tim was at work and I was not there Danielle would have to wake the littles up and drag them out in the cold, then wait for the bus.

Besides for the fact they did not live in the safest of neighborhoods for a young mother with a female toddler and female infant to walk back home alone after depositing the kids on the bus. Another consistent issue is that most of the time the non-school age girls would stay up WAAAAAAY past bedtime and one if not both parents would stay awake with them meaning that a great deal of the time someone would sleep through the alarm or boys would turn off their alarm and WALLA they missed the bus. So if I was not staying there I would get the call asking for a ride. By being right there that saved everyone time and saved me a bunch of gas making things way more convenient.

A few years ago when Aspen was in kindergarten the family lived in the hood and walking him to the bus was a must. Then after school, someone would also have to be there As far as I know that morning routine never changed.

I have no idea how they did things when they lived in Florida for a few months, but when they lived with grandma they were to close to the school to qualify for a school bus but they lived too far to walk alone. At that point, they found a way to buy a vehicle and got the kids to and from school daily somewhat easily. Again as far as I know the routine never changed. ALARM, GET DRESSED, RIDE TO SCHOOL. This system was working great even when they got their own house on the south side. The system was working until one fatal day when a Milwaukee street pothole took out the front axle and they did not have the money for the necessary repairs so the car sat for days which turned into weeks and soon was creeping up on months that grandpa drove them to school.

From the jump, I told Danielle she needed to call the school and get those kids on the bus. I was told there were no buses available for that area to that school. So trying to weigh my options of being a good grandpa or an asshole parent I decided it was much better to be a great grandpa and by doing so I got up for weeks and drove from my house to their house drove the young ones to school which was about 7 minutes from my place but by the time I made the round trip I was on the road a tad bit over an hour. As I said I did this for a couple of months, it was either that or the kids would be transferred to the ghetto school a block and a half away from their house and easily within walking distance. Or so I thought. One morning after waiting for the young ones to get ready because as I was there to pick them up nothing was stirring not even a mouse. I waited in the car for a good 10 minutes and then went to knock. A minute or two of knocking and Tim finally answered the door and said; "They are not even up, give me a few minutes."

Needless to say, I was pissed. Here I am waking up, driving there, and then taking the kids to school and they have the balls not to have them ready. The good news is that it only took them 7 minutes to wake up get ready then out to the car. Thankfully we made it on time so they still got to eat breakfast.

As I said I was pissed but I have been trying really hard to watch what I do or what I say to the kids because they are memory sponges so what you say soaks in and stays there. They are only young kids and it took me a long time to understand that one harsh word at the wrong time can and sometimes does stick with a kid for life.

So instead of yelling and screaming so, they felt as it was their fault we had a discussion about being late for school and how it was unfair if the whole class had to wait because someone was late. I then explained that I would understand that because I don't like to be kept waiting either. Then instead of getting angry I somehow realized that they are kids and the responsibility for getting up and ready for school falls on the adults in the house not them so the rest of the ride we talked about how proud and impressed I was that they were able to get up get dressed and get out in 7 minutes.

I could feel the shift in my emotions and I knew they would have a much better day knowing they did something good instead of feeling it was their fault for being late. As I pulled up to the school I thought just for giggles I am going to see if there is a bus that they could take because not only am I spending 100s of dollars in gas but getting up this early is starting to take a toll emotionally.

Well, the answer was one I DID NOT WANT TO HEAR. There is and has been a bus they could have been taking this whole time. I am not sure if I was lied to or she just assumed and never called. After I went to the school and confirmed a bus ride. I told my daughter she had 1 week to get them registered and taking the bus. Again she knows all and said the school had to set it up, check availability and it would take weeks. However I knew different, the office lady told me with a phone call and a signed slip they could be on the bus in a day. As I said I was driving them for a couple of months and when the week was over I did not show. Of course, I got the "so you're gonna make the kids suffer" speech. But my defense was then and still is now "they are your kids, and getting them to school is your responsibility as their mom not mine as their grandpa" so they all missed Monday and Tuesday but by a miracle of God had a time a location and route number and found a way to be on the bus Wednesday morning.

Believe me, when I say not showing up Monday morning was one of the toughest things I have ever done. I struggle with that a lot. Do I sacrifice sleep and personal health and wellbeing to get up early to make sure they get to school? Or do I stick my guns because by no stretch of the imagination am I responsible to get them to school?

AT THIS TIME I WAS NOT EVEN STAYING THERE BUT SOMEHOW IT WAS THEIR HOUSE, THEIR RULES.

RULE 2. MEAL TIME.

When I was a kid no matter where we would eat be it my house if we were invited by grandma for meals or if it was up north visiting my grandpa we always had a set and established time to eat breakfast and dinner. However, lunch was always a crapshoot. Most of the time you would fend for yourself make what you could or if there were leftovers, we could eat those.

When in school my family got up a half-hour before we had to leave for school so mom always had at least a bowl of cereal ready to go. Dinner never changed for us my brother and I got home from school then my dad got done working at 3;30 and my mom would have dinner on the table at 4 sharp. If we would go by grandma for Sunday dinner..it never varied dinner started promptly at 6 P.M. Every so often we would be invited to my grandpa's house for Saturday night dinner and wrestling and again there was no question on what time, if I was out playing ball with friends or doing something away from the house I was expected to be home by 4 some we were on time for dinner by 5. If we spent the night by grandma either on the weekends or during vacations breakfast was always at 8 A.M. And whoever was there be it just me, me and a cousin or 2, and even when the kids she babysat for spent the night everyone that was there would be at the table. If you are in our house you are at our table so we all ate at the same time every day. Another rule we had was if you put it on your plate you needed to eat it ALL gone no matter what house we were eating at.

When I was older and had my own family things remained pretty much the same. We would eat at a certain time, the kids were expected to eat everything on their plates. However, at some point, I met a woman who completely changed my thinking about food and mealtime. This lady explained to me that kids are little humans and have a different metabolism. Just because dinner is scheduled for 5:30 does not mean everyone will be hungry at 5:30 also if you are having pork chops, potatoes, green beans, and ice cream Not everyone's taste buds are going to be the same. so Johnny may not like beans as much as Suzy and visa-versa. Also if they like a certain food today taste buds are always changing so they may not like the same food today the same way they liked it last month.

So as my kids got older we did not make 4 different dinners to feed them what they wanted, however, we did start eating dinner a bit later so we knew everyone would be hungry and we allowed them choices of sides and quantity so yes they had to eat everything but the everything was their choices.

These past few months of living with my daughter and her family I find myself impressed with the way mealtime/family time is run. What I mean by that is when mom and dad are both present for meals, they have very strict and specific rules. When they are home while dad is at work the rules are VERY different and that bothers me because the rules are made and enforced by MY DAUGHTER-THEIR MOTHER which begs the question "WHAT KIND OF AN INFLUENCE & IMPACT DID I MAKE AS HER FATHER?" The rule is VERY clear no eating in the living room or upstairs PERIOD. These rules only apply when Tim is home. If I am there and come down and try to enforce the rules Danielle will jump in and say it's okay, because she said so. Danielle does not enforce shit either because she breaks the house rules herself of she does not want to deal with screaming kids. Either way, it is not right.

IT IS DEFINITELY NOT THEIR HOUSE THEIR RULES. WHEN SHE IS QUEEN IT IS HER HOUSE HER RULES (and that is exactly why those kids are confused and have very little respect for her).

Rule 3. ELECTRONICS.

There is absolutely no doubt that all electronics have a home and an owner each kid has a switch each has access to a T.V. The boys have a television to watch. The girls have a T.V. In their room and the main television in the living room. The chain of command amazes me. The kids all know as well as Danielle does who bought and paid for things and who has access to what and when. As long as Tim is home he has total control over the living room T.V. NO MATTER WHAT. He sleeps in the living room because the baby sleeps with Danielle so the living room is off-limits to the kids while he sleeps so if they want to watch a show or play a game on the big screen they cannot.

They would be told they have a television up in their room to play on. It's their T.V. And I was shown that without question. Now in a normal house if someone is watching a show or movie unless that person has been binge-watching a show for hours the decent and courteous thing to do would be to let the show or movie end then ask for THEIR T.V. Not here. I was upstairs in the room watching a movie Ethen & Aspen were downstairs watching Tim play a game. He would not allow them to play with so Ethen decided to come up and play on the upstairs T.V. But I told him no I was watching a show. He went whining downstairs saying I wouldn't let him play completely mentioning I had been watching a movie that was almost over Tim came storming up - snatched the remote and turned on the game and walked away. That night at dinner "I BOUGHT THAT UPSTAIRS T.V. FOR THE BOYS."

They also have a Nintendo switch that they share and when it runs low on battery plugs into the T.V. They also like to watch Youtube videos and the t.v. Has the ability to play Youtube. Harlow and Violet also have a T.V. In their room so with all that being said As long as one of the household members want to watch a show or play a game if I am using the T.V. Or not they simply swoop in and do what they want.

WHY? BECAUSE IT IS CLEAR WHEN IT COMES TO THE ELECTRONICS THEIR HOUSE, THEIR RULES.

MARCH 31, 2020, This story could go in several different chapters but I decided to put it here because as a guest I have no house rights but as their grandpa, my responsibilities change daily whatever suits the situation to make them look good. On this particular day, the "ADULTS" in the house needed to do some errands which included grocery shopping and laundry. At the time they still did not have a family vehicle and needed to use my car. Also, there is not enough room to bring ANY of the young ones so not only are they using my car but I am babysitting ALL 5 kids.

Okay, here we go... First of all the errands were only supposed to take 3-4 hours. Starting at the laundry mat to drop the wash off, go to the grocery store, drop off the food at home, then back for the wash bring it home and maybe run another errand or two. That was the plan that I agreed to.

Things started just fine the laundry was loaded in the car, kids were all in the living room watching paw patrol videos. They were all fed. the two in diapers were changed and clean. The time 11:20 A.M. And off to the laundry mat. The plan was in motion and things were going along nicely. 1:30 P.M. Walking through the door with a good number of grocery bags. So laundry in(check) grocery shopping is done and put away(check) on the way back to the laundry mat to finish laundry(check) so far so good but around 4ish things took a bit of a downhill turn.

"How is it going? You guys have been gone quite a long time."

"Yeah, the laundry is taking way longer than we expected."

The time now is 5:10 P.M. And they are walking into the house with the wash. But please keep in mind the kids have not eaten since before 11 this morning and were asking for food. Not knowing when they would be home to fix dinner I gave them all snack packs of crackers to hold them over until dinner. With that being said the baby has to sit in a high chair to eat and none of the older kids like listening to rules so instead of eating in the kitchen like they are supposed to the went to the living room and decided it would be more fun to smash the crackers on the floor than to eat them and in the kitchen, the baby had similar thoughts but because of her milk allergies she can't eat crackers but decided she would share her cup of oranges with me by throwing them all over the floor. The time 4:55 P.M.

By now I AM PISSED. They have been gone 5 hours the kids are not listening and destroying the house. I had just finished picking up the orange slices and was grabbing the broom to sweep up the crackers when the door opened and... "HOLY CRAP WHAT HAPPENED IN HERE? JESUS DAD WHY WOULD

YOU LET THEM EAT IN HERE? YOU ARE THE ADULT. THEY NEED TO EAT IN THE KITCHEN" after her rant, she went and got the broom and swept up the crackers. The time now 5:35 P.M.

I was FUMING and wanted sooooo bad to tell her to go to hell but here were 3 problems with that First, she is my daughter. Second, don't disrespect the parents in front of the young ones, and Third, I didn't want to live in my car, so yes I kept my mouth shut, then came the kick in the testicles - "We'll be back, we still need to run to Menard's and will be back soon to make dinner." WOW!

All I could say to myself is WOW. And out the door, they went. TIME 5:55 P.M. After they left I asked the kids to find a Disney movie we could watch until they got back. We all agreed on MOANA. TIME 7:15 P.M. Movie is almost over, kids are asking for dinner and no sign of the "PARENTAL UNITS" 7:20 P.M.

I decided I would be a nice guy and make the chicken she had out for dinner. I opened and rinsed the chicken, sliced off the fat, set the oven temp, put the chicken on A COOKIE SHEET, and stared the rest of dinner which included mashed potatoes and gravy. I also made a can of corn or green beans, their choice. TIME 8:10 P.M. I finally get a text;

"We can't find what we are looking for and are running to Walmart. Do you think you can make mac & cheese and hot dogs?"

"The veggies and mash taters are done and the chicken only has about 10 minutes"

"You made dinner? WOW THANKS!"

BUT AS THEY SAY, NO GOOD DEED GOES UNPUNISHED. Dinner turned out great the young ones all ate and even the baby liked it. It however was a long day and I have never watched this many kids this long EVER so yes it was along. stressful day for me but the worst was yet to come. TIME 9:55 P.M. - I receive this text "We didn't find the sewing machine we were looking for at any store so we ordered it online. On our way now are the kids in bed?"

They were not. They were all crunched into a cardboard box playing like it was a fort watching sponge bob. I simply answered "nope" - TIME NOW 10:10 P.M.

And they are finally walking in the door after being gone almost 11 hours BUT instead of hearing what I expected which was; "THANKS FOR WATCHING THEM DAD WE'RE SORRY IT TOOK SO LONG."

OOOH no, NOT HERE - within seconds of walking in the door started barking orders. At this point the young ones were all overtired and cranky not even asking to watch the rest of sponge Bob but screaming and whining and here's where Tim jumped in, "YOUR MOTHER TOLD YOU TO GET IN BED NOW GET IN BED. AND BOXES ARE NOT TOYS", and with that started tearing the box apart. To keep the kids safe and not to start a physical altercation where someone would have been hurt or at the very least arrested, I scurried up to my bed and let him finish his rant. But he was not close to finished from my area I could hear him yelling at Danielle...

"JESUS CHRIST DANIELLE HE LIVES HERE FOR NOTHING, LETS THE KIDS DO WHAT THEY WANT WHEN THEY WANT, THEY TRASHED THE HOUSE AND HE DOESN'T HAVE THE COMMON SENSE TO COOK CHICKEN IN A PAN INSTEAD OF A COOKIE SHEET".

Yes, you read that correctly. They had my car for 11 hours. I watched the kids for 11 hours. Thought I was doing a good thing by making dinner because they were out looking for a SEWING MACHINE and he had the balls to bitch a little grease dripped off the cookie sheet on the bottom of the oven. What was I gonna do? I left my living space to help with the young ones and fell short by their standards so I had only two choices; I could go down and punch him in the throat or I could keep my mouth shut & simply accept the fact **THEIR HOUSE, THEIR RULES** (in case you are wondering I went with # 2).

MAY, 24, 2020, The problem remains on the home front with an Alpha male that needs to control everything and make sure everyone in the house knows he is king and this is his castle. ALL the bills are paid from his paychecks and this is his kingdom. Grandpa is JUST a guest and in his world my authority means nothing. House rules are house rules until they are not. What I mean is if it is convenient for the "ADULTS" then rules are bend or mostly broken. There has always been a long-standing family rule NO PHONES OR ELECTRONICS AT THE TABLE WHILE EATING.

This rule just applies to me and the kids I guess. So anyway, today we are eating dinner and Danielle's phone was at the end of the table. So she asked for it. I did pick it up and gently shook it at her and I jokingly said; "NOT AT THE DINNER TABLE remember no electronics at the dinner table." Tim then stood up and snatched it out of my hand and handed it to her like I was one of their kids (if looks could kill he'd have been a dead man). Both boys at the same time started to say "NO PHONES AT THE TABLE Mama. AND GRANDPA SAID..." but before they could finish that sentence Tim yelled; "IT DON'T MATTER WHAT GRANDPA SAID, WE ARE THE PARENTS HERE, NOT YOUR GRANDPA. WE MAKE THE RULES NOT YOUR GRANDPA!"

HE COULD NOT HAVE MADE IT CLEARER "THEIR HOUSE THEIR RULES."

MAY 31, 2020, last night was family movie night and the boys came upstairs to bed way later than normal. A few minutes later, Tim came up to say good night and caught them trying to sleep in their tent. They were both told NO tent tonight so he sent them to their bunks. I don't know for sure but I would assume everyone else in the house also went to bed late. With that being said family movie night is always on a Saturday night then Sunday morning mom & dad get up to make a big breakfast. Flavored pancakes, bacon, and fruit. This Sunday morning Ethen & Harlow were both hungry both came up asking for Nutella toast but I said no explaining "YOUR MOM ALWAYS MAKES YOU SUNDAY BREAKFAST."

Well, last night Aspen was told mom would be up cooking breakfast at 10. SHE WAS NOT so Aspen said he would start making breakfast because Mama showed him how and it would be ok. So with a little help, he started making breakfast.

In a normal family, mom would get up and be grateful someone was up starting breakfast so her kids were eating at a decent time... not here. Both Tim & Danielle were sleeping when we started cooking but Danielle found it necessary to wake up walk into the kitchen and complain we used the wrong mix. Tim wasn't even all the awake yet looked in the kitchen bitchin there was a plastic bowl on the stove when in reality it was glass. Tim was on the way to the bathroom and overheard me complimenting Aspen for making a perfect pancake but again instead of just walking by or better yet agreeing on a perfect pancake he found it necessary to tell us there was to much oil in the pan.

WHY? FOR ME THIS WHOLE BOOK WAS WRITTEN TO HELP GUILD AND ENCOURAGE THE YOUNG ONES SO I just went back upstairs and let Danielle take her kitchen back. While she was finishing breakfast the boys were upstairs watching videos waiting for breakfast. Tim for whatever reason instead of just finish cooking the bacon came up to intentionally start some problems. WHY? He went right to the tent and accused them of going back there after he told them NO. Aspen was pissed and Ethen tried to explain they DID NOT sleep in the tent and were in their beds all night. I saw them both and KNEW for a fact they were in bed. Usually, I keep out of things but he was wrong and they were being unjustly accused so I said; "dude they both slept in bed. They were both in their beds when I went to the bathroom this morning."

Aspen was like "Yeah, we were in bed not in the tent".

"SO YOUR PILLOWS AND BLANKET WALKED TO THE TENT ON THEIR OWN...
YEAH OK I BELIEVE YOU."

It was a hypothetical slap to my face. For some reason, he thinks that I allow
the kids especially the boys to break his rules and undermine his authority so
he takes every opportunity to take his sarcastic shots to make me mad.

A few hours later Ethen and Harlow were having a major battle over a game
(Ethen was having a very bad day today) the kids were told to clean because
a friend was coming over and Ethen pitch a bitch like he has not done for
months (he needed a nap) He started kicking chairs and tossing toys. Then
he and Harlow started a physical fight about the game and Harlow smacked
him with a controller. Ethen fired back and they took off running. I was just
about to grab Ethen and bring him downstairs but they took off. I thought the
fighting was over so I sat back down to continue working. They were on the
other side of the attic where Ethen was dragging her across the floor by her
leg. No screaming. No crying. I had no idea they were still even upstairs.

They have a very bad habit of doing this. They only see part of the action
or worst yet see none of the action and listen to the young one who is
downstairs whining they got hurt when the reality is they start stuff someone
fights back and that person who fights back gets punished in some form or
another. Today Tim just happened to walk up at the exact moment I sat back
down and Ethen was dragging her across the floor not seeing the whole fight.
Another good opportunity to make me look bad, instead of saying something
to me directly he ran downstairs to tell Danielle they were fighting and I was
just sitting there doing nothing.

*WHY? I SOMETIMES WONDER IF IT BOTHERS HIM THAT ALL THE KIDS AND
PROBABLY DANIELLE SHOW ME MORE RESPECT THAN THEY DO HIM. IF SO,
BELIEVE ME, I AM WELL AWARE THAT IT IS YOUR HOUSE, YOUR RULES*

JUNE 8, 2020; Everyone has a breaking point and today I found mine. Yesterday
a friend of mine needed help moving so we had plans to go help for days.
Aspen and I were gonna go help but at the last minute, they decided he could
not go because a family friend was coming over with his son and they were
having a small party for Tims birthday with Aspen being the oldest and part of
the family preferred he stayed there instead of helping me. That reasoning is
both acceptable and understandable to me.

Later in the day, my daughter asked me what time I would be leaving
to go help. Then she told me she didn't get anything for cake or even
presents so she wanted to go before I was leaving. Well, I was planning

on leaving around 8 A.M. driving my car in case we needed more room to move small boxes or whatever. She does not wake up until at least 10:30 A.M. So to get up by 6 to go to the store was not happening. At this point for her, it was either get up and go or the party would have to go without cake or presents. Knowing my daughter and there is no chance of her getting up me being the nice guy I am called my friend to tell him things changed and I needed to get picked up. So there you go, now she will have access to my car for the entire day and this will inconvenience both me and my friend but do you think she will acknowledge the sacrifice? Of course not. It was almost that she was pissed I wanted my car and leaving it there was expected.

So I worked moving my friend for about 11 hours and got back to the house exhausted. Now please let me clarify before I explain what happened this was a very emotional day. As we loaded the truck my friend's 87-year-old father in law came outside thinking he could either help or even worse bark out orders and point out what we were doing wrong. He was let us just say POLITELY asked to go back in and let us work. But as he was struggling to get back in the house he must have slipped because he fell and scraped up his arm pretty bad. There were only the two of us loading, packing, and moving so as you may have guessed by the time we loaded the truck then drove to the other location we were both very tired and stressed out. But unfortunately, the stress had not even begun. As we were pulling up to the new house Karl looked in the driveway and was like "what the heck is in my driveway?" pulled the truck up a few feet "JESUS CHRIST THOSE ARE DWAYNE'S FEET!"

So, I jumped out of the truck and ran up to his father-in-law and the old man was OUT COLD. I stood there looking down at a motionless body completely freaked out thinking he was dead. Then as I was yelling that he was out cold his daughter came out of the house started calling him and thankfully he came to but had a gash on the back of his head and VERY severe scrapes on his arms. I was freaking out because I thought he was dead at first so I can't imagine what was going through their minds. With all that being said the stress level increased by 10 but we still had to unload. Dwayne ended up going to the ER and as I write this story days later he is still in the hospital.

We finished the move and I was dropped off at 11 P.M. Stressed out and exhausted just wanting to take a hot shower and flop into bed. As I walked into the kitchen I saw the empty box that my cards should have been in. Then I went upstairs to get some clothes and take a nice hot shower while everyone was asleep I was VERY wrong and VERY upset.

First of all both boys were up playing video games. Next, the kids ALL know it's my stuff and they need to leave it alone unless they have permission. I know a deck of cards may sound petty, but I do play games almost daily myself or with the young ones so if the cards are lost, ripped or damaged no more games. Also beside for my cards being gone, there was a box of leggings that were up on a shelve that unless kicked down or pulled off by me would not have fallen but I was told Harlow pulled a pair of legging and dragged the whole box down which is almost physically impossible for a little girl. also, my books and papers were thrown all over the room so it would appear that if I am not here to protect and watch my stuff it is fair game for whoever wants to mess with it.

Instead of pitching a fit at 11 o'clock at night, I decided to sleep on it and deal with it in the morning. After a night's sleep, I decided that if they don't respect their things how can I expect them to respect mine. So, I put my leggings back in the box found my cards then picked up the rest of my stuff and decided to start looking for a place to move.

Monday morning I was still sore and tired but new my friend would probably need help again so Aspen & I got picked up again because Tim had my car to go to work. Today we got done around 6:30 P.M. And I fed him dinner then went back to the house. Once there dinner was just being put on the table for the rest of the young ones to eat. After dinner, I was asked if I would watch the kids so Danielle could ride along with Tim to go to Menards because they closed at 8 and wanted a chance to look around. Again they needed my car and left before 7. thinking it closed at 8 they would be home around 8:15 AGAIN I was way wrong. They came rolling in about 9:30 and while they were gone I made sure the young ones all finished dinner. After dinner, they all asked for dessert which was some leftover birthday cake. Earlier today I put the leftover cake in the fridge so young picking fingers would not get into it. In theory that was a great idea but apparently while I was gone the cake ended up out of the fridge and Violet's little picking fingers destroyed a good portion of the cake.

What I did not know was Tim was bringing cake tomorrow to his co-workers and nobody was to eat the cake. It is very hard to know they can't have cake unless I am told but Here it is VERY easy to point fingers and shift the blame. Danielle walked in the house and as ALWAYS started to complain that the cake was not to be eaten and that I should have called to get permission. So I was pissed and said;

"How the hell am I suppose to know if no one says anything?" Then Tim and his wise-ass piped in "WELL YOU COULD HAVE KEPT VIOLET FROM DESTROYING IT."

When I say at this point I would have loved to tell him to completely go screw himself all the kids were standing there and didn't need to here that also I could almost guarantee things would have turned physical and if things did I am certain Aspen would have gotten involved maybe getting hurt so I simply said "that happened way before we even got back." Danielle admitted she let the girl get at it so he stuck his head out of the door "YEAH DANNI." Just like every other morning the boys and I were up around 8 while Danielle slept downstairs with the baby and about 10 Harlow started yelling for someone to open her door. So again like every other morning I went downstairs to make the young one's cereal. This morning however was just a bit different Danielle was up before 11. The boys finished their food, Violet was asking for her 2nd bowl and Harlow was also. Now getting up with the young ones every day I knew Violet would easily finish her 2nd bowl and Harlow would simply waste hers. 5 minutes later I went back downstairs and one bowl was all gone and the other full and sitting. So I tried to explain to Danielle she would waste a whole bowl of cereal and milk but HERE mother knows best so I went back upstairs. In a few minutes, I went back down to check things out because Danielle says she was vomiting and not feeling well. Violet is a very independent 2-year-old who was attempting to pour Harlow's bigger bowl back into her much smaller bowl and missed. I walked by chuckled a bit and told "mom" her daughter made a mess.

Now yesterday I was told that I needed to call to get permission to give them cake for dessert suggesting that my ability and judgment was not up to par as an adult or as a babysitter but yet today less than 12 hours later I told her not to give another bowl of cereal because it would go to waste but when I walked by I kind of gave her an "I TOLD YOU SO" look.

They don't like it when their wrong because I was told I am an adult and capable of helping around the house and cleaning up kid's messes. So guys what is it? Living there is driving me insane it is like living with an ex-wife only times two.

I CAN'T EVEN SAY I AM A HOUSE GUEST BECAUSE MY RULES AND RESPONSIBILITY CHANGE DAILY. I AM SURE THEY WANT ME GONE AS MUCH AS I WANT TO BE GONE BUT UNTIL THEN THE FACT REMAINS "THEIR HOUSE, THEIR RULES"

JUNE 7, 2018, The boys have been in TKD for a few months now. The change in their attitude has been very noticeable. They have better behaved at home and school officials, teachers, and even the principal have pulled me aside to comment on Both boy's behavior.

I pay for the class, I pay for testing and anything else they need that is related to TKD and don't ask for a penny as far as money goes however I do expect them to be able to go to class. They are both elite members and could go daily if they wanted so to miss days that would be considered extra I certainly understand but days they are scheduled for means they will either learn new material or practice what they recently learned.

Today was a challenge. The boys had a belt promotion coming up soon. Aspen had all the requirements needed to test but was very close to the required attendance he would also need. Ethen on the other hand needed a technique stripe and he also was very close to his attendance requirement so every scheduled class is VERY important. So Ethen had an issue on the bus today getting written up. Whatever that means for a 6-year-old on the bus I don't know. Anyways I was just going to leave to be on my way to grab them for practice then go to class when I got the call neither one of the boys could go to class. I probably should not have asked why because her answer made me very upset. She told me Ethen was naughty on the bus and Aspen had a wise comment about Ethen not being able to go to class.

Both Tim and Danielle know the boys both enjoy TKD so they use that as a tool and try to leverage better behavior by threatening to keep them home from class. When I signed them up for class the rules were schoolwork first then house chores needed to be done AND NO USING WHAT THEY LEARN ON THEIR SISTERS.

So, when I was told they COULD NOT go and found out why I explained to her that going to TKD was EXACTLY what they needed. The school teaches DISCIPLINE, RESPECT & SELF CONTROL.

Then this conversation ensued –

"I TOLD THEM NO."

"You do know that testing is coming up and at this point every class is essential."

"I ALREADY SAID NO AND I AM NOT GONNA LOOK FOOLISH BY CHANGING MY MIND AND LETTING THEM GO. THEY NEED TO LEARN WHEN WE SAY NO WE MEAN NO."

At this point, a thousand nasty things were running through my head I wanted to say but I have learned to think about the consequences of my words and actions especially when the kids are involved. I knew if I brought up money and saying I paid asking if they are going to reimburse me for time missed or if I mentioned what I think of her parenting skill the boys would be the only ones who would suffer because they would be yanked out of class. So before I responded to her I did think it through and simply said;

"YES DANIELLE YOU ARE CORRECT WE WILL TRY AGAIN TOMORROW THEY ARE YOUR KIDS AND THAT MEANS YOUR HOUSE, YOUR RULES."

JUNE 12, 2020; Today was an enlightening day for everyone. Tension in the house was at an all-time high for several different reasons. like they want me gone as much as don't want to be here. Plus with this quarantine nonsense, everyone is getting on everyone's last nerve. Tim would come home from work complaining that he works for 10 hours and come home and needs to take the trash out or dishes some other type of housework that a working man should not have to come home and do. He feels that two adults in the house and 3 young ones old enough to do chores bags of trash or recyclables just sitting by the door and not taken out is just lazy if you can take it out of the bin and tie it then take the additional 2 minutes to run it to the alley. Just don't leave it by the door for someone else to take out.

A few days ago at dinner, I was asking the boys about TKD and wanted to know if they are still wanting to go. I also found out that they had 4 months before they lost their belt rank. This was the conversation that started the "when is your dad leaving" movement. Danielle was sent up to have a chat with me but being my daughter she finds it somewhat hard to scold me so that plan didn't work. Tim didn't want to talk with me that day either because he thought I would say something to get him upset then I'd get upset and things would escalate to a point of no return and nobody wants that. THE logical thing to do was wait a few days then have a MAN 2 MAN conversation. That was a VERY good idea because some misconceptions were cleared up and ironed out.

One of the big ones is the fact that I thought I was asked to stay here because of the convenience of driving the young ones to school. Then I would drop my daughter at work and head over to Starbucks for a while. Somedays I would have side jobs to do and other days I would spend most of my day at Starbucks until my daughter got done working pick her up then depending on the time wait for the kids at the bus stop. Most of the time they had homework so go to the house get them something to eat get their homework done then head to TKD. Making it more convenient for everyone a WIN-WIN SITUATION FOR EVERYONE… THAT'S WHAT I THOUGHT.

Their reason for asking me to move there was WAAAYYYY different than I would have ever thought. When Danielle was going to her appointments, I was asked to stay there for that week so I could drive her and then watch the kids and pick her up afterward. THE week went as planned and when she was finished I was getting my stuff to go back to my room, she got the vibe I didn't want to go back because I was behind in my rent and didn't want to deal with that. Tim was working that Saturday and when he got home asked what I was still doing there. They went on to have a conversation that she felt I did not want to go back because of my rent. So they agreed to let me stay with them until I got back on my feet. A total shock to me but something I needed to hear so I understood where they were coming from.

The next thing was the conversation I had with the boys about TKD. Why did an innocent conversation start so much hoopla? Again thankfully we were able to put the cards on the table and clear the air. What he heard that night was a guy that didn't have a regular job and sat around basically watching T.V. Not even looking for a job not offering to help with the rent or bills but yet was planning on taking the boys back to class or worse get the boys thinking they were going back and didn't have the money to follow through getting them excited and he would have to pay for classes. Either way, he felt like he was being taken advantage of. THAT'S WHAT HE THOUGHT.

In reality, I send letters every week looking for real estate deals. I also write every day and work on selling my products on market place and craigslist trying to earn enough money to at the very least get a room to live and give them their house and privacy back. As far as the boys and TKD class he completely misunderstood that conversation and we ironed that out also.

The last major issue we had to work out was house rules. He will get up leave for work at 7:30. Most days the boys would get up shortly after that watch videos for a bit then go downstairs and eat breakfast with mama and the girls. He also assumed that the house rules of no food in the living room was be followed by everyone while he was working. Trask and recyclables were being handled by the boys so they could earn good points. THAT'S WHAT HE THOUGHT.

Reality is way different. Yes, the boys do wake up shortly after he leaves for work and watch videos but when they get hungry I am the one that takes them downstairs to feed them and if the girls are up, feed them too. No eating in the living room is a joke. Today Ethen came into the living room with a pop tart and I kind of got loud telling him NO FOOD IN THE LIVING ROOM and of course, Danielle was like "it's ok I gave it to him".

So I ask you how are the kids supposed to learn and respect the house rules when the co-parent breaks the rules at will and when grandpa, the house guest, tries to help by enforcing the rules is shot down.

Danielle was not happy with me because if I am getting accused and blamed for things in the house. I am certainly gonna take credit for what I do and feeding the kids while she stays asleep is one of those things. Being concerned about their safety when I move is another one. If I leave and the boys get up make breakfast for themselves and their sisters and something happens not even something serious say for example they drop and crack the galloon of milk which results in milk all over the floor. They definitely will not wake her up in fear of getting a bad point. Mom is not gonna get up with the attitude "oh well they tried why cry over spilled milk" is she gonna get up and take responsibility because as MOM she should have been up caring for her kids. NO, she is gonna get up bitching and complaining that kids should have known better. Making it very hard for the boys to grow and try new things because now they are afraid to make a mistake or have an accident. After our conversation, Danielle will be waking up as Tim leaves and will be there to make and feed them breakfast. At this point, the baby stays asleep but all the other young ones are woken up with the intension they will be on a summer schedule and the shift to a school schedule in fall will be much easier. The fact that kids are allowed to eat in the living room will be addressed. House rules are made for everyone to follow.

SO REMEMBER THAT YOUR HOUSE...YOUR RULES DISCIPLINING THE GIRLS
The boys and I have a bond and mutual understanding. They know if they want to spend time doing something with me like playing cards or if they want to go to the dollar store they must be respectful and ask nicely. Even though I am here both Danielle and Tim know the influence I have on the boys so if they hear me yelling upstairs they know that they did something significant to set me off so in most cases they leave it alone and let me handle it.

The girls on the other hand are untouchable discipline wise. If at dinner Ethen or Aspen makes a comment or shows dislike or are unappreciated the meal I can explain why that is wrong or disrespectful. If Ethen is bouncing around or is using his hands to eat instead of his silverware I am allowed to correct him. If they are done eating and ask to be excused I can release them from the table. Harlow has complete control of Danielle in all areas of the house but when home without Tim being here she runs the place. During mealtime, she won't eat if she asks for mac n cheese and is served a peanut butter and jelly sandwich (a meal she does like) That girl will scream she wanted mac & cheese and refuses to eat. I would find it necessary to put her in her room until she got hungry but Danielle's answer to a spoiled screaming 5-year-old "OH JUST LEAVE HER BE, SHE'LL EAT WHEN SHE'S READY"

That may be true but to give in to a screamer does 3 things to the family dynamic:

1. It teaches her that mom has absolutely no authority and makes it harder for dad to discipline when he comes home

2. It shows the other kids screaming for what you want or don't want is OK.

3. It makes the boys feel like a lesser part of the family because they would get disciplined for the same behavior.

At dinner time 95% of the time Tim is already home from work and discipline is a bit different. If Harlow would try to pull that crap with Tim him she would get disciplined however Violet is a completely different story. She is by far the most independent 2-year old I have ever met. If she is hungry and the fridge is unlocked she will get what she wants and take it in her room. A whole carton of strawberries... GONE. A large piece of leftover cake... GONE. A couple hotdogs left... GONE.

If the fridge is locked she will crawl up on the counter and open cupboards to grab things.

When she is hungry I have seen her open and eat 6 or 7 slices of bread or even a package of soft taco shells and munch 3 or 4 of those. She will never get a hand raised to her or even a voice raised because she is 2 and that shows creativity and independence. On some level, I can see that and respect it.

However, mealtime should be mealtime and all the young ones should be subject to the same rules. Maybe not as strict as the others but she should have some of the same rules. What do I mean? At mealtime mostly breakfast or dinner when everyone eats together Violet is allowed to get up from the table and run around. If I was to pour her a bowl of cereal she would be allowed to start eating and get up at any point and take off. She could go anywhere from watching cartoons in the living room to upstairs playing in the boy's room or she may just head to her room and lay down. She does the same thing at dinner, her plate is prepared and placed down in her spot she will eat a little and take off unless she likes what is being served then she may stay and eat. The point is for awhile she was made to sit and eat. That was going very well until mom decided it was OK to let her run around during breakfast and instead of correcting her allowed her to run and finish when she wanted.

The problem that I see is not necessarily at home but when they want to go out at a restaurant or they are invited to someone's house for dinner but Violet has been taught and conditioned that running around instead of eating is *OK.*

AGAIN, TRYING TO HELP BY ENFORCING HOUSE RULES THAT ARE ALREADY IN PLACE IS VERY TOUGH WHEN THE ONE BREAKING THOSE RULES IS THE PARENT IN CHARGE. THE LONGER I STAY THERE THE CLEARER IT BECOMES THEIR KIDS, THEIR HOUSE, THEIR RULES.

DON'T TALK BAD ABOUT OTHER ADULTS

Being a GREAT GRANDPA requires you to realize there are little ears EVERYWHERE. You need to be aware of where they are and what they may hear. When I was growing up my parents always told me "If you have nothing nice to say don't say anything at all."

These words of wisdom have even more significance if you have young ones that could be in earshot of a mean, sad or angry conversations.

As I said before kids are sponges and they have a remarkable talent for remembering EVERYTHING. They eves drop to hear what or where they might be going. They eves drop on phone calls and learn personal things about friends and family members sometimes you think you are having a private conversation but inquisitive noisy little ears are listening to everything being said. Again some of the most damaging and hurtful things are overheard and never meant for the ears they went in. Sometimes things are said in a sarcastic manner that was never intended for young ears. As my girls were growing up their mother and I made it a very common practice to smack talk to each other which affected the kids. As young kids, they felt like they had to take sides. As young adults, I am very glad that they never had to go to serious therapy because we did not have the common sense to keep our negativity and comments to ourselves. My feelings towards their mom which is now the young ones grandma DID NOT CHANGE, however, the kind of woman she was as a wife and mother is much different than the woman she is as a grandma. My negative feelings and dislike for her should not and never will be spoken intentionally in front of these kids. To them, she is GRANDMA an old lady that lets them play computer games, play with her bunnies, and always has snacks and kool-aide on hand when they visit. Letting them know my feelings for her would do absolutely no good for ANYONE so I make a very conscious effort to keep my mouth shut and my opinions to myself.

The big one for me is their X#@#$. Unfortunately or fortunately for my grandkids (depending on how you look at it), their biological sperm donor (I will NEVER use the term father), is a complete and useless piece of garbage.

Some may say these kids had a rough start to life and that might be true. He was around for the first 2 years but so was I The very first time I saw him was at the mall and as I was walking on the upper lever I looked down to see Danielle sitting on his lap. FROM THE SECOND I SEEN HIM MY FATHER SENSES WERE TINGLING. I hated him before I even knew his name. There were times when there were physical altercations that friends kept me from kicking the crap out of him. The worse thing that I did in front of the kids (and thankfully they are too young to remember) is Aspen was less than 2 years old and he smacked him across the head and I flipped out and threw him into the wall and told him "YOU HIT THE BOY, I HIT YOU!"

Thankfully, my common sense kicked in before my temper and I walked out and went for a walk for a couple of hours otherwise I would have killed him. Most of this book was written in June of 2020 and at the time of these writings Harlow has never met him, Ethen knows he has a dad other than Tim. Aspen remembers bits and pieces and if he is asked by someone about his "DAD" his reply is always the same "I don't see Tyler and Tim is my dad." There are only two people in this world that get my hands shaking in anger that I truly say I HATE and their SPERM DONOR is one of them but my personal feelings for him doesn't change the fact he is their FATHER and someday although very doubtful may grow up and want to talk with them.

I MADE THE DECISION A LONG TIME AGO TO LET THEM FORM THEIR OWN OPINIONS OR LEARN WHAT THEY WILL FROM THEIR MOTHER AND NOT SPEAK BAD ABOUT HIM.

The second person on that truly hate is my ex-mother-in-law; their great-grandma. I will never speak out loud in front of the young ones how I truly feel about her because in their eyes I am a very kind and fair person hearing OUT LOUD how I truly feel about her would certainly change that. In their eyes, she is a NICE OLD LADY that hands them money whenever they visit. To me, she is a vile old bag that just thinking of her turns my stomach and stirs up emotions I'm certainly not proud of.

SHE IS PART OF THEIR FAMILY   NOT MINE SO WHAT POSSIBLE GOOD COULD COME FROM BAD MOUTHING HER N FRONT OF THESE KIDS

MARCH-MAY, 2020; as most people are aware the corona-virus scare of 2020 closed down the entire world for months and completely changed the lifestyles of the American public. The most dramatic impact it had on me was the fact that at the time I agreed to live with my daughter and her family so I could drive the kids to school every day but with all schools being shut down due to the pandemic that was not necessary.

The school however did supply the kids with chrome books so they could keep up with school work. The theory of the school officials is that the parents would be responsible enough to schedule a time and teach the kids at home and make sure they are online for those scheduled classes.

The first couple of days worked the way they should have. The kids would get up come to me for breakfast, I would feed them while Danielle stayed asleep with the baby. Then after breakfast, she would let the baby sleep get up and do some sort of schoolwork. Aspen needs to practice writing he can read at an advanced level, excellent math skills but his penmanship is substandard, and he needs practice. Ethen has just started all the basic learning skills so from a teaching standpoint he needs to practice everything but especially reading. Harlow is up to her age level and beyond so basically, she just needs to practice so she does not slip backward. The irony of this section is today is June 1, 10:20 A.M. and as I'm sitting here writing this the young ones are asking for breakfast.

"Where is your mother?"

"Sleeping"

"What would you guys like?"

So, I took their orders made and fed them breakfast then came back to my desk to continue. It is currently 11:24 A.M. And she is still asleep. Did the kids do any schoolwork? NO

Is it my responsibility to make sure they do schoolwork? NO. They are all sitting watching videos until noon when they are allowed to play video games for one hour which now is their allotted time per day.

The rule is supposed to go wake up, school work, eat, school work, until noon... then should be allowed to play videos for an hour than some type of fun time that they would do at school like art or exercise time.

I would have no idea what would be going on if I had my own space but living here I see every day the way these kids are schooled and the problem is THEY ARE NOT. In my opinion, it is VERY wrong that she allows her kids to do nothing except watch videos and then video games ALONE for hours why she sleeps. Today as I was making breakfast I was intentionally and purposefully loud trying to wake her or the baby up with no luck. In my mind, I said to myself "This is truly pathetic" Who do I talk to? Bring it up to her and she has "reasons" the baby is teething... we were up late...blah...blah...blah.

Bring it up to Tim? First, off he probably wouldn't care and secondly, I would get "IF YOU DON'T LIKE IT, MOVE." So I do keep my mouth shut and just let it slide and certainly don't say anything negative or disrespectful directly to the young ones and I make sure they are not within earshot if I am bitching to someone on the phone. If I have issues that IS my problem and the kids certainly don't need to hear it.

SO NEVER TALK BAD ABOUT OTHER ADULTS.

NOVEMBER 15, 2019; TKD has been a great experience for both boys they have learned a great deal about respect, rules, self-respect, and generally how to be a better person. The problem is that sometimes adults find it necessary to trash talk other parents and that completely undermines and contradicts what the school stands for and teaches. As I said I feel TKD is a very good and positive influence on the boys. So every time they attend a class I try to be there to watch and if they need to practice a movement for form or something to improve their techniques I try to follow up with their instructors or other black belts so they are ready and improved by the next class. However, at times there are other students that clown around for the whole class time or worse yet there are students that clown around and the parents are never there to watch to see that "little Johnny" is a class clown but when confronted "Oh that can't be possible, my little Johnny would never do that."

There is one student in particular that more times than not is in problems with the instructors. He has had his belt taken on 2 or 3 occasions just in the short time the boys have been in class. This kid has problems keeping his hands-off other students so he gets called out for that. Well, I believe he started quite a while before Aspen but with practice and not missing a testing cycle they were soon the same belt rank. This quick movement up the ranks infuriated his mother. MOM would brag on "little Johnny" like he was the next Bruce Lee. We heard stories of how "little Johnny" was in a class that the instructors would send him to the front to demonstrate movements and that he was so skilled he was asked to take advanced classes. These were all stories I heard while Aspen was a couple of belt ranks lower. He became a higher belt and "little Johnny" did not make the requirements to test things became very clear that his mom was a big blowhard. She is the type of mother that made it a point to point out the flaws of other students while making sure it was followed by "my little Johnny already got his stripe for that" or "my little Johnny can do that perfect."

After a very short time, it became very clear to me that LITTLE JOHNNY was an only child. His mother is an Xtra large woman and is not physically fit by any stretch of the imagination. I felt that she put a great deal of pressure on her son to live through him to make up for her shortcomings. I feel that the school not only teaches students how to be better people than you also should be prepared to practice what they preach. In the beginning, I tolerated this woman but as time went by I found myself more and more disgusted with her bullshit boasting. For months I was able to stay away from her but one busy Saturday morning I had the misfortune of coming in late and the only chair left was right next to hers. During class, her son and my grandson were partnered together for a technique exercise. Well her son was clowning around and Aspen was there to learn and be serious so when "little Johnny" wouldn't step back like he was supposed to he got smoked with a pretty hard roundhouse kick. The instructor barked out "SWITCH" and LITTLE JOHNNY thought it would be funny to clip Aspen hard. Let me preface this by telling you Aspen is a much better practitioner a harder, higher kicker and if kicked intentionally he will kick back. With that being said LITTLE JOHNNY tried but could not connect and again the instructor barked "SWITCH" this time before they could reset into the fighting stance LITTLE JOHNNY through a cheap shot and nailed Aspen in the back. Without thinking and I believe by pure reflex he stepped down and NAILED LITTLE JOHNNY square in the chest knocking him off his feet. Luckily one of the junior instructors witnessed the whole thing Both boys were brought off to the side wall to explain to master Corey why they were making contact during practice. After a minute or so they were separated and allowed back in class.

"LITTLE JOHNNYS" mom had a few bad things to say and the whole audience heard. I just chuckled a bit. Then she turned her snide rude comments at me. There was a time in my life I would have laid into that fat POS wonderful woman but as I said you need to practice what they teach. I simply took the high road and turned the other cheek and said nothing. Then on the drive home as frustrated and angry as I was the young ones certainly didn't need to hear about her. So we stopped had our dinner at Wendy's drove home and *HER SON IS A FRIEND AND FELLOW TKD STUDENT. TALKING BAD ABOUT HER IN FRONT OF THE BOYS DOES NO GOOD FOR ANYONE SO I DID NOT TALK BAD ABOUT ANOTHER ADULT.*

FEBRUARY 14, 2018, I have been aware for years now and trying very, very hard to watch what I say to the young ones and most of the time I try to make an effort to not only watch what I say to them I try to watch and monitor what I say around them. Today being Valentine's day I was pissed off at the world and feeling sorry for myself. February 14, the birthday of the guy my ex-wife left me for. On February 14 a couple of years ago I slipped on the sidewalk and shattered my ankle and now have 2 plates and 5 screws in my leg. Let us just say that every year for the past few years something unpleasant occurred on February 14 so I am not a fan of Valentine's day.

Well, today I was feeling especially alone and bitter because I was asked to babysit so my daughters could cook and clean in peace so they could prepare a romantic dinner for their fellas. I did agree because I thought maybe spending time with the young ones would lift my spirits but I was wrong. I stopped to pick them up and every one of them got in the van climbed in the correct car seats then buckled. My negative energy was pouring out of my body and they knew just to get in and keep quiet. After about 6 or 7 minutes someone finally asked "so grandpa where we going?"

"I DON'T KNOW."

The silence continued for a couple more minutes then I asked "where did you want to go?"

"Can we go to the mall?"

"SURE GUYS, WHY NOT."

At the time it was somewhere around 2 in the afternoon so the roads were not crowded with after-work traffic to be honest not much traffic at all. Yet on the way to the mall, I found it necessary to cuss out someone at every stoplight we stopped at. With the young ones in the car for a long time now I have been carefully choosing my words trying very hard. Today though today was rough. I heard myself calling other drivers "idiots, morons and fools" then an older lady crossing the street, I said to myself but it was out loud; "COME ON YOU OLD BAG MOVE IT!" After we got to the mall my mood didn't improve until this happened.

The young ones were playing and a MALE PARENT went to help one of my grandkids up who simply slipped and fell while running around and this guy was just checking to see if he was alright. I ran up and flipped out "KEEP YOUR F!#KING HANDS TO YOURSELF YOU PERVERT. YOU MAKE IT A HABIT COMING TO THE MALL TOUCHING LITTLE BOYS?"

On and on I went I tore into that poor guy until he was almost in tears and grabbed his son and left the play area. That was the first time no other kids wanted to play with my young ones because of the other parents telling them to stay away. A few minutes later Aspen finally just bit the bullet and took his chances to say "GEESE GRANDPA THAT WAS MEAN. WE WERE PLAYING WITH THAT BOY NOW HIS DAD TOOK HIM AWAY AND NO ONE ELSE IS ALLOWED TO PLAY WITH US. WHY ARE YOU BEING SO MEAN TODAY?"

As they say... **OUT OF THE MOUTH OF BABES.**

The boy not only dared to tell me that I was being an asshole. He told me to keep my mouth shut and more importantly, he told me to watch what I say when there are children around not only the ones I am responsible for but ALL children. I was trying hard to monitor my words before but after being scolded by my 7-year-old grandson. The reality of what they hear and remember hit me like a ton of bricks so I try even harder not only when with the young ones but as a lifestyle practice ***EVERYBODY SLIPS UP AND HAS A BAD DAY BUT I DO TRY VERY HARD NOT TALK BAD ABOUT OTHER ADULTS.***

AUGUST 2, 2018, Unfortunately, there will be "GROWN Ups" who will be around on a fairly consistent basis but by no stretch of the imagination should be considered a good influence or role model. On this particular day, grandmas boyfriend Charlie many times had said he would be there to take the boys on a trail ride along the lake. Let me just again preface this by saying this man has been in the picture and part of their lives for a LOOOONG time. Long Before the grandkids were born and my kids were still kids this guy made promise after promise. He was very good at making promises like; "Kids I'll be there Sunday and I will take you and your mom to the zoo" only to be a NO SHOW or "I will be there this weekend and will have a family BBQ" and again another NO SHOW. The one that broke the proverbial camel's back is when he promised to take the family to Six-Flags GREAT AMERICA.

All the kids were ready, their mom was ready, lunches packed and the excitement level through the roof. He never showed and never even bothered to call so from that day forward when he promised anything it was taken like a grain of salt. So when he promised to take the boys on a trail ride, they were there waiting but not shocked when he didn't show.

We skipped a Saturday TKD class so they could go so they were a bit disappointed not to go but they were more upset they missed a class. They called me to say he did not show could we go to a later class. "No can do boys there is only a 9:30 class on Saturday and we missed it but if you can go I will take you to the arcade "THEY WERE ALLOWED TO GO TO THE ARCADE. On the way there it would have been very easy to bash someone who did not show seeing the boys were pissed and disappointed anyway. But 2 things happened on the way to the arcade - I made sure the boys knew that they could count on me for ANYTHING. I made sure they knew Charlie was a truck driver and maybe something happened to his truck or he may have been stuck in traffic.

EVEN THOUGH HE HAS BEEN UNRELIABLE FOR YEARS THE KIDS ALL LIKE HIM AND I GAVE THEM A REASON TO GIVE HIM THE BENEFIT OF THE DOUBT. I DID NOT TALK BAD ABOUT ANOTHER ADULT.

JUNE 30, 2020 The in-home orders have been very relaxed but still, some people are wearing masks some are not. Some restaurants are open for business and others have completely closed their doors while others still try to struggle through and keep the door open enough to stay afloat until the government or their elected officials give the all's clear and life as we knew it resumes. Today I took the boys to drive through Cho's parking lot to get a reaction if they got excited to gauge how bad they wanted to go back. We also stopped at the dollar store for ice cream sodas and Pokémon cards, en-route we passed by a couple of panhandlers on the corner. This was only the 6th time I have been out in the past 2 months. People were driving through red lights panhandlers still holding up signs asking for money and a couple of people walking around in public places wearing masks but way more not. With this Corona virus rearing its ugly head to threaten another wave that could potentially be more devastating this time around I find myself thinking the more things change the more they remain the same.

When you make an effort to try and be a nice person things you need to do intentionally changes. For example driving: people are still idiots and drive as such. But to verbalize that in the car with young ears near you makes no sense. Why call others names and cuss while driving either learn to completely keep your mouth shut or try hard to find good things to point out. Panhandlers: Why drive by and completely bash someone who may or may not be homeless you don't know for sure and by planting the seed of mistrust in their heads while driving say it enough and have more people confirm it they start to believe it. What if you simply changed it to: "I hope that man has a place to sleep tonight", can you imagine what that simple shift in words would do to the way the kids look at people. And finally, the mask debate. I think this whole virus scare is a bunch of garbage but their mother and other relatives think it is necessary going into certain stores a mask is required the kids are very impressionable at this age but are old enough to have an opinion.

SO, THE ONE THING I HAVE LEARNED THROUGH ALL OF THIS IS THAT PEOPLE ARE PEOPLE AND TALKING BAD ABOUT OTHER ADULTS DOES NO GOOD FOR ANYONE, SO DON'T.

EXPLANATIONS. Kids are extremely curious and do ask a ton of questions especially when they are with me and I talk to them about being nice to people and grandpa makes a very hard effort to try to be nice to people even in the worst of situations. We have been by great grandma for birthday parties, Christmas, or other family gatherings and the young ones have seen pictures of their aunt Michelle and have met their auntie Jenny. A couple of times they asked who she was and she just answered, "Auntie Jenny."

There are underlying family reasons why I don't make an effort to see my daughters. When Aspen was very little He and Danielle lived with me. One day I received a call from my older daughter saying she lost her apartment in Tennessee a few weeks ago and her boyfriend and their cat has been back in Milwaukee and living in their car for the last couple weeks wanting to know if they could stay with us for a while. My first knee jerk reaction was HELLLLLL NO! But, she is my daughter.

I should have stayed with my first thought of why me? Her mother, her sister, and her grandma all have houses why would she want to stay with us in a small apartment. The answer should have been obvious and it was... EVERYONE ELSE SAID NOOOOO. For the sake of keeping our family together, I should have said no. She may have been pissed for a while but at least she would have been more of an active part of our family but it is what it is and we don't talk.

When she first came to stay with me I was on crutches because a couple of weeks beforehand I slipped and broke my ankle pretty severely. The bathroom in my apartment was way on the other end of the house from my bedroom so instead of struggling through the small apartment on crutches I used a large gallon container and emptied it once or twice a day. Jennifer thought that was disgusting. At the time I also had my own business which was buying trinkets on line by the 100s and selling them online for a profit again she did not like that according to her I should have a job to make sure I could pay my part of the rent and finally she thought Danielle and the boy should move to make more room. Now keep in mind she was living in her car just a few short weeks ago and wanted to dictate our living arrangements. I said no so how they handled it was amazing. Again, keep in mind this is my daughter and her boyfriend. On the next rent cycle, she convinced the landlady to allow her and her boyfriend to put the lease in their names and told the owner Danielle did not pay and needed to go and that I was not paying my half and I needed to be evicted.

I told them in no uncertain terms to get the hell out of my apartment and that is when they sprung it on me it was their place and I had to get out. One day I was working at a friend's house and they changed the lock. I knew from being in real estate they had no legal right to change the locks so I took a shovel and pried my way in at which point they called the police and landlord both parties had told them they had no legal rights to change locks and they had to wait until I was legally evicted. Well as can imagine the tension was not worth it so Danielle and her boy went back to live with her mom, and I ended up living in a men's shelter for a couple of weeks.

Now when the young ones ask who Jennifer is I could explain she is my daughter that lived in her car, moved in, and got me thrown out of my apartment while at the same time throwing away over $10,000 in product. I could also say her boyfriend is a sneaky lying piece of dog crap but at some point, they may want to know her and because she is their aunt my personal feelings for her or her boyfriend should not judge their opinion and **TO TALK BAD ABOUT OTHER ADULTS DOES NO GOOD FOR ANYONE, SO DON'T.**

TIME AFTER TIME. More and more often I hear of kids being in a situation that people are fight or talking crap about someone behind their backs. The young ones have a hard time figuring this out. They get confused and it is hard to see and even harder to fix especially as they get older. They hear mom and dad fight calling each other very nasty names. Sometimes resulting in someone crying other times escalating into very loud shouting still other times things get thrown and broke. Now in most families, I am guessing that this is a relatively common occurrence in most families but for the young ones it happens maybe once a month. Sometimes more sometimes less sometimes just an argument sometimes things get thrown.

Some of you may be thinking once a month that's nothing and you could be correct. Now even if they try to keep it away from the young ones and they don't see the argument there is a good chance they will hear it. So let us do the math. Aspen is just over 9 and maybe arguments did not happen with parents but they did happen and sometimes worse than between parents. His mom and grandma got into some doozies. So 9 years old for this discussion let's say 1 major disagreement a month, 12 months in a year 9 years old 12 x 9=72 major arguments in his young life. Do you think that as he grows up he may think that arguing is a part of a healthy life? What if every time he sees a fight there is a nice meal or gift of some other prize or present afterward you believe that he will not grow up thinking this is normal? What if he meets a nice girl and she was brought up in the old fashion ways the man is the man and she is content as a mother and wife, at some point will he start an argument because for years that is what he was taught to be life.

Now as a grandpa how do I explain that? When he is with me and we are driving and someone is going slow and he is screaming they are a bad driver or when we are in the store and an adult is taking his or her time looking at something and I hear him under his breath "come on you idiot hurry up" and for me the thing that bothers me more than anything else is when they are arguing amongst themselves and the verbal name-calling begins. They are brothers and sisters and I do understand that and I also understand that this is a LEARNED behavior that is very, very hard to be untaught. From a very young age as a matter of fact from the time they are born if you want to raise respectful, happy healthy kids you must make a very conscious effort to watch your words and if you are grandpa *TALKING BAD ABOUT OTHER ADULTS, OTHER KIDS AND EVEN OTHER FAMILY MEMBERS DOES NO GOOD FOR ANYONE...SO DON'T*

KIDS TOO? One of the hardest things for me to remember is kids are kids and what you say about someone in their mind may translate to every kid or worse yet they might find similarities in certain actions and think you may be talking about them. Several kids in the TKD class are an extreme pain in the butt to watch and I can't even the patience it takes to instruct these kids. But there is one young boy who is a complete nightmare. This kid comes in late. He will keep his street close on and toss his uniform over it. During classes, I have seen him sit down or even lay down on the floor saying he was tired or sore and could not continue. He has argued with instructors and questioned the way they are teaching. This kid is a kid that is a very low belt and a relatively new student questioning a master instructor in front of the rest of the class. He has been disciplined in many different ways from taking his belt to making him sit against the wall facing away from the rest of the students.

There is another student who is Ethen's age but Aspen's rank and this kid is a handful. He is so often disciplined that after class his father will ask Aspen if his son behaved that day. He is a decent kid and tries when he needs to but he is the class clown and the big problem is keeping his hands off other students. He is a very touchy-feely kid and in a TKD class that is not a good thing. This boy also has had his belt taken away on several occasions he also has been seated facing the wall to try and get him on track all of which to this point did not work. Both these boys are still problematic in class but for me, the problem is Ethen has had his belt taken away and both the boys at one time or another have had to sit against the wall. So who do I talk to? I can't tell the boys what I think of the other two students because I don't want them to draw any sort of parallel between their all the time behavior and the boys every once in awhile behavior. I can't talk to their mom because during that conversation both boys would be within earshot and may hear what I had to say and again think it was about them. I can't speak to the instructors because neither of the other boys is my concern and they will simply say they are handling it. I can't talk to anyone else because frankly, no one else cares *SO MY ONLY OPTION IS "IF I CAN'T SAY SOMETHING NICE ABOUT SOMEONE DON'T SAY ANYTHING*

AT ALL" SO I DON'T.

JULY 14,2020; Today I took Verne, Amanda, and the boy to the grocery store and it was a very eye-opening experience. Warren is only two and a half but he knows the difference between right and wrong. We were on our way from their house to pick up my friend Verne who is completely blind and needs assistance getting in the store, while in the store pick out a product and they paying either with cash or his debit card. Today I learned lessons about life from two separate sources and they were both opposite events one good and one not so flattering. We were in Festival foods today and Verne is a huge fan of chocolate and more specifically he likes dark chocolate brownies. So today the bakery had a real nice sale on one whole container of brownies but they were not cut into sections. We went to the bakery counter and asked the manager if he would be willing to cut these 2 tins of whole brownies into 8-10 pieces because it would be very difficult for Verne to do it at home. Now for whatever reason, I thought he would say no maybe it was against policy to open then reseal the package maybe he didn't feel like it but I did expect a NO. and I was wrong not only did he do it he did it with a smile and saying he was happy to do it. Warren seeing how happy we were yelled "thank you, sir", ***ON THE WAY OUT I MADE SURE TO STOP AND TELL HIM AGAIN HOW IMPRESSED WE WERE HE DID THAT. I ALSO MADE IT A POINT TO INFORM HIS SUPERVISOR. HE MADE OUR DAY BETTER SO WE TRIED TO DO THE SAME. SO IF YOU FIND YOURSELF IN A SITUATION TO SAY SOMETHING GOOD ABOUT SOMEONE, DO IT!***

Smile a grateful smile at someone and I can guarantee they will find a way to pay it forward. On the ride home, we were sitting at a red light that had just turned green and some female behind me was honking away just a split second after the light changed. I usually just take off and let it go but today I felt the urge to slowly take off and as I did flip her the middle finger. In response, she flew by us honking and returning the single-finger salute. Verne sitting next to me in the passenger seat could not see what was going on so he asked: "What was that all about?" "Nothing, just some impatient bitch in a hurry to get through the light."

Amanda asked; "Did you say impatient bitch? Yeah she was."

Then out of the mouths of babes, "Mama that is not nice at all. You know mama that was even kind of mean." Warren said.

I heard my little grandson scolding his mother for saying something bad about someone we did not know. We had no idea why she honked. She may have had to use the bathroom bad, maybe she got a call and had to get somewhere quick or maybe she was just an impatient bitch we will never know but what we do know is my two and a half year-old grandson has more common sense than me or his mother in that situation which is ***YOU CAN NEVER KNOW WHAT IS GOING THROUGH SOMEONE ELSE'S HEAD OR WHAT THEIR SITUATION MAY BE. SO***

DON'T TALK BAD ABOUT OTHER ADULTS BECAUSE YOU JUST NEVER KNOW.

12 TO 1, SO WHY NOT BE THE 1. I remember when I was in college I was in a marketing class and there was a statistic that has stuck with me for years. That stat would be this...for every one compliment, a business gets they get 12 complaints. Years ago when Ponderosa Steakhouse was still open I was there with my family and the place was PACKED. We were seated promptly when it was our turn, the waitress was very polite and the steak was very good. The service was so outstanding that my girls even commented.

I would have to assume that the reason places only receive negative feedback before they receive the good is that most people look at it the same way I do. They are doing their jobs and if someone or something negative happens to a paying customer that customer feels cheated and calls to complain but on the other side of that coin if a paying customer receives service over and above what is expected that server or business is just doing a good job. If the server is lucky they may get a little extra in their tip with no other recognition.

Well this particular day I wanted to change that but the place was still very busy when we left so I waited to get home and until after I felt the dinner rush would be slowing down then called and here is how that conversation played out "Hello, can I speak to the shift manager please?"

"He is currently on the floor but this is Jack the store manager how can I help you?"

"Hi Jack, my family and I were just at your restaurant"

Although I could not see his face, I could hear the despair in his voice and just the tone of his voice was NOW WHAT?

"Yes sir, what can I help you with?"

"We were just there and the place was packed so I just wanted to call and say the waitress was very polite and prompt, the food was exceptional and you and your staff did a great job...THANK YOU!"

I mise well had been calling to tell him he just hit the lottery because the change in his voice and attitude was amazing. I could feel his face light up and instantly stood up straight with a renewed pride in himself, his job, and his staff. WHY? All because I took 10 seconds out of my day to let someone know they are appreciated and doing a good job ***SO WHENEVER POSSIBLE...BE THE 1 OUT OF 12 and TAKE THE TIME TO MAKE SOMEONES DAY.***

FUN STUFF

I had a conversation with the young ones and asked them; "WHY DO YOU GUYS LIKE HANGING OUT AND SPENDING TIME WITH ME? AND WHY DO YOU THINK I AM A GREAT GRANDPA?" Without missing a beat they all at the same time said "BECAUSE YOU TAKES US TO FUN PLACES!"

"REALLY? LIKE WHERE?"

"**ASPEN** YOU FIRST. WHERE HAVE WE GONE THAT'S FUN?" I Asked.

ASPEN:

BOUNCE MILWAUKEE	HELIUM TRAMPOLINE PARK	CHILLIS
GRANT PARK		
	CHO'S	

ETHEN:

THE MALL	THE CUPCAKE STORE	OLD COUNTRY BUFFET
RED'S GARAGE	GARCADE	

HARLOW:

THE ZOO	DOLLAR STORE	HALLOWEEN STORE
GREAT GRANDMA'S		

EVERYBODY

CHUCK-E-CHEESE	BRISTOL RENAISSANCE	THE PARK
MONSTER TRUCKS	FAIR	
		SWIMMING
7 MILE FAIR	THE GYM	
		4TH OF JULY
PUPPY STORES	SKY ZONE	
		CHINESE BUFFETS
DINOSAUR SHOW	HUMANE SOCIETY	
		TRAIN RIDES
SUMMER FEST	STATE FAIR	
		WRESTLING MATCH
FROG HUNTING	SPEED LITE ZONE	
		GREAT AMERICA
WISCONSIN DELLS	FLYING A KITE	
		TRAIN SHOW
	VESCOSE SPEEDWAY	

Part of being a GREAT GRANDPA is the ability and desire to take the young ones to fun places this final chapter is places we went and the explanations they gave me why they liked it there HOPEFULLY AS A GRANDPARENT READING THIS CHAPTER YOU GET SOME IDEAS YOU MAY NOT HAVE THOUGHT OF.

ASPEN'S PICKS

BOUNCE MILWAUKEE

My school took me there on a field trip and we had a great time. We had to do the buddy system so we were with a buddy for the whole field trip so basically we had to agree on where to go and what to play on. So my buddy and I worked it out so we went 15 minutes where he wanted and then 15 minutes of what I wanted to do. What I liked better when you took us is we could go where we wanted. I got to play in the bounce houses way longer than with my school trip. Plus you bought us pizza and drinks. I remember you even said they have yummy pizza for a trampoline park. When we were there I had a chance to do rock climbing and we got to stay in the laser tag game because it was slow that day they had a birthday party and the party go'ers allowed us to stay and play. I also liked the fact it was a birthday present for both me and Harlow so that means Mama could come and so did my baby sister.

HELIUM TRAMPOLINE PARK

I liked it here a lot more than the other trampoline parks because it is way bigger. It has a lot of the same stuff but here is bigger. Like when I got to rock climb all the other places were really easy to get to the top here I fell off a couple of times before I made it to ring the bell. Also, they have many more games. I mean like video games. When we are at other places we have to pay extra cash money to play video games at this place we showed our wrist band and could play as many games as we wanted. Then go back and jump around on the trampolines for however long we want and we could go back, show our wristband to play more videos. We were allowed to do that as many times as we wanted during the whole time we were there which is cool. I also liked the balance beam with the padded Q-tip things we used to battle. I could hit Ethen as hard as I could and he could hit me too we didn't get in trouble and it didn't hurt and was fun.

The workers there were cool too. They would tell us how things worked and then we'd try. If we tried a couple of times and didn't make it one of the guys would show us how. We try again most of the time we made it but if not someone helped us. I am talking about a TALL WALL that was at the end of a long narrow trampoline that looked like a bowling alley. How to get up the wall you had to run as bestest and fastest you can down the trampoline alley jump as hard and high as you can on the end then scurry up and grab the handles on top the wall to pull yourself up. Two boys worked there that showed us how. When I didn't make it one jumped down to show me again then again. I made it on my fourth try. Ethen was next to me with the other boy he kept jumping down but Effers kept falling off. He is my brother and he didn't quit he was mad he wanted to sit on the top of the wall. He tried a lot and couldn't do it. Then the boy said he'd boosted him up but Effers said NO. I laid on my tummy to try and grab his hand but couldn't reach. The boy that helped me reached down and now I was shouting, the boys were shouting, and a couple of other kids were watching and started to clap and chant

"YOU CAN DO IT...YOU CAN DO IT...YOU CAN DO IT"

"COME ON ETHEN YOU GOT THIS...YOU GOT THIS"

"COME ON LITTLE MAN RUN, BOUNCE AND JUMP"

By now I heard all the cheering so I had to walk over to check things out and there is the tiniest of toons trying to scale a 10' wall and a dozen people cheering for him so naturally, I had to "COME ON BUDDY I GOT A BUCK IF YOU MAKE IT THIS TIME."

He looked back to see if it was me that said that I pulled the dollar out of my pocket, snapped it, and held it up for him to see. That boy had the biggest shit-eating grin I have ever seen and took off like a rocket. About 2 ft from the end JUMMMMMP, bounce and he reach up grabbing Aspen's hand to help pull him up. That boy had more pride in his eyes and the smile on his face you would have thought he just won a GOLD medal. I guess when you are 5 years old and accomplish something like that you did win a medal made not a physical medal that you can hold in your hands but an emotional medal that you hold in your heart.

CHILLIS

"Ok buddy we have been to a lot of different restaurants. What is it about Chillis that makes your fun place to go list?"

"There are a couple of things, grandpa, first we always go on Tuesday which means that before we go eat we were at TKD. The food there is great. Remember the first time we all went I had a cheeseburger and fries Ethen tried the chicken tenders and you had a steak with soup and a slice of garlic bread and we all got chocolate milk. The reason I remember is we all shared each other's stuff and it was really good. I like going there to when your friend Katie is working because she brings us extra goodies like more fries or orange slices. The best thing I like is you let us play on the tablet and the games they have are fun and when Ethen and I are not playing games we are on the trivia section playing against other people and it is neat when we win but even more than the tablet I like going to Chillis because YOU take us, grandpa"

GRANT PARK

I know Grant park is one of many parks we go to but I remember things that I have done there so every time you say we are going to play at the park in my head I say I hope it's Grant. The most fun thing about Grant park is the play area that has the obstacle course. I love trying to beat the times I have and improve. I know it seems weird but when I am there I always think about TKD and doing better. Another thing I like is every time we go when we leave we stop at Dairy Queen because DQ is right there at the end of the park. Even though we don't know how to golf yet we do know how to putt and you take me and Ethen to the putting place to practice, The bestest most coolest thing though is that is where you taught us how to jump and skip rocks. I remember we were walking around the play area and saw a trail. We followed that trail and it took us to a very high hill and from the top of the hill we could see the lake Michigan I think that's what you said lake Michigan. Then we took a hike down the hill what ended right next to the water. Remember grandpa you found a rock and tossed it in the water and it bounced on the top. We stayed there for a long time until both of us could bounce rocks on the water at least 3 or 4 times. The last thing I like about Grant park is they have a beach that has a pier way out in the water and sometimes we would have extra bread from fishing then go way out on the pier to feed the seagulls. I think that is neat too.

CHO'S TAE KWON DO

"There are a lot of reasons I like Cho's. Mostly I can't wait to be a black belt. I think being a black belt will be awesome and once I earn my black belt I want to be on the demo team. You have seen the demo team grandpa they are the students at testing who put on the show at the beginning that wear those real cool red uniforms. They do all kinds of board breaks and weapons and fighting and board breaks and ALL kinds of cool stuff.

I like my teachers. Master Corey is very smart because he has to teach everyone he knows how to teach little kids and he also teaches the other instructors so he has to know everything. Madam Monique is a good teacher too. Sir Josh teaches us when we are lower belts and kids Ethen's age and he is a big scary guy but I like him too. But I like when sir Will teaches the class the most cause he is a very high black belt and works on the demo team. I am not for sure but I think he is just a little older than me. He lets us do more challenging stuff too. Like when we are doing warm-ups on the obstacle course if there are 4 bags to jump over and I ask to try 5 he puts another one out and says "GO FOR IT" All the teachers show us how to do things and If we make a mistake the show us the proper way and no-one yells.

You already know I love dodge ball and fireball and black belt tag. I like the extras too.

Like being an elite member me and my brother get to go to the Halloween and Christmas party. We got to watch a movie after class a couple of times too. I like it when I am High belt in class and run to the front when called and lead the class. I like it when we learn new movements and forms because then we have to practice for stripes. After all, getting stripes is the only way to earn my next belt.

Weapons class was pretty cool but so far I only got to do that once. I like the uniforms. The blue uniform that the elite members get is awesome. what is the best and most fun is sparring. When I spar that tells me in my head how good I do. If I spar against a lower belt and smaller kid and win that is OK but I like when Master Corey puts me up against a taller kid or higher belt because then when I win I feel really good. But the coolest thing about sparring is the headshot bet that I have with you, grandpa. If I am sparring and score a head kick you pay me $2 if someone scores on me I owe you. (BTW you still owe me 16 bucks) Winning trophies at the tournament was pretty cool too. OH and I forgot it was because of TKD I was able to get my ears pierced and dye my hair blue.

ETHEN'S PICKS

SOUTHRIDGE MALL

I like going to the mall and play with my brother and sisters but I like it more when you and I just go. I like going with you because we stop for samples. Remember grandpa they have a place where we can try different cookie dough flavors. I liked the mint and you did not even have any. Then we went for a walk in the mall and got sample ice cream and they had mint too. My most favorite is the frozen yogurt and we put M&M pieces and reeses pieces in it and that was yummy I like the train to grandpa most of the time we don't ride the train cause it costs too much money but the time I went with you you let me ride by myself cause I am old enough. When I got on the driver man let me sit upfront because I went by myself and he said I was a big boy and got to ring the train bell when we were driving around the mall. I think that was the day I saw kids from TKD and waved. When I got off the train the driver man gave me some candy, a sticker, and a picture page to color. That was nice.

THE CUPCAKE STORE

I like going to the cupcake store because we only go there for one reason we always stop to get energy before TKD class. So I know if we are at the cupcake store we are going to the park to practice than class or we are going from the store straight to class. When you take us sometimes you just give us money and let us go in and get what we want. I like the different flavors of popcorn they have. When you come in you always get water for the car and extra bread to feed the deer, oh yeah I forgot bread for the deers and geese and squirrels that are pretty cool too. We can get what we want some if we go in with money we have 5 dollars and I always get popcorn we get a bag of doughnuts to bring home Harlow gets a fruit pie Then Aspen gets a carrot cake. Sometimes they have extra that the lady will give us samples and sometimes she gives us suckers or candy but that's why I like the cupcake store

OLD COUNTRY BUFFET

I love going to OCB. Every time we go they always have ALL my favorite food. We go after class for family night on Thursday which is fun. I know when we go they have 3 different kinds of chicken that is my favorite. Then after the first plate, you let me have orange teriyaki chicken and pudding with an icee and chocolate milk. I know what Aspen likes too grandpa. He will go and have steak and a chicken taco and then like me he has orange chicken with rice and he gets a cherry ICEE and chocolate milk and I forgot to say I mix all the ICEE flavors. But you grandpa you go for the steak and pork chops, right? I know you eat lots of steak then sometimes you even have soup I think you said you like the soup and veggies.

But like I like the games best. On family night we get to sit at the table with other kids and the lady helps us with projects. Sometimes we make cards for or mom and dad. Sometimes we color pictures with crayons. sometimes we paint and they let us keep the paints. One time we built puzzles and she let us take them home.

My most favorite part is when we play games for prizes. Sometimes we would play SIMON SAYS and whoever is the last kid standing wins. Remember grandpa the time I won a spiderman color book, with a box of crayons and stickers? Sometimes we play MUSICAL CHAIRS. I don't like that game so much cause I never can get a seat but Aspen likes it cause he is a very good sitter. The lady that runs the games is very nice because we go after TKD and our sisters ain't there cause we don't have time to drive home and then drive back so the lady always gives us extra popcorn and extra bags of cotton candy and extra balloons for our sisters. I like the games and fun on family nights but sometimes we go after Saturday class and get breakfast. ALL the bacon I can eat with pancakes and chocolate milk YUMMY.

RED'S GARAGE
I like going with you to sell stuff by Red's garage because when we leave you will have money and then we will either go for pizza or maybe Wendy's for food. Maybe the dollar store for Pokémon cards. If you sell a lot you take us to both. The thing I like there is at home we play HIDE-SEEK but there are only a couple of good places to hide. When you take us by the garage and we play there are way more places to hide. Member the time Asper & me both hid in the garbage cans and you had to count again cause you couldn't find us and gave up? When Aspen hides he likes to climb up by the ceiling and hide by the doors and hoses then he is very hard to find. My favorite place to hide is under the trailer. Hahahaha, nobody ever thinks to look under there and someone else always gets found first.

I think you got mad at us because you had to count and me and Aspen found a door high up and went to hide on the roof. Do you remember that one grandpa? I like went Harlow comes with too she finds some hard places to hide and when its hard to find people that makes the game FUN.

THE GARCADE

This place is GREAT. The lady who owns it is very nice and she knows who we are and I like that a lot. I like playing games over and over and over trying to do better every time. I know how to do pinball now because you showed me. Me and Aspen are very good at air hockey and I like playing that because I can use a stool and reach the top and I know how to hit the disk thing hard and bounce it off the walls to make it hard for people to hit. Remember that game you and I play together? I don't remember what it is called but it has the 4 colored boxes and I either play you or we team up and me and you play against the cool game. I like teaming with you cause you are good at that game and we win a lot. I know I am small and can not reach most games but they have the little white stools that I carry around so I can play all the games. The most fun thing we all do is the motorcycle or car race games. We can all sit on a different game and we race each other I think that is completely cool. Plus when we pay we get a band on our hand so I can play what I want s many times as I want and not get in trouble. If another kid is waiting we can take turns...Right grandpa? So far I have made friends there that like playing the same games as me.

I know you said you like the fact we can pay and play for hours and hours then leave and go eat and come back and play more but don't have to pay again. I like that too grandpa but I like that we can just walk down a few stores and there is a Domino's pizza that has tables. We can eat and then go back. THAT IS WHY I LIKE THAT GAME PLACE.

HARLOW'S PICKS

THE ZOO

I LOVE the zoo cause of all the animals. I like going with my school but I like it more going with you and mama. When we went we got to the zoo we can stay and watch the animals we like. My teacher says we have to hold our partner's hand and keep walking. You and Mama let us look for a long time at the animals we like to look at. Remember grandpa we watched that great big mama elephant tear the stuff apart(a bail of hay) and feed her baby. Then we got to ride on the camel. Me and Effers rode on the same one and he was tall. The most favorite thing was when we went and petted the goats and baby sheep they were nice and soft and after the food was all gone they licked my hand and that tickled.

DOLLAR TREE

You always take me and my brodders to the dollar store for presents. On mamas birthday we went and bought her flowers and a card and chocolate. You let us have snacks and a puzzle and Pokémon cards. Every time we go we get to buy a couple of neat things and if my baby sisters are not with us I buy stuff they will like and bring it home for them. I know you like ice cream and Mt. Dew from the dollar store and the ice cream I like is the sour patch popsicles because if you buy 1 box there is enough for all of us to have 1. another thing I like to buy there is gummy candy we get a bag and all the kids get some. And the bestest thing at the dollar store is the dolls. I like dolls and I like to bring my baby sisters' dolls so we can all play together. My brodders always buy Pokémon cards and get me some too so we can Pokémon battle.

THE HALLOWEEN STORE

It was really scary there. I don't like scary stuff like zombies and scary movies because I am afraid that when I go to sleep something will get me. At the Halloween store, you showed me that the bad people in the movies were only fake and not really and wouldn't hurt me but I was still scared. But the Halloween store had pretty masks and not scary stuff like Disney princess costumes and Anna and little mermaid things but my most favorite thing was I got to say hello to Queen Elsa then she gave me a bag full of really yummy candy and said I should come back soon.

THE MUSEUM

We all went to the museum there was me Harlow, you grandpa, mama, Auntie Da, my brodders, Violet and Warren. We all went first to see what things were like in olden times. I know the kids all waited in a line and we got to pick out candy. You waited with Auntie Da and violet and Warren cause they are too little for candy. Then we went to a place that had BIG dinosaurs and that was kind of scary cause I thought maybe they'd get us but they were only machines and left us alone. There are lots of neat things we looked at but my most favorite thing was the butterfly room. We had to wait in the little room before we got to go in so no butterflies got loose and fly around the museum. Mama told me to stand still cause I wearing a very pretty pink shirt and I looked like a pretty bright flower and butterflies liked pretty pink flowers so they would like me and land on me. I had lots and lots of butterflies landed on my arms and one even landed on Violet.

GREAT GRANDMA'S HOUSE

Great-grandma is always fun to go by with you. My most favorite thing to do there is playing the hot/cold game with great-grandma and my bodders. It is like hide and seek but instead of hiding kids, we hide pieces of a toy and then tell you if you are hot or cold. Another thing about great grandma's house is cookies she always has the best cookies and fruit snacks we always get to eat fruit snacks by grandma. At Christmas when we go to visit she has a tree that turns on when you clap our hands that's always neat.

HERE IS WHAT THEY ALL LIKED

CHUCK E CHEESE

Whenever we go to Chuck E Cheese we have a great time because it is for either one of our birthdays or we are invited to a party. Sometimes you take us just because. Most always we go because of a party and that means we can get lots of tokens to play lots of games of ride on lots of rides. If It one of our birthdays we get extra tokens to try and win tickets for candy. Sometimes we even get to take a picture with Chuck E. We always leave with nice presents and the pizza is yummy and cake whenever we are there we ALWAYS get cake. So yeah CHUCK E CHEESE is a cool place to go.

THE PARKS

Grandpa you know we go to a bunch of different parks. They are all cool because we go to different parks for different reasons. We go to parks by the lakefront when it is hot because it is always cooler by the lake and there are beaches so if it is REAL hot you let us jump in to cool off. Sometimes we go to the park before TKD so we can practice and because it is close also because it has some cool playgrounds and hiking area. We go to other parks because of small lakes and ponds to go fishing and turtle and frog hunting.

SWIMMING

Swimming is OK when we go to the lake but we like it much more better when we go to a pool. We don't mean a pool like at Margaret's house that is only a small little pool that we jump off the deck and it's not even deep. We mean a pool that has slides and tubes and waves and life jackets and guards and long lines like a water park yeah swimming with you is fun but we meant a water park like GREAT WOLF LODGE OR KALAHARI

THE GYM

We all like going to the gym because there is a ton of fun things for us to do. We can play tag with other kids. Some days we are allowed to sit at tables and color pages with crayons and paints and we can take our art home for mom and dad. Other times when nobody is using it Ethen and Aspen can go in the total body fitness area and work on low, medium and head kicks with the free-standing bag they have. Another time Harlow was allowed to go to a dance class and dance and exercise with mama and Antie Da. Ethen gets to practice wall e ball in the volleyball court and Aspen got to try tennis against a serving machine, why we like it the most is we are never bored. There is always something fun and different to do and there are always different kids to play with. But if we get lucky and no other kids are playing we have the gym to ourselves to do what we want when we want and that is awesome.

SKY ZONE

We never had a chance to enjoy SKY ZONE to its full capacity because when we were there something happened and we had to leave but the man gave you a ticket that we could use anytime. But while we were there we got to play trampoline tag which is very hard but very fun. Running fast across a trampoline floor might sound simple but even Aspen as fast and athletic of a kid he is was having trouble staying up. We also played trampoline dodgeball and we were just about to go on the obstacle course when we had to leave. But the stuff we did do was great the stuff we have seen and are going on next time will be fun so if it is like the other few trampoline parks we have been to IT WILL BE EXCELLENT

TRICK or TREATING

You have taken us trick or treating for the past few years cause Mama is afraid to go because of the neighborhoods we lived in but when we go with you, you take us places that have safety first posters all over and we know what houses to look for that are safe houses and will be giving us candy. Plus you take us because most of the time before Halloween night you are the one to take us to rummage sales and buys the cool costumes. We like going with you cause you just don't drop us off on the corner and drive to the next corner you park the car and walk with us. The best part of walking with you that you keep the youngest child on your shoulders to make sure they get candy.

PET/PUPPY STORES

All of us want a pet of some kind. I know Ethen wants a bird, Harlow has her heart set on a kitty named Elsa and Aspen would like any pet. He says fish or a mouse maybe a couple of rabbits like grandma but when asked to narrow it down to 1 animal and what he would like first he always drifts back to a puppy. Not just any puppy but a solid black male German Shepard. Now I am not sure if he truly likes Shepards or if it is because grandpa's favorite dogs are Shepard not just any Shepard but an old black boy Shepard. At the moment everyone in the family that wants a dog lives in places where dogs are not allowed so we go to 2 or 3 different pet stores that sell puppies that allow us to play with them. The best place is when we drive for a while the puppy store in Racine. That store lets us have any puppy we want in a small room so it can play with us with their toys and some like to pull shoelaces some like to tug a war with a rag and some just like to jump and play with us. The store also has birds, and rabbits and ferrets that we can hold but what we all like most is CHARLIE a great big tortious that walks all over the store and for 25 cents we can buy some pellets and feed him.

THE HUMANE SOCIETY
We like this place because grandpa and our Auntie Da used to volunteer here and they told us how they save hurt animals and if people find sick or hurt babies they can bring them here to get fixed and healed. We went there a couple of times when they were feeding baby birds and baby squirrels. we didn't know that when a baby bird doesn't have a mommy to feed it the workers here feed it and they eat with a medicine tube just like the one mama uses to give us medicine. If it is a very little baby squirrel they use the same thing but if the baby is a bit older they eat formula from a baby bottle. When we were there once someone was bringing in a box full of baby geese and the lady said someone accidentally ran over the mama so they put the babies in the box and brought them there. Small young baby geese are very soft and fuzzy and LOUD they were loud and the man told us they were just hungry so they brought them into a room and let us watch through the window while they fed them. The best part is knowing that sick and hurt animals have a place to go and get better and when we go fishing the fish we catch go there to help feed baby geese and baby raccoons.

They have pets here too. People don't get to take wild animals home they get healed or when they growed up and are big enough they are let back in the parks so they can find other members of the family. We go sometimes to look to see the kitties and dogs the have. We like going there cause they are nice to animals.

SUMMERFEST
We go here a lot in the summer because grandpa gets tickets for us from a friend that performs there so she gets tickets free for friends and family to get in. We like going because there are some water areas that we play in when it's hot. We go and when we walk around there are different places to hear different music. One day we were walking around and there was a bunch of guys banging on barrels and pipes things that looked like trash that sounded kinda neat and grandpa said that is why their name was THE JUNKYARD DOGS. The bands that we saw that we all enjoyed so far are 5 finger death punch, KISS, and Alice Cooper. With the 2020 season being canceled we will have to

wait until next year to see what shows will be next on the list.

STATE FAIR

The animals are the best part of the fair but the rides are cool too. The other part that we like is some of the strange food we can get. We have been to a lot of different restaurants with our grandpa and his friends but we can never get the stuff outside as we do at the fair. There is a pretty big ride area that looks like it would be fun but every time we go we can never go on the rides cause we are there for the food and the animals that the rides are WAAAY too expensive and if we use all our money for rides we could not buy things like fresh milk, milkshakes YUMMY!!

BRISTOL RENAISSANCE FAIR

Sometimes even as kids they know things may be fun but expensive is expensive. We were here only twice the first time I was invited by a friend who was performing so we did not have to pay for admission but I did not realize prices for food, fun, and drinks would be so incredibly expensive so we were there but did not get to enjoy things the way they were designed to be enjoyed. The next time I took them we went on opening day so admission was free and the attractions were half off and we did bring a budget this time so all the young ones were able to do a pony ride, they got a chance to battle the evil knight in a sword fight, we watched a jousting match and we ate and drank hardily. We also were able to come home with souvenirs. This place is VERY cool but not high on our go back to list.

7 MILE FAIR

We have been to the 7 mail fair (and it ain't no fair) both helping our grandpa sell stuff and we have been there a few times looking to buy stuff. Grandpa has some cool things that we sell. He has t-shirts and some earrings last time we had a couple of boxes of stuff to sell. But the more fun times are when he takes us to buy stuff. If we are good for the whole week and we go on Saturday we have a budget so we can buy what we want but we need to make sure that is what we want because they have a rule once you give them your money you can't get it back. So before we should buy anything grandpa says we should walk around and look at everything and then go back for what we want. The best thing about going here is the animals. There are a lot of people that sell chickens and ducks outside but there are people indoors that sell cool things like snakes, lizards, and spiders. Some day we will buy a lizard not a spider or snake cause Mama is afraid of those.

MONSTER TRUCKS

We have been to the truck races with the boys a few times Grandpa, uncle Ryan, Effers and Aspen. We have never brought any of the girls, 'cause I don't think they would like it and it is VERY, VERY loud. As their grandpa, I do try to be as fair as I can but it is my money and to spend $30 bucks for tickets on an event I am quite sure neither of the female young ones would enjoy makes no sense to me. Now the boys on the other hand have both already been and both enjoy if. What they tell me they like the best is the crushing of smaller cars. Both told me that when the truck flies off the ramp and lands dead center and flattens a car is cool. The next thing is what they said is a 1-1 race. two trucks start side by side and race around the track flying up in the air and sometimes they flip on the side and once we even have seen one flip over on its head. At the end of the race, the winner goes around and around either on the concrete or in the dirt and that makes a HUGE cloud of dust or smoke and then drive to the top of the mountain and wave. The most surprising thing for me was that we bought a flag and at the end of the show the drivers were all at a table in the hallway and both boys wanted to have the flag signed and they were both excited to talk to these guys and ask them questions about driving such a big truck and having them sign our flag. Someday I hope that they will be able to sit in the cab or behind the wheel of a monster truck cause that would be something they could tell their grandsons.

4TH OF JULY PARADE
Working out at Cho's has been both a challenge and an honor for both boys. They have both worked very hard to not miss a test and they both rose through the ranks quickly. They both find themselves as role models in class and they were both asked to be in the front line of the Cho's students for the annual Greenfield 4th of July parade. This is a position of honor because it shows the other students your hard work and commitment is recognized by the master instructor and other teachers. It also shows the people in the crowd that you are committed to the school and what it teaches and most importantly you are one of the few students that can throw candy to the crowd.

CHINESE BUFFETS
My family and friends make a joke about the fact that I am a Chinese buffet expert by their standards. I have been to every buffet in this area and judge them by 3 criteria: price, selection, quality, and taste.

There are buffets I go to because of each of these criteria but the young ones like Chinese food at the mall or so they THINK they like Chinese food but teriyaki chicken someone hands you from a sample tray is by no comparison to authentic Chinese food even from a buffet. So one day I had the young ones and we were hanging out with a friend of mine who was the person who turned me on to Chinese food so his expertise is more solid than mine. The kids asked if we could go to the mall because they wanted "Chinese food" We both had to chuckle because Chinese food did sound amazing, but the mall? We think not. So with a somewhat disappointed look on their faces, the kids buckled up and prepared for a 35-minute ride for a Chinese buffet that fit all 3 of my criteria. To this day I don't know the name of this place but I do know how to get there and I do know I have brought friends and family there and not one person has ever complained. As far as I know, everyone I have brought went back at least once. Ask the young ones about it and they will all tell you the same thing. They would drive there for the teriyaki chicken but when they finish eating and are allowed desert there is not a place anywhere else that has a selection like this place. 4 kinds of cake, pies, cupcakes, jello, and chocolate bars yes, they even have a HUGE hunk of chocolate they can break off and have a chocolate bar for dessert. They loved it the first time we went and want to go back.

WRESTLING MATCH
This particular event should just be Aspen's because I went into a play it again sports with him and the owner was there and he happened to be a sponsor of a local wrestling event and we happened to walk in minutes after they dropped off their complimentary tickets and we just happened to be there looking for TKD equipment and the owner just happened to ask us if we would like free tickets to this upcoming event. AND Aspen just happened to say SURE. But the man only had 3tickets and usually for something like this it is either 2 or 4 of us that go but the owner would not give us just the 2 because he would have had to find someone willing to go alone so for us it was all 3 or none so we took all 3. Because it was very close to Uncle Ryan's birthday we decided to ask him first and at the time Effers was a little too young to enjoy a live event anyway.

We were there very early and the seating was first come first seated and it was a very small intimate venue anyway so no matter where we would have been seated it would have been great but we were the first in line and the first row was the only assigned seating but anywhere in the 2nd row and back was a free for all. So we got 2nd-row dead center seats and the action was less than 10 feet away. After the first match started there was a lady in front of us in the front row that said her husband was not coming Aspen was welcome to his seat. What a night for that little man FRONT ROW RINGSIDE. The action that came out on the floor on our side of the ring was inches from him at one point during a woman's match a female wrestler yelled at him to move and she slammed her opponents head in the chair Aspen had barely moved from. We got pics, autographs and a signed masked from a Mexican wrestler at the end of the night. This was a situation that from walking into the store we were at the right places at the right times and this is a night he will remember for a long, long time.

TRAIN RIDES

The young ones have been fascinated with trains for a very long time. Not only the boys either. Harlow has been intrigued by trains too. When they were small they would watch a cartoon called Thomas the train which was about several different trains that were responsible for different tasks. They spend hours each week watching that cartoon but they finally had a chance to ride a somewhat real train at the mall and more of a real train when we went to the zoo. All 3 of the young ones ask when we are going back to the zoo because as a little one the zoo train is as real as it needs to be but for me, I am waiting until they get a little older so I can take them on the amtrak to Chicago spend the day at navy pier and the train back home. Then they will be able to tell their friends about grandpa and the train ride. A couple of years back there was a train show at state fair park here in Milwaukee. There were no real life-size trains or even train cars but there were the national champion toy train builders. Some of these guys had scaled-down cities so realistic that if you have never been there you could see the eagles eye view and figure out how to get around the city. For me, it was OK for the young ones that like trains it was EXCELLENT

DINOSAUR SHOW

We have all been to the zoo seen the dinosaur section which the additional entrance fee is 3 bucks per person and there are maybe 8-10 mechanical dinosaurs some moved some roared some spit water but overall a very nice somewhat realistic exhibit for an additional 3 bucks. At the museum, they have a dinosaur exhibit that is only a few dinosaurs but the one they do have are very large and real looking so although limited a very nice section. This dinosaur show was promoted as a MUST SEE for any dinosaur enthusiasts. I figured this was a once a year event and the commercials and the hype made it sound very appealing. So I bit the bullet and took the young ones. I was VERY disappointed after paying over a 100 bucks to get in. yes, it had everything they advertised they would have but nothing more. They had life-size dinosaurs but so does the zoo. They had a fossil dig but so does the museum. They had a dinosaur ride race...for an additional charge. The young ones must have had a memorable time because this made their list but unless someone gets me free or extremely discounted tickets I don't believe I will be taking them again.

FISHING, TURTLE & FROG HUNTING

We have been a lot of places fishing and caught lots of fish but the thing we like the most is we get to take turns. When we go to the lake and we go with grandpa. Mama and Auntie Da. Grandpa will take the fish pole and show Aspen how to hold it and throw it out in the water then watch if the bobber goes down and JERK the pole to catch the fish. Mama sits with the babies and auntie Da walks around the edge of the lake with Effers and Harlow looking for frogs & turtles. Then if Aspen catches a fish or we walk back Autie Da watches the babies Mama takes her turn with the fish pole and lets Harlow hold it then waits for the boober to go down and try to catch the fish and grandpa walks around looking for frogs. We like it when we go with grandpa because he sees frogs more than anyone else and he catches a lot. One time we went to a different lake that was very hard to get down next to the water but we saw real many turtles that day. The good and bad part of that day was we were fishing for fish and using nightcrawler so when we tossed the line out we could see the turtles swimming toward the bobber and after they found the boober dive down and eat our worms. We catch 7 turtles that day and thankfully we did not hurt any of them. They did not get hooked they just clamped on the worm and would not let go. Grandpa says this was one of the strangest things he has ever seen while fishing. He said he has been fishing 100s of times and catch 1000s of fish but never before brought in a turtle and today reeled in 7.

FLYING A KITE

Today at the dollar store we were looking for something new to do at the park. Being a cool spring sweatshirt wearing kind of day we did not want to play frisbee or throw around the football it was kind of windy for either of those activities so as we were looking down the toy aisle there was a box of kites. KITES, of course, a bit windy and a tad nippy perfect kite flying weather but the problem is I have not flown a kite for years and the young one never have either. I asked if they were willing to learn how to fly a kite. Just like everything else they jumped at the chance to try something new and different. So we picked out 3 kites and 3 rolls of string and headed to the park. No, what never occurred to me was these were dollar store kites and the quality may not be the best in the world. We did make it to the park we did make it to the picnic table and we attempted to open the spiderman kite and as we took it out of the package we saw the sticks were snapped in half. Ethen was very sad. So we opened the lightning McQueen kite and as we put it together we noticed the paper kite had a slit completely down the center and could no way fly. Aspen was very sad. So we had one kite left and it was Queen Elsa so we took her out of the package very carefully. No rips in the paper, so we carefully pulled out the sticks, both OK, and we proceeded to put together our last kite. Although it has been years since I flew a kite I did remember a good kite needs a tail so we went in the car and found an old T-shirt ripped it up and made a tail. Connected the hook at the end of the string to the hook on the kite. We were ready for take-off and I asked the young ones to tell me which way they thought the wind was blowing and away we went. The first attempt we went up about 15 ft and came crashing down and they all thought that was the greatest thing ever. They did not realize the kite was supposed to fly. I tried a couple more times with similar results but on the 4th try I ran against the wind threw her up in the air and caught a wind sheer and skyrocketed to the end of the 75 ft of string. Although we only had 1 kite left and 3 rolls of string we all took turns holding the string and flying our kite. The wind stayed pretty steady for over an hour letting all the young one have a very nice turn for flying the kite.

BEING A GREAT GRANDPA DOES NOT ALWAYS MEAN SPENDING GOBS OF CASH EVERY TIME YOU SEE THEM. WHAT IS DOES MEAN IS ENJOY THE TIME YOU HAVE BEEN GIVEN. IF YOU HAVE THE MONEY AND CAN AFFORD TO TAKE THEM FUN PLACES every time THEN DO THAT BUT IF ALL YOU CAN AFFORD IS 5 DOLLARS AND A FEW HOURS GO FLY A KITE!

ALWAYS HAVE THEIR BACK!

Being a GREAT GRANDPA means you completely understand and accept the fact that they are kids and sometimes kids stretch the truth and sometimes even straight lie to your face to stay out of trouble. Sometimes kids might say hurtful things to brothers and sisters. Sometimes kids will say hurtful and disrespectful things to their parents, teachers, and friends. Yes, sometimes kids will even disrespect their grandpa. No matter what they do or what they say, I will always be their grandpa and they need to know: **THAT ANY DAY FOR ANY REASON AT ANY TIME DAY OR NIGHT I WILL ALWAYS HAVE THEIR BACK!**

There are several ways and definitions to HAVE THEIR BACK. Believe in them, listen to what they say and if they find themselves in trouble be it at home, in school, on the bus if they say they did not do it UNLESS you see it hear them out listen to their side of the story and then judge the facts just don't jump to conclusions because an adult tells you the story, you may not have an interest in say video games or school stories they are writing, something that happened in class or on the playground deep down you don't care, but they came to you, believe me if it is important to them it should be important to you know where they are ALWAYS. If you are babysitting or taking them shopping, playing at the park, riding in the car, or taking the dog for a walk KNOW WHERE THEY ARE AND MAKE SURE THEY ARE SAFE ALWAYS!!!

Don't disrespect them by calling them names if they do something find the reason and the possible good then focus on that correct them without criticism.

Miss the bus, overslept maybe they fell or got hurt and need the ER It is important that they know WE CAN CALL GRANDPA FOR A RIDE.

JUNE 11, 2020; Today was a special day for me. Today was the day that everything came together and the universe showed me why I am a GREAT GRANDPA.

I was just sitting at my desk working then came an unexpected surprise Amanda and her son Warren stopped by for a visit. At the moment Warren is an only child so he spends a great deal of time being taught so he has a very large vocabulary and very articulate for a two-year-old boy. He is also a very active kid which keeps his mom and dad moving. However, when he comes to visit his cousins be prepared for ALL HELL TO BREAK LOOSE.

From the second he gets here to the second he leaves he is running, chasing or playing with someone. Sometimes Aspen, maybe Violet but more times than not they are ALL playing together. Today they were playing some kind of TAG game. The other kids know their house that if they come running up the stairs they can make it to the top bunk they can either stay there where they can't be touched or if they're being followed can jump off the back of the bed to escape. Well, today Warren was the chaser and playing with Ethen and Violet.

As I am watching the game Here comes Ethen up the stairs on the bed and sat there... A second later here comes Violet with Warren right on her tail. As she started climbing the ladder Ethen jumped down and took off. Violet made it to the top and so did the boy. The difference was Violet just sat and waited to climb down the ladder but Warren wanted to follow his cousin and JUMP (that must be a boy thing).

Anyhow I was sitting a few feet away and Warren asked "GRANDPA I WANT DOWN." Before I got up he had his foot on the edge ready to jump. He had absolutely no doubt in his mind I was there to catch him. He jumped as far as he could. I caught him, set him down and the game continues only now Violet is it. A few seconds later Up the stairs comes Ethen up the ladder across the bunk and jumps...Warren is right behind him "GRANDPA HERE I COME", I wasn't exactly sure what that meant so I got up JUST IN CASE. Here he comes, climbed the ladder ran across the bunk and JUMPED. He did not even look, he just jumped.

HE KNEW AT THAT MOMENT AND FOR THE REST OF MY LIFE. THAT THEY ARE MY GRANDKIDS AND I WILL ALWAYS HAVE THEIR BACKS!

MAY 11, 2018; As you may have guessed by now Aspen is a very independent and confident young man. He has not been in TKD very long at this point but he enjoys class a lot. Like any normal 7 year old he likes to talk about it to his friends and like most normal 7-year-olds he is friends with most of his class. Most of the time if the young ones have issues at school the teacher or secretary sometimes even the principle himself will call or Email mom. I am on the approved list to pick up or drop off but discipline problems I don't want to deal with I feel it is not my place. Besides that, if I know about it I am obligated to keep them out of TKD class, so what I don't know won't hurt them.

Aspen's teacher knew he was in TKD and she also knew we used this as leverage to keep him on track at home and school. WE USE IT FOR LEVERAGE NOT THE SCHOOL & CERTAINLY NOT THE TEACHER. Today I was asked to pick them up after school because no one would be home to let them in off the bus. So I am sitting there waiting for the bell to ring and I notice here comes Aspen walking out with his teacher. She knew who I was and she knew I was the one who would be there for them today.

She walked up and gave my window a tap; "How are you doing Mr. Grandpa? Can I talk to you for a second?"

"Sure. What can I do for you?"

"Aspen tells me that he is a new student in TKD"

"Yeah. So what can I do for you?"

"Well he has a friend in class and he and Aspen don't want to listen. They are continuously talking about TKD and refuse to stop when I ask them to pay attention. I tried to separate them but the kids I sit them next to start asking them questions about TKD. This has been going on for a few days now. I have reached out to their parents and nothing has changed so I wanted to make you aware because I know you take the boys to TKD."

"I told Aspen if he DOES NOT STOP DISRUPTING CLASS I WOULD HAVE NO CHOICE BUT REACH OUT TO HIS INSTRUCTORS TO SEE WHAT THEY CAN DO. TO HELP. I also told him I was going to move him by Jimmy because Jimmy listens, follows instructions and is a good student so they need to act more like him"

As I said I would normally just tell her to contact his mom or bring it to the principle but seeing she brought me into this and what she told me got me incredibly angry I decided to get involved. Now Aspen was standing right next to her so I had to choose my words carefully but also make sure she knew I was dead serious about what I was saying;

"FIRST OF ALL LET ME SAY I AM GOING TO HANDLE THIS RIGHT HERE AND NOW WHEN MY FIRST REACTION IS TO FILE A FORMAL COMPLAINT WITH THE SCHOOL BOARD OR THE VERY LEAST THE PRINCIPLE AT THIS SCHOOL. SECONDLY, I AM NOT HIS FATHER SO IF HIS MOTHER DID NOT HANDLE THINGS YOU AS A TEACHER YOU SHOULD HAVE TAKEN THIS UP WITH YOUR SUPERIORS."

"WHO DO YOU THINK YOU ARE THAT YOU CAN THREATEN HIM WITH CALLING HIS INSTRUCTORS AT TKD. THAT IS AN OUT OF SCHOOL ACTIVITY AND NONE OF YOUR BUSINESS. IF HE IS TO MISS CLASS OR HIS INSTRUCTORS NEED TO BE

SPOKEN TO SOMEONE IN HIS IMMEDIATE FAMILY WILL DO IT NOT A TEACHER FROM SCHOOL. NEXT ASPEN IS ASPEN HE IS NOT BOBBY, HE IS NOT JIMMY HE IS ASPEN WHICH MEANS HE IS A CONFIDENT, TALKATIVE AND SOMETIMES DISRUPTIVE STUDENT AND IF YOU EVER COMPARE HIM TO ANOTHER STUDENT IN FRONT OF CLASS MAKING HIM FEEL INFERIOR I WOULD SUGGEST YOU START LOOKING FOR ANOTHER PROFESSION BECAUSE I WILL RAIN HELL DOWN ON YOU."

"Aspen get in the truck."

"Do you have any questions for me miss white?"

"No sir."

"GOOD, now you have yourself a wonderful afternoon."

I got in the truck and we left. On the way back to his house I told him we would have a conversation with Sir Josh about his behavior and he needed to be grounded but I made sure he understood that I was speaking to his teacher ADULT to ADULT and that did not give him an excuse to misbehave in class and that I would reach out to his teacher in a day or two for a report, Two days later I did reach out and emailed miss White explaining that we as his family are dealing with the problem and wanted a report from her. She did respond very quickly saying the past two days he was very respectful and much better. Now I am hoping that is true and she was not just afraid to say the wrong thing.

EITHER WAY, HE KNOWS THAT ON THAT DAY AND FOR THE REST OF MY LIFE, I HAVE HIS BACK!

JULY 19, 2014; This day pushed the limits of how far I would push the limits of being a GREAT GRANDPA. Aspen had the flu and at 30 years old some types of flu are no joke but at 3 years old to say we were concerned would be a LARGE understatement. He was a very sick little man for a very long time. We watched him closely for days to make sure his flu did not turn into pneumonia. He was Danielle's firstborn and my first grandson so yes we were scared. Well after his flu symptoms finally went away. A couple of days later he was developing red pimples and rashy patches all over his body. We called and thankfully got him into his pediatrician that same day. When we arrived she looked at his medical history show that he recently had the flu, checks his rash, and immediately called for an ambulance and off to children's hospital he went. His mom and grandma rode with him in the ambulance. To this day he still remembers that ride saying how COOL it was having no clue how sick he was. He was diagnosed with Idiopathic Thrombocytopenic Purpura or ITP for short which a decease that affects the platelets in your white blood cells. A normal 3-year-old should have a platelet count between 250,000-400,000 Aspen was at below 100,000 but steady. He was there for about 6 hours and his count was fluctuating between 100,00-150,000 not dropping below 100. So the doctors decided to send him home with the strict instructions if he felt dizzy, suddenly got pale or vomited we were to bring him back IMMEDIATELY. Well, not even halfway home he power barfed and I turned around and flew back. My daughter was in meltdown mode and thankfully her mom was there for her but Danielle was in no condition to comfort Aspen so that is where I would come in. The nurse on duty was like; "I am sorry sir but it is hospital policy that only two visitors at a time are allowed back"

"WELL THEN LADY YOU BETTER CALL A COUPLE SECURITY COPS AND BRING HANDCUFFS BECAUSE THAT IS THE ONLY WAY YOU ARE KEEPING ME AWAY FROM THAT BOY."

We were all allowed back and when they did his platelet count it was at less than 100 and dropping fast. I had no idea what ITP was but I did know he was a very sick boy. Platelets in the white blood cells cause an open cut or scrape to scab-up and stop the flow of blood. In other words, if he was playing, fell, and bloodied his knee or cut his hand even a bloody nose without white blood platelets to scab the wound he could bleed to death. When I heard that I knew exactly why his mother was in meltdown mode her little boy was at ZERO platelets and we were on our way home.

We ended up staying in the hospital for 2 days in which time he had a medicine IV drip and a continuous blood transfusion. After a day on the IV, his platelet count was at 200,000 and rising on its own. He was taken off the medications and monitored for the next 24 hours. His platelet count was at 380,000 and steady for 24 hours and the red pimples and rashes were almost completely gone. So they sent us home reassuring me that he will be just fine and grow up to be a healthy young man.

There is always a way to put a positive spin on anything and you can always find something to be thankful for. TODAY as weird as this may sound I was thankful he puked in my car because if we would have gotten him home and he played hard or even accidentally got hurt by the time we realized the bleeding wouldn't stop and we went to the hospital it may have been too late. Being with him in the hospital saying silent prayers and no sleep for two days he may not remember being in the hospital or his mom, grandma & grandpa being with him but on that day and for the rest of my life, *I WILL ALWAYS HAVE HIS BACK.*

NOVEMBER 30, 2016 For the last week or so I have been battling a very nasty stomach flu and have not even attempted to stand up let alone leave the house. For the past week, my only traveling was from my bed to the toilet and back to my bed. I have been sick before but this flu was kicking my ass like nothing I have had before. About 2 o'clock in the afternoon, I get a call; "I know you don't feel well dad BUT today is the last day we can get the stuff for the kids from toys 4 tots. Do you think you can take me?"

I knew that money was tight and if she was unable to get there the kids would have a very disappointing Christmas. Now with that being said, I do realize that Christmas is not about getting gifts it is and should be the holiday to celebrate life, love, and family but as very young kids they didn't understand that. I called back and spoke with the young ones or at least tried to ask what they wanted for Christmas.

Even over the phone, I could hear the smiles on their faces as they told me about Santa and they were being good so they expected Santa to bring either this present or that surprise. I knew I could not let them down so I drank as much water as humanly possible and waited a few minutes I knew that it would be coming out one end or the other or both. If it was just Danielle she is a big girl now and Christmas should not be a time of expectation but a time of thanks and reflection but the young ones. How could as grandpa let them down. So after the water did its job I called to let her know I would try. I would be there in 30 minutes wait in the car and go back to her house to drop stuff off and back to bed. I was taking a big chance of shitting my pants and I will wait for 1 minute after I hook and if not out SORRY. It must have been important to her because she was outside waiting and ready to go. THE pick-up time for her was between 2;20-2;40 and we arrived at 2;15 she went to the building showed her ticket then got right in. I never have been to toys 4 tots before so I didn't know how long I could expect to wait but thankfully the process was quick she received from VERY nice things for all her kids and with presents from me and other family members, the young ones had a VERY GOOD CHRISTMAS. They still talk about living in a shelter and how Santa found them and gave them the best Christmas ever. They have no idea that Santa was fighting a very severe stomach bug that year but Santa knows that even the flu and vomiting will not keep him down when the young ones need me *I WILL HAVE THEIR BACKS THROUGH SICKNESS AND INJURY FROM THAT DAY AND FOR THE REST OF MY LIFE.*

SCHOOL HALLOWEEN DANCE. Mama was gonna take us, remember grandpa? But she didn't feel well so you came to get me after my brodders had TKD. I remember cause I dressed like a zombie and my brodders wore their uniforms and I remember you played a song on the way on your phone and you said they would play it at the dance so we could dance, "Remember grandpa? It was the monster song remember?"

"Yes kiddo I do the name of the song is THE MONSTER MASH and I remember you and I went dancing, and it was fun."

Who would have thought that taking 3 young kids to a school dance with a few dozen screaming kids could actually be fun? I know why. Because they thought they couldn't go because their mom was gonna take them and couldn't we danced, we sang, they ran around with friends, collected candy and we bought hotdogs chips and cookies at the school bake sale.

I step into something knew I did not want to do and their mother couldn't.

THEY ALL KNEW FROM THAT NIGHT AND THE REST OF MY LIFE, I WILL HAVE THEIR BACKS.

OCTOBER 18, 2017; Today my daughter had to go to UMOS to fix a problem with her food share. Both boys were at school and I did not want to drive her to the appointment, drop her off, drive back to her house to watch Harlow for a very short time and then go back. I thought the easiest thing to do would just go with and wait in the car while she was in her meeting. I did not want to go anywhere and have to walk because a was in the middle of a severe case of gout and the slightest pressure on my toe and foot made it extremely painful to simply stand let alone try to walk. That would have been ok but Harlow wanted to go in with Mama and that too would have been OK but Harlow was very rambunctious and wanted to run around. Danielle was not feeling well so chasing the kid was not possible without the chance of puking all over the office so I got to bite the bullet and chase after her on one foot. The pain was almost unbearable and being a HE-MAN I had to hide the pain and roll with it. The Umos office she was at was in a strip mall and at the end of this mall was a CHUCK E CHEESE so after chasing her around for a few minutes I can to the conclusion that if I am going to be in pain anyway the least I could do is bring the young one to play and have fun while mommy was in her meeting.

So, I grabbed her put her up on my shoulders and hobbled over to C.E.C. And let her go nuts. Now I had a few bucks in my pocket and I knew she liked the pony ride so I briefly got to rest my foot while she rode the pony ride. Thankfully her meeting was quick and she came over and kept her occupied for another ½ hour or so before we took off for home. *I ALWAYS WONDERED WHAT KIND OF GRANDPA I'D BE WHEN IT CAME TO THE GIRLS BUT AFTER TODAY I KNEW I WOULD BE THERE TODAY AND FOR THE REST OF MY LIFE.*

PLAY VS PRACTICE. Both boys know that I consider TKD very important and enjoy taking them to class. We practice hard and try very hard in class because they enjoy it when people come up to say how good they are and at times how much they improved. Part of the issue is that sometimes I feel like I am living my life through them. Yes, I was in TKD with Amanda as a young man. When I was in TKD I worked at being flexible daily. I would stretch and do the splits and even went as far as to buy a jumping jack /split machine. I would stretch the backs, fronts, calves, and hamstrings. But the harder I worked the more frustrated I became. I could never do even close to the full splits and never could touch my toes. The first time I left I was in a tournament and attempted a wheel kick and ended up flat on my back and was so embarrassed I left the tournament and quit classes.

Years later I tried again but this time Amanda and I joined Cho's. Again I had massive power in my punches but my legs were like brittle wood that could not and would not stretch. I made it to a green belt in Cho's and watch how easy it is for both of them to stretch and do the splits and I find myself wondering do they like it or are they doing it to please me? Just exactly where I am with the boys. They made it to High red and red belts but had to quit because I ran out of money. But when we did go and I paid for everything was it fair of me to push because I wanted to see them do well? Or was it really that I wanted them to do well or did I simply like the title of being a good grandpa because I took them to class, tournaments, and testing. Just because I paid they had to want it I had no right to make them practice and keep them from playing in the park because at times they would rather play than practice.

THE MOMENT THEY TOLD ME THAT THEY REALLY LIKED CLASS BUT ARE KIDS AND SOMETIMES WANT TO TAKE A BREAK AND PLAY FIRST. I KNEW FROM THAT MINUTE THAT NO MATTER WHAT I WOULD HAVE THEIR BACKS THEN, NOW AND FOR THE REST OF MY LIFE.

Now during this chapter, I have never told you how often I go to the gym or my workout routine. So for informational purposes, I go to the gym 4 days a week. Play basketball 30 minutes, lift weights for 90 minutes, 20 on an elliptical machine and finish with 10 minutes in the pool. I am 5'10" and weigh 210lbs, not a big guy but not small either and never really considered myself physically intimidating until today. We were playing at the playground and I was away from the boys keeping my eyes on the girls watching to make sure they were okay.

Aspen came over with a scrape on his knee and said that some kid pushed him so he pushed back. In my world that is completely, fine kids will be kids and as long as it stays fair I have no problem. But today however a father thought it necessary to put his hands on Aspen and gave him a shove and told him to keep his hands to himself. Now I try to keep a cool head because I have a very bad temper and a violent streak that I cannot control. Aspen had told this guy that he was going to get his grandpa and he was gonna kick his butt. Well apparently the term grandpa and kick your butt was funny to this clown because he shoved him again and said sarcastically;

"Yeah you do that...go get your GRANDPA"

This guy was about 24 years old and weighed about a buck 30 soaking wet maybe 5'6" so when the kid said he was bringing his grandpa He probably visualized a 70 something old man that he could verbally intimidate and make himself look good in front of his son.

As Aspen was telling me this story I could feel myself getting angrier by the minute so before we went over to chat with this guy I made sure I put my Harley jacket back on with my work out gloves fully prepared to throw down with this guy not knowing what he looked like or how big or small he was until I got over there. When I did come back with Aspen I made sure I started taking my coat off before I said a word and tossed it on the ground.

"SO WE HAVE A PROBLEM HERE? YOU FIND IT OK TO PUT YOUR HANDS ON A BOY? NOT JUST ANY BOY, BUT MY GRANDSON." His eyes went right to my tattoo and the wife-beater I was wearing. "No, no we don't. Just a misunderstanding amongst the boys."

"You okay then Aspen?" I asked.

"YES SIR GRANDPA, I'M GOOD"

And with that, I went back to my table *AND HE KNEW FROM THAT DAY I WAS WILLING TO BEAT AN ASS OR MAYBE TAKE AN ASS BEATING BUT IF SOMEONE EVER LAID A HAND ON HIM HE KNEW FROM THAT MINUTE AND FOR THE REST OF MY LIFE I WOULD HAVE HIS BACK.*

NOVEMBER 29, 2015 Today I got a call that both of the littles were sick. They were throwing up and had high fevers. To be honest I don't remember where they were living at the time but I do know it was not with me. Honestly, I think they were living in the family shelter at the time because I remember getting a picture of both boys looking very sick and I remember thinking to myself I wish I could go stay with them awhile. But living in a family shelter no men were allowed to visit for any length of time. They were sick. scared and alone with daddy to protect them from the dreaded boogie man. Mama tried her best to comfort them but she was young and scared herself. I felt really bad for them but what could I do? I lived in a rooming house at the time and house rules were adults only so even if I wanted to bring them back with me I couldn't. I could go grab them and take them out for a bit but that almost seemed very counterproductive because they were sick and dragging them out made no sense. So I did what any good grandpa would do. I BOUGHT THEM STUFF TO FEEL BETTER.

So the littles were 4 and 2 not feeling well and scared what would make them feel better? As I was on my way to the store I made the list in my head of what to get. First a matching pair of soft and comfy footy pajamas. Ah yes, Spiderman Pjs perfect. Next, they needed a movie to watch to keep their minds off being sick so the obvious choice was Spiderman. I know they both like chocolate milk but being sick milk of any flavor would not be the best idea so I went with cranberry juice and white soda with saltine crackers. Medicine the correct medicine that would be age-appropriate and help them feel better was the most important thing.

When I finally did get there I could see in their faces they were sick but seeing me their faces lit up like a Christmas tree *BUT KNOWING THEY KNEW THAT I KNEW THEY WERE SICK AND LONELY & THEY KNOW THAT GRANDPA WOULD BE THERE NO MATTER BAD WEATHER, COLD OUTSIDE OR EVEN IN THE MIDDLE OF THE NIGHT FROM THE SECOND I WALKED THROUGH THE DOOR THEY BOTH KNEW I HAD THEIR BACK AND WOULD FOR THE REST OF MY LIFE.*

MARCH 20, 2018; Birthdays in our family have always been very important. For me, I prefer to do something fun and memorable and I try to do it on the exact birth date. My girls like to schedule parties either for the weekend before or after a birthday so working family and friends can make time on their days off to come to the party. I completely understand and respect that but I think a birthday is an important date and do something on that date. However this year on Ethens Bday I would be out of town at a real estate convention so I decided to take him to Country Springs Hotel A local hotel that has a very nice indoor water park he has been asking to go to for months. He was 3 years old going on 4 and his brother was 6 so a day in a water park would be a perfect present and hopefully one he'd remember for a lifetime. YES he will remember today but for all the wrong reasons;

We made a call asking about prices and it is free to enter the park if you are a guest of the hotel. For non-registered guests, it was very expensive on the weekend but if you went during the week it was kids free with a paying adult admission, and kids under 2 are free. I paid for Danielle and I and the boys were free and Harlow was under 2 at the time so she was free also. The place had very few people using the park simply because it was a Tuesday morning and not a lot of people jump up out of bed and head to a water park so we had most of the place to ourselves for most of the morning.

We as a family rode the lazy river on the tubes, we did the long slides together, he went up did the curvy slide as long as me or his mother and the lifeguard was at the end of the tube tunnel waiting. The kiddy pool was only a foot and a half deep and at the time we walked right by the life jackets not realizing they had them to use. Ethen for the most part stayed with us the whole morning until that split second he didn't. One second he was standing next to me while we watched Aspen and his mom walk up the stairs to the water slide the next second he was gone. It took about 30 seconds for them to get to the bottom of the slide but in my head, it took close to an hour. I was sick to my stomach and panicked. We started walking around looking for him and believe me when I say that was the longest 3 minutes of my life. As I walked around the slide a lifeguard was carrying Ethen coming the other way looking for us. He went to the side of the lazy river and jumped in trying to grab the rafted and missed. He went under the raft and scared the crap out of the family riding in it. The mother without hesitation rolled out of the raft and grabbed him bring him above water. Then she went to the side of the river and calmly handed him to a guard. She found us and explained what happened. I hit my knees and thanked God then we found the mother that pulled him out and thanked her again and again.

She was the one that showed us where the life jacket stand was. From then on any time we are near water ALL the young ones are wearing vests. **I WAS SCARED AND ANGRY BUT HE WAS ONLY 3 AND THE WAY I HANDLED THIS WOULD NO DOUBT LEAVE A MARK ON HIM FOR THE REST OF HIS LIFE SO I DID NOT SCREAM AT HIM. I SIMPLY AND CALMLY TOLD HIM THAT HE NEEDS TO STAY BY US & I WOULD HAVE BEEN VERY SAD IF I WAS NOT THERE TO PROTECT HIM SO HE KNEW AS WELL AS I DID FROM THAT SECOND ALWAYS BE AWARE OF WHERE THEY ARE IF YOU ARE RESPONSIBLE AND ALWAYS HAVE THEIR BACK TODAY AND FOR THE REST OF YOUR LIFE.**

JUNE 26, 2020 A couple of weeks ago I was helping a friend move. during the move, I was told that everything in the house was up for grabs because the move was from a house to an apartment and most things were going in the trash so I took a 44" & 32" T.V. For my daughter for gaming systems. I also found a nice bike in the garage I brought for my grandson and knowing the weather was going to get hot soon so I took a couple of rotary fans. But my most prized possession from the day was a hand-carved wooden pirate sword. I had planned on hanging it on the wall in my new house and use it as the centerpiece for a collection I was hoping to start. I did not want to keep it in my car because it may get damaged so I put it in the house hidden behind a board nailed to the wall. The only part of it you could see was the handle and that was covered and hidden by a piece of poster board.

Now I do know the boys have no respect for their things and a couple of months ago Tim bought and set up a tent upstairs telling them they could go camping as long as the tent did not get broke. It took longer than I thought it would but busted it is and camping is not happening. They cannot keep anything nice even for something they would enjoy. Pokémon cards have been thrown away Bae Blade equipment broken and trashed then thrown away, but my stuff especially something I told them I liked and wanted to hang on a wall I thought they would have enough respect for me that they would leave it alone. I was wrong. I was downstairs and Ethen came running down with a chance to tattle on his brother (something ALL the young ones enjoy) to tell me Aspen broke my sword. At first, I was furious and prepared to beat his ass with the busted half of the sword. That had two issues... Firstly, being that mad I would have hurt him and hurt him bad. Secondly, hitting kids as punishment is not my style anymore. Calmly I just went upstairs to let him know I was very upset and then the "grandpa it was an accident" set me off.

NO, I DID NOT LAY A HAND ON HIM. I simply explained in a very loud voice that it was impossible to be an accident because of where it was and how it was broken the only possibility was he lifted a little and pulled snapping the handle from the blade.

I continued to let him know I was extremely disappointed and thought he had more respect for me and my things and that he should not ask for anything. Don't ask for my phone, don't ask to use my computer nothing more from the dollar store don't ask grandpa for another thing. I made it a point not to call him names or cuss at him but I was loud and he knew I was mad and disappointed. Being 9 years old he ran away crying knowing he screwed up. At times I may take things a bit far and don't mean to but I am who I am and changing is a long slow process but I am trying.

A very short time later his brother came to me asking for help reading a book we are reading together. Aspen came to be involved but I very coldly asked him to get away from me. He looked shocked and very hurt walking away in tears. Later that night as we read again I invited Aspen to help his brother sound out some words he was having trouble with.

IT WAS ONLY A WOODEN SWORD THAT CAN AND WAS GLUED. HE IS A VULNERABLE YOUNG MAN WHO'S FEELINGS CANNOT BE GLUED TOGETHER WHEN BROKEN SO WHATEVER THEY BREAK BE IT A SWORD, A WINDOW OR A FAMILY HEIRLOOM THOSE ARE ONLY OBJECTS, THINGS WITH NO FEELINGS. LET THEM KNOW NO MATTER WHAT YOU HAVE THEIR BACK NOW AND FOR THE REST OF YOUR LIFE! WORDS ARE WEAPONS.

Words are weapons; your tongue and your mind can be more deadly than any gun or knife you can hold in your hand. As far as the young ones go some of them would probably prefer to get their little butts paddled than be told some of the things parents have a tenancy pounding in their heads. I have read stories and studies time and again about parents telling kids they are dumb or they are worthless years of this kind of verbal bashing has a very deep and lasting impact on a kid. What if as a youngster they studied for a test I mean studied and mom or dad help them for weeks and they just didn't get it and every wrong answer they were continually reminded of how stupid they are. I can guarantee that the test results would be well below average. This same kid did something wrong in school and now he is being told he is not only dumb but a miscreant. 7th or 8th grade he gets in trouble for shoplifting and now he is dumb a troublemaker, and now a thief.

At 19 years old this kid ends up robbing a store and shoots the owner on the way out. In jail, he gets a visit from mom and dad confirming that they knew from the time he was little he was no good.

There are situations like this in every family every day. That is why I try very hard when the young one does something wrong I try to correct it and try very very hard not to slam the point home. The example I am talking about is for months now Ethen has been disrespectful and very sneaky. He has been lying to our faces and just continues to do something wrong when he is told with no doubt to stop. As an example, he is a very little guy and when his baby sister is crying he will go pick her up and carry her around. Now he has been told way more than once not to lift and pick her up and try to carry her but yet he will simply ignore instructions and commands just keep going like he didn't hear. During groundings, he is not allowed to watch videos or play video games. But he will sneak into a remote area and hide to play. The issue here is he is a very sneaky little lier that needs to be corrected. So the challenge is correcting him without deeply rooting the idea he is sneaky and a fibber. It is very hard and **EVEN WHEN THEY ARE HAVING DIFFICULTIES TELLING THE TRUTH AND FOLLOWING THE RULES ALL KIDS MUST KNOW THAT NO MATTER WHAT YOU HAVE THEIR BACK NOW, AND FOR THE REST OF YOUR LIFE!**

DECEMBER 8, 2017; DANGER, DANGER. Is there danger in today's unpredictable world? You bet the kids today have much more to be concerned about then we did back in the day. The availability of automatic weapons and going to school worried there is some nut job kid they may shoot the place up, being at the mall at the wrong time or getting snatched up and sold. So no matter where you are and what you are doing always be aware of where they are. Today Warren turns 3 months and I was asked to take his mama and uncle Ryan to the video store to look for a new game. I am not a fan of video games so I decided to stay out int the car and wait. I dropped them off in the front of the store and made my way around the corner to find a place and parked. Now I have been 100s of places with Amanda but most of the time if not every time we go in together because she does not like going in alone but this time she had her brother and she did not want to bring her son in so we waited in the car.

I have been a grandpa many times over and for many years but for Amanda, this was her first child and for me, I was still trying to get used to the fact that she was a mama and she had a son. He was asleep in his car seat and I was sitting there in the car listening to a CD and when the CD ended I thought they have been in there quite awhile I should probably go check on them and see if all is well. So I turned off my car, grabbed the keys, and took that minute walk into the store.

"How you guys doing in here?"

"UMMM, WHERE IS MY SON?"

I did not say a word to answer I simply turned on my heel and bolted out the door and run back to my car. I was not used to Amanda having a baby and I accidentally left him in the car alone.

Let me tell you as a grandpa my stomach dropped and I ran out to my car like I was on fire. I was gone for less than 4 minutes and he was sleeping soundly in the car and will never have any knowledge that I left him as an infant in the car and **FROM THAT DAY WHEN HE IS WITH ME I WILL KNOW EXACTLY WHERE HE IS AND HAVE HIS BACK NOW AND FOR THE REST OF MY LIFE!**

EVEN TOUGH GUYS SHOULD SHOW FEELINGS For years my kids have said that when I walk I walk like a tough guy and that is why people don't approach me or smile as they walk by because I look like I will bite their head off. This is a good thing I guess when walking alone or in a not so great area people may think twice before approaching me with not so nice intentions. But it is not such a good thing for a grandpa the kids need to know they can come to me with problems or concerns. I am not an emotional person and I rarely cry. I think if my family truly thought about it they could very easily count on 1 hand the number of times they have seen me cry.

One day I was parked in the front of the school waiting for Aspen because both the other littles were homesick and a friend of his came up to me saying Aspen was in the school crying. A couple of seconds later another kid comes up to me saying the same thing. I have no idea what's going on. My head went to the worst scenario right away that he's in there getting whooped and I was about to go to jail for beating some grade-schoolers ass. Another minute or so went by and I was just about to head into the school to see what was going on when his teacher from last year came up to me and explained that his bestie Maxwell was moving to Texas and Aspen was extremely upset. Now I was there alone and as far as I knew both thought of me as the same as my girls that I walked around like a tough guy and Aspen was trying to compose himself before coming out to the car because in our world tough guys don't cry & he was a TKD kid so that had to make him a tough guy. Although I am not an emotional man feelings and emotions are part of life so I was preparing myself for when he came out. Another few minutes past and he came running out with a smile trying to hide the pain of missing his friend.

"Hey buddy how was school?" as he turned away from me and said "fine."

"What took so long for you to get out today? I thought maybe something happened."

He lost it and started crying "MY BEST FRIEND MAXWELL IS LEAVING FOR TEXAS AND TODAY IS THE LAST TIME I WILL SEE HIM."

I have no clue how to console a crying little boy so I simply let him cry in my shoulder explaining that with computers and technology he would be able to face time his friend whenever he wanted. I do wish his mom would have been there but under the circumstances, I think I did an O.K. job.

SO AS A TOUGH GUY AND PROTECTOR OF THE FAMILY WHEN THEY NEED YOU TO BE EMOTIONAL AND UNDERSTANDING MAKE SURE THEY KNOW YOU HAVE THEIR BACK THEN AND FOR THE REST OF YOUR LIFE!

DECEMBER 7, 2019; FRIENDS & FAMILY. Today was a very important day for all of us in more ways than one. Today was belt promotion day for both boys, They have both been working and practicing very hard to earn this belt because red and high red put them in the advanced class. They are both proud and worked very hard to get where they are but One and two steps away from black belt is very impressive.

For whatever reason, it was just us going today. Mama could not come and believe it or not that turned out to be a blessing in disguise.

I doubled checked the time and route made sure everything was in their bag, uniform – check, belts - check and headed out to pick them up. On testing days I never know who is more excited them or me. They were both ready and waiting so away we went. One-stop on the way, we needed gas. Pulled in the first gas station, shut off the car, paid, pumped, and got back in to take off to testing turned the key and NOTHING my car was completely dead. I tried again and again nothing.

Normally I would be in panic mode but studying the law of attraction I felt like this was just a test and everything happens for a reason. Aspen did not feel he practiced enough and this was just a sign from the universe telling him he wasn't ready yet. Ethen on the other hand was very confident and wanted to go and was visually upset my car wouldn't start. Now myself I have been the type of person that would rather be somewhere an hour early rather than 5 minutes late and seeing the boys wanted to get there early to watch and practice before their time slot we had plenty of time to figure out a solution. I popped the hood and we made sure the battery was connected ..it was and the headlights and radio worked but no clicking and the starter was not spinning so the natural assumption was the starter went bad. But I have never heard of the starter going bad with no warning.

THINK...THINK...THINK what could I do? I knew my folks would come to give us a ride but they lived too far and we would never make it on time.

So I called my friend Red. Red is 92 years old and would not want to drive an hour to take us to hang around for hours watching something he was not at all interested in but perhaps he would let me use his truck. That is exactly what happened. He came to the gas station we tried jumping my car with cables just to be certain it was not just my battery. It wasn't, so we drove him back home transferred for his Explorer to his little pickup and headed to testing. On the way, I made sure to continue to drill into Aspen's head that he is more than ready and the universe wants him to test because we have friends that will help us get there and we have plenty of time.

About half way there we realized that we grabbed their uniform bag but we left their sparring equipment in the trunk. Do we go back or do we go and hope to find equipment to borrow? We had to continue and have faith because we simply didn't have time to go back.

"See grandpa the universe is telling me I am not ready"

"No buddy the universe is trying to show us that you are so ready no matter what obstacles are thrown our way we will figure it out"

We did get to testing with plenty of time to spare but another obstacle was presented. The boys were scheduled to test at different times so when we found one set of gear to use when finished his brother could step in and use it next. The challenge now was that they are both testing at the same time, both needing gear and will not be able to share.

When we first arrived I spoke to madam Monique who is an instructor at our branch and she found someone willing to borrow us their equipment and it was a female student so it would be a better fit for Ethen but that still meant Aspen had no gear. As we were trying to figure things out another lady who is the grandma of a few students came walking back through the door because he grandkids tested way earlier but forgot something and she needed to find it before leaving. Now Aspen being a true believer in the law of attraction and how the universe looks out for people this woman's grandson is exactly Aspens size, he is a deputy black belt which means he has to hold that rank for 4 months to test and was just there to watch his sisters and cheer not needing his gear because he was not testing today. Besides for all of that they drove grandma's car and not his mom's and his gear was in her trunk. The boys are friends and it was VERY clear the universe wanted him to test because she was more than happy to borrow me her grandson's equipment.

Both of the boys passed with excellent scores. They learned that they had to have confidence in themselves and if it is meant to be no obstacle is too big to overcome but most importantly they know without a shred of doubt that **I WILL ALWAYS HAVE THEIR BACKS AND IF I CANNOT DO IT ALONE I HAVE FRIENDS & FAMILY THAT HAVE MY BACK SO I CAN HAVE THEIRS**

JULY 8, 2020; Better safe than sorry. Twice in the past 12 months, the boys were playing and Ethen jumped off an elevated surface landing on Aspen's arm. Today they were playing with their baby sister and his arm was between the crib mattress and the metal frame when Ethen thought it would be funny to jump off the dresser and land on the mattress wedging his brother's arm between the two. It was not funny and his brother screamed in pain. This was the 2nd time the same thing happened only the first time I was not staying with them so when I did get the call it was late in the night and they feared he may have fractured his arm so when asked I got up got dressed and took him to the ER. We sat there for hours just to be released with the doctor saying he just had a nasty bruise but no breaks and he will be fine.

The 2nd time I was, however, staying there and I heard Aspen shriek all the way upstairs so I ran down to check. As they explained what happened I took hold of his arm and it was mobile from side to side but very sore and tender to the touch. In my opinion, there was nothing wrong but as always somebody else knew better and it was explained to me that it may be a hairline fracture or worse so we need to take him in. However, the problem was we didn't need to take him I needed to take him in.

I had a feeling this would have and was a complete waste of time especially with the corona crap going around and the wait time at the hospital would be unnecessarily extended. I did not want to waste my time but I did ask him how bad it hurt and his response did convince me to take him in. Although I knew this was going to be a waste of my time I certainly did not say that to Aspen.

HE WAS HURT AND FELT THAT HE NEEDED MEDICAL ATTENTION SO INSTEAD OF SAYING WE WILL BE WASTING OUR TIME I SIMPLY SAID "IT'S ALWAYS BETTER TO BE SAFE THEN SORRY" AGAIN AND AGAIN HE KNOWS NO MATTER THE SITUATION I WILL HAVE HIS BACK THEN AND FOR THE REST OF MY LIFE.